China and International Law

China and International Law

The Boundary Disputes

Byron N. Tzou

PRAEGER

New York
Westport, Connecticut
London

Library of Congress Cataloging-in-Publication Data

Tzou, Byron N.
　　China and international law : the boundary disputes / Byron N.
Tzou.
　　　　p.　cm.
　　Includes bibliographical references.
　　ISBN 0-275-93462-4 (alk. paper)
　　1. China—Boundaries.　I. Title.
D737.T96　　1990
911′.51—dc20　　　　89-23098

Copyright © 1990 by Byron N. Tzou

All rights reserved. No portion of this book may
be reproduced, by any process or technique, without
the express written consent of the publisher.

Library of Congress Catalog Card Number: 89-23098
ISBN: 0-275-93462-4

First published in 1990

Praeger Publishers, One Madison Avenue, New York, NY 10010
A division of Greenwood Press, Inc.

Printed in the United States of America

The paper used in this book complies with the
Permanent Paper Standard issued by the National
Information Standards Organization (Z39.48-1984).

10　9　8　7　6　5　4　3　2　1

To
My Family

Contents

	MAPS	ix
	ACKNOWLEDGMENTS	xi
1	Introduction	1
2	International Law: A Means of Foreign Policy	7
3	Border Policy	23
4	Boundary Disputes and Settlements	45
5	Unequal Boundary Treaties	77
6	Boundary Treaties	91
7	Determinants of Boundaries	113
8	Methods for Settling Boundary Questions	125
9	Conclusion	139
	SELECTED BIBLIOGRAPHY	143
	INDEX	155

MAPS

1	The Sino-Soviet Disputed Boundaries	46
2	The Sino-Soviet Disputed Area in the Pamirs	51
3	The Locations of the Sino-Soviet Disputed Chenpao/Damansky Island and Hei-hsia-tzu/Bear Island	53
4	The Sino-Burmese Disputed Boundary	57
5	The Locations of the Sino-Indian Disputed Boundaries	61
6	The Sino-Indian Disputed Boundaries: Western and Middle Sections	62
7	The Sino-Indian Disputed Boundary: Eastern Section	64

ACKNOWLEDGMENTS

There are a number of people to whom I am deeply indebted for support, assistance, encouragement, and guidance in completing this book. First there is my teacher, Professor C. Neale Ronning, who closely read the entire manuscript. He provided me with invaluable suggestions and careful corrections, and without his wisdom and guidance I could not have completed this work.

I also owe a deep debt of gratitude to Professor Stanford Lyman. He taught me to gear theory with practice, and provided me with invaluable resources. I remain indebted to Professor Jacob Landynski whose exacting methodology prepared me for the academic world.

A special debt of gratitude goes to Professor Adamantia Pollis, whose continued encouragement led me to complete my studies and whose warm concern helped me throughout this endeavor.

Special thanks, too, to Professors Jerome A. Cohen and Hungdah Chiu who stirred my interest in China and international law when I was doing research at Harvard Law School. Both have enriched my life as a scholar.

My thanks also to Tom Lane, freelance writer, and one of my best friends, who helped with organization, style, and general editing. His tireless counsel and patience are greatly appreciated. I am indebted, too, to Ms. Lilian Solzman, who substantially improved the final manuscript. Despite their help, inevitable errors remain, and for these I take full responsibility.

Last but not least, my indebtedness goes to my family: to my parents whose love and expectations have always motivated me to achieve; and to my wife, Joan, with two small children, who gave me understanding and support, and endured many domestic hardships so that I could complete this work. To her I will be forever grateful.

China and International Law

1

INTRODUCTION

One of the most intractable issues in the People's Republic of China's (PRC) foreign policy has been her boundary questions. As each nation may have its own peculiar questions regarding its boundaries, China has her own. How has China worked to settle her boundary disputes and how successful has she been?

Scholars may approach China's boundary questions through different perspectives. They can examine China's cultural heritage and historical status because the Chinese empire before the middle of the nineteenth century controlled a large part of the Asian continent, extending from Siberia all the way to Indochina. Scholars have found that nationalism is a supremely important factor, contributing to contemporary China's determination of boundary claims.[1] The Chinese have never lost their fundamental conviction that they would ultimately dominate Asia.[2] Harold C. Hinton said that "the Chinese seem traditionally to have been unwilling to concede that territory once gained by the Chinese empire could ever be permanently lost, even if it was formally ceded to a foreign power."[3] Therefore, China's effort to consolidate her territorial integrity has been termed, by an Indian writer, "territorial Sino-centralism."[4]

The Chinese territorial grievance was demonstrated in a map published in a school textbook in Shanghai, 1954, showing China's lost territories comprising of Siberia, Outer Mongolia, Korea, Ryukyu, Indochina, and islands in the Indian Ocean.[5] This map raised intense academic interest. A. Doak Barnet, for example, observed:

> It is difficult to predict what other territorial claims Communist China might attempt to assert by force.... Peking has not made any official claims to other territories

which China has controlled or claimed at sometime in the past, including parts of Vietnam and Korea, Outer Mongolia, and the Soviet Khabarovsk and Maritime provinces. It seems unlikely to do so now, but it might decide to put forth irredentist claims to some of these areas in the future.[6]

This historical and cultural approach reveals the nationalistic feeling of the Chinese people. Barnett's observation implied that China might go to any lengths to settle boundary disputes in her favor. Only the lack of military strength has kept her in check to date. If China puts the slogan of "recovering the lost territories" into practice, then, she will work to change the status quo of the world order and will definitely be condemned as an imperialist.[7] A. M. Halpern has criticized this a priori condemnation of China:

> The "Middle Kingdom" thesis: The real policy of CPR[Chinese People's Republic] is to restore traditional Chinese suzerainty is a defined portion of Asia and nothing more, this thesis seems clearly not to correspond to the record. If it were true, it would imply that Chinese Communist foreign policy is not oriented towards the international system that now exists, but towards one that expired over a century ago.[8]

The 1954 map was also read as "designed merely to convey the PRC's sense of historical grievance vis-à-vis the imperialist West and Japan," and not as a project of irredentism.[9]

Writers also have studied diplomatic history to discover China's intentions regarding her boundary questions. They have seen the Sino-Indian border conflicts as the result of ideological[10] and power struggles in Asia.[11] The Chinese-Soviet border conflicts in the Ussuri River they saw as a by-product of ideology,[12] a conflict of nationalism,[13] or a fusion of ideology and territorial demand.[14] They have concluded their studies branding either Russia,[15] India,[16] or China as the aggressor.[17] They have used the same sources but have drawn different conclusions.[18]

Diplomatic historians have also discussed the formation of China's present boundaries in general studies of international relations[19] or monographs on China's boundaries.[20] From their studies, we know how the present Chinese boundaries were shaped; which boundaries were defined, uncertain, demarcated, and undemarcated, and what the problems are.

The second approach to the study of the Chinese boundary questions is to view the questions from the perspective of international law. Socialist states have argued that traditional norms of international law were formed among capitalist states in order to meet the needs of a capitalist world order. Scholars of international law severely criticized the capitalist concept of territorial acquisition.[21] Early statements made by revolutionary government and articles published by scholars of international law have raised questions as to whether or not traditional norms of international law would be accepted by the emerging socialist segment of international society.[22] Studies of socialist attitudes toward international law have provided some of the answers. This study seeks to shed additional light on the matter.

Early study in the 1960s of Communist China's general attitude toward international law was provided by Hungdah Chiu, who observed that "China's past experience . . . has some influence on the view of the Communist Chinese towards international law,"[23] and that "Communist Chinese theory and practice with respect to the conclusion of treaties is different from that of the West."[24] Both in theory and practice, James C. Hsiung concluded that the PRC accepted "certain norms of the established code of international conduct but rejected others."[25] Still another scholar observed that "while it [the PRC] showed no desire to be confined by legal technicalities, the Chinese government did not demean international law as a regulator of interstate behavior or attack it on ideological ground."[26] No study specifically deals with Chinese boundary questions except a few paragraphs in James Hsiung's book.[27]

After the Sino-Indian boundary disputes accelerated, the legal advisor to the Indian Ministry of External Affairs, R. Krishna Rao, discussed the entire Sino-Indian boundary questions based on international law,[28] and an Indian writer published his own "perspective."[29] Undoubtedly, the legal arguments they presented were one-sided in favor of advancing Indian boundary interests. Yet another writer accused the PRC for violating international treaty obligations.[30] The Chinese, too, denied the legal binding force of the so-called McMahon Line.[31]

There are unbiased observations of the Sino-Indian boundary disputes written by Western scholars of international law.[32] But these works have dealt with the Chinese boundary questions in a partial manner. None of them has ever systematically analyzed the entire Chinese boundary question taking all her neighbors and international law into consideration. This book examines how the Chinese have employed international law to protect their boundary interests; it includes an examination of boundary claims, border policies, boundary settlements, boundary alignments, and armed conflicts. In order to do this, we have to first understand the Chinese Communists' attitude toward international law in general. Chapter 2 approaches this task. Chapter 3 analyzes China's border situations and the border policy in light of international law. Chapter 4 looks at the shaping of some of her boundaries, the troublesome frontiers, the disputes and some settlements. Chapter 5 specifically deals with the issue of the unequal boundary treaty; its legal problems and the ways to solve them. Chapters 6 through 8 discuss the technicalities of the boundary settlements in detail; namely, the attitudes toward the old boundary treaties, the practices involved in concluding new boundary treaties, the tangible elements determining a nation's boundary lines, the means to solve boundary questions, and the armed conflicts. Chapter 9 returns to the assumption set forth in the Introduction.

This study focuses on China's land boundaries, excluding maritime boundaries, which belongs to another field: the law of the sea. Thus, the status of islands, such as the Sino-Japanese disputed Tiao-yü-tai Islands, the Sino-

Vietnamese disputed Spartly Islands and Paracel Islands is not covered in this book. Yet Chapter 4 discusses the status of Outer Mongolia (the Mongolian People's Republic) including its adjacent territory, Tannu Urianghai, because the Nationalist government in Taiwan cancelled her recognition of the independent status of the Mongolian People's Republic and has been claiming Outer Mongolia as Chinese territory.[33]

Boundary values for the Chinese have continuity in spite of changes in governments. This study deals with both the Nationalist government and the People's government, and in places even with the Ch'ing dynasty, but the main emphasis is on the PRC. Since its inception, the Peking government has had ambition and has been anxious to settle any boundary disputes with China's neighbors. Therefore, most of the sources in this study are those produced after the founding of the PRC. The sources are primarily in the English language. If a source in the Chinese language has been cited, the translation is this author's or as otherwise indicated. All Chinese personal names and places are romanized in accordance with the Wade-Giles system except in popular usage. Personal names are arranged in Chinese order, which is family names preceding the given name.

NOTES

1. Albert Teuerwerker, "Chinese History and the Foreign Relations of Contemporary China," *The Annals of the American Academy of Political and Social Science* 402 (July 1972): 1–14; Harold C. Hinton, "Conflict on the Ussuri: A Clash of Nationalism," *Problems of Communism* 20, nos. 1–2 (January–April 1971): 45–59.

2. John Rowland, *A History of Sino-Indian Relations: Hostile Co-existence* (Princeton, NJ: D. Van Nostrand, 1967), p. xii.

3. Harold C. Hinton, *Communist China in World Politics* (Boston: Houghton Mifflin Co., 1966), p. 273.

4. Gondker Narayana Rao, *The India-China Border: A Reappraisal* (London: Asia Publishing House, 1968).

5. This map was reprinted with English translation in Dennis J. Doolin, *Territorial Claims in the Sino-Soviet Conflict* (Stanford: The Hoover Institute on War, Revolution, and Peace, Stanford University Press, 1965).

6. A. Doak Barnett, *Communist China and Asia: Challenge to American Policy* (New York: Harper, 1960), p. 78.

7. Regarding the definition of imperialism, see Hans J. Morgenthau, *Politics Among Nations*, 5th ed. (New York: Alfred A. Knopf, 1973), p. 54.

8. A. M. Halpern, "China in the Postwar World," *The China Quarterly*, no. 21 (January–March 1965): 44.

9. Samuel S. Kim, *China, the United Nations, and World Order* (Princeton, NJ: Princeton University Press, 1979), p. 44.

10. K. S. Shelvankar, "China's Himalayan Frontier: India's Attitude," *Foreign Affairs* 38, no. 4 (October 1962): 477; Mohan Ram, *Politics of Sino-Indian Confrontation* (New Delhi: Vikas Publishing House, 1973), p. v.

11. Hinton, *Communist China in World Politics*, p. 281.

12. Doolin, *Territorial Claims in the Sino-Soviet Conflict*; Tai Sung An, *The Sino-Soviet Territorial Dispute* (Philadelphia: The Westminster Press, 1973), pp. 73–76.

13. Hinton, "Conflict on the Ussuri," pp. 49–59.

14. Leonard Schapiro, "Communists in Collision," *Studies in Comparative Communism* 2, nos. 3 & 4 (July–October 1969): 122.

15. David J. Dallin, *Soviet Russia and the Far East* (New Haven, CT: Yale University Press, 1948).

16. For example, Neville Maxwell, *India's China War* (New York: Doubleday, 1972).

17. For example, Margaret W. Fisher, Leo E. Rose, and Robert A. Huttenback, *Himalayan Battleground: Sino-Indian Rivalry in Ladakh* (New York: Praeger, 1963).

18. This phenomenon was illustrated in Graham T. Allison, *Essence of Decision: Explaining the Cuban Missile Crisis* (Boston: Little, Brown, 1971), pp. 14–15.

19. For examples, Vincent Chen, *Sino-Russian Relations in the Seventeenth Century* (The Hague: Martinus Nijhoff, 1966); Alastair Lamb, *Asian Frontiers: Studies in a Continuing Problem* (New York: Praeger, 1968); George N. Patterson, *Peking Versus Delhi* (New York: Praeger, 1964); John Gittings, *Survey of the Sino-Soviet Dispute: A Commentary and Extracts from the Recent Polemics 1963–1967* (London: Oxford University Press, 1968); Dallin, *Soviet Russia and the Far East*; Tien-fong Cheng, *A History of Sino-Russian Relations* (Washington, D.C.: Public Affairs Press, 1957).

20. For a few examples, Peter Berton, "The Border Issue: China and the Soviet Union, March–October 1969," *Studies in Comparative Communism* 2, nos. 3 & 4 (July–October 1969); W. A. Douglas Jackson, *The Russo-Chinese Borderlands* (Princeton, NJ: D. Van Nostrand, 1962); Alastair Lamb, *The China-India Border: The Origins of the Disputed Boundaries* (London: Oxford University Press, 1964); An, *The Sino-Soviet Territorial Dispute*; A. R. Field, "Bhutan, Kham, and the Upper Assam Line," *Orbis* 3, no. 2 (Summer 1959); George N. Patterson, "The Himalayan Frontier," *Survival* 5, no. 5 (September 1963); Alastair Lamb, *The Sino-Indian Border in Ladakh* (Canberra: Australian National University, Asian Publications Series, 1973); John W. Garver, "The Sino-Soviet Territorial Dispute in the Pamir Mountains Region," *The China Quarterly*, no. 85 (March 1981).

21. A writer, Ying T'ao, of the PRC wrote: "Occupation, cession, subjugation, accretion and prescription are methods imperialists use to seize territory from the weak, small and defeated states." Therefore, the capitalist concept of territorial acquisition cannot be accepted by the weak states, see his "Ts'ung chi-ko chi-pen k'ai-nien jeng-shih chih-ts'an chieh-chi kuo-chi-fa ti tseng-mien-mu" (Recognizing the True Face of Bourgeois International Law from Several Basic Concepts), *Kuo-chi wen-t'i yen-chiu* (Studies in International Problems), no. 1 (1960): 42.

22. H. Arthur Steiner suggested in 1950: "Communist China is motivated by a revolutionary ethic thoroughly incompatible with the existing structure of international law and relations." See his "The Mainsprings of Chinese Communist Foreign Policy," *American Journal of International Law* 44, no. 1 (January 1950): 89. In 1963, India accused the PRC of being "the first state which has defied all rules of international law and international behavior after the second World War," *India Calling* (official publication of the Indian Embassy in Peking, April, 1963), quotation in a Chinese note to the Indian embassy in Peking dated June 3, 1963, printed in *Notes, Memoranda and Letters Exchanged and Agreements Signed Between the Governments of India and China; White Paper* (New Delhi: Ministry of External Affairs, government of India, 1963), 9: 165.

23. Hungdah Chiu, "Communist China's Attitude Toward International Law," *The American Journal of International Law* 60, no. 2 (April 1966): 266.

24. Hungdah Chiu, "The Theory and Practice of Communist China with Respect to the Conclusion of Treaties," *The Columbia Journal of Transnational Law* 5, no. 1 (1966): 13.

25. James C. Hsiung, *Law and Policy in China's Foreign Relations: A Study of Attitude and Practice* (New York: Columbia University Press, 1972), p. 315.

26. Arthur A. Stahnke, "The Place of International Law in Chinese Strategy and Tactics: The Case of the Sino-Indian Boundary Dispute," *Journal of Asian Studies* 30, no. 1 (November 1970): 95–120.

27. Hsiung, *Law and Policy in China's Foreign Relations*, pp. 128–30, 195–98, passim.

28. K. Krishna Rao, "The Sino-Indian Boundary Question and International Law," *International and Comparative Law Quarterly* II, part 2 (April 1962): 375–415.

29. Surya P. Sharma, "The Indian-China Border Dispute: An Indian Perspective," *The American Journal of International Law* 59, no. 1 (January 1965): 16–47.

30. R. S. Arora, "The Sino-Indian Border Dispute: A Legal Approach," *Public Law* (Summer 1963): 196.

31. Wei Liang, "Ts'ung kuo-chi-fa chueh-tu kan su-wei McMahon hsien" (From the Angle of International Law to Look at the So-called McMahon Line), *Kuo-chi wen-t'i yen-chiu* (Studies in International Problems), no. 6 (1959): 47–52.

32. Lamb, *The China-India Border*; Alfred P. Rubin, "The Sino-Indian Border Disputes," *The International and Comparative Law Quarterly* 9 (January 1960): 96–125. This study was evaluated by Harold C. Hinton as "the most detailed and objective account of the historical and legal aspects of the [Sino-Indian boundary] dispute," see his *Communist China in World Politics*, p. 275, 3.

33. See Chapter 4 of this book.

2

INTERNATIONAL LAW: A MEANS OF FOREIGN POLICY

Modern international law had its origin in Christian civilization. It emerged from the natural-law tradition of Western Europe and was confined originally to those states. China after the nineteenth century gradually accepted the norms of international law[1] and utilized it for protecting her national interests in international relations.[2] However, after the founding of the People's Republic of China, her attitude toward traditional international law has been something different from former governments.[3] In accordance with the orthodox Marxist point of view, international law is the instrument of bourgeois nations to perpetuate their favored positions in the world.[4]

The PRC's foreign policy has been influenced by a mixture of traditional culture, political reality, nationalism and Marxism-Leninism. Among them, nationalism has been the most important element.[5] It is a common feeling of the Chinese that their country was reduced to the status of a semicolony after the middle of the nineteenth century.[6] China was forced to cede and lease territories, to give up control of maritime customs, salt tax, and other economic and industrial privileges, to grant extraterritorial jurisdiction, and to accept foreign troops in her territory.[7] It is understandable that both the Republic and Communist China's basic foreign policies have been striving for political independence, territorial integrity, and equality with other nations.[8]

To achieve these goals, the PRC urged that a proletarian science of international law based on "the principles of peace and democracy" should be established to serve her national interests.[9] Ho Wu-shuang and Ma Chun specified:

After the liberation, we must in principle deny the bourgeois science of international law . . . only in this way can we gradually establish a science of international law agreeing with our country's concrete situation and make international law compatible with serving our foreign policy.[10]

In 1957, eight years after the founding of the PRC, Ho and Ma reported: "In new China, the proletarian science of international law, which differs from the bourgeois science of international law in principles, has finally been established as primary."[11] The establishment of the proletarian science of international law was made by, on the one hand, denying the bourgeois "absurd" theory of international law, and on the other hand by presenting new "progressive and democratic" principles of international law.

Based upon their denials and proposals, we will in this chapter examine in detail their attitude toward the system and definition of international law, national sovereignty, the models of territorial acquisitions, state equality, and in the end discuss the utility of international law.

THE SYSTEM OF INTERNATIONAL LAW

The system of international law had been discussed among Marxists even before the Bolshevik Revolution in 1917.[12] In China, the discussion about the system of international law began in 1957, when Professor Chiu Jih-ch'ing of Fu-tan University at Shanghai wrote of two systems of international law: socialist and general. The general international law adjusts relations among bourgeois states, and between bourgeois and socialist states; the socialist international law adjusts relations among the socialist states alone. The former has the capacity to adjust relations between socialist and bourgeois states because it includes "those Leninist principles relating to the equality of nations," but it is unable to adjust relations among socialist states because the principles of proletarian internationalism are not included.[13]

A year later, Lin Hsin argued that there are two totally different systems of international law. Since there are two economic and social systems, there are two types of international relations. Accordingly, there must be two systems of international law to adjust relations among bourgeois states and among socialist states respectively.[14]

However, some writers argued there is only one system of international law binding upon all states, whatever the economic systems are.[15] Chu Li-lu wrote: "I consider that there are a number of norms of international law which are generally recognized, basic and common; they are equally recognized by and binding upon bourgeois states and proletarian states."[16]

The question of how many systems of international law was not resolved, even in the "great debate" (a symposium held in Shanghai and sponsored by the Shanghai Law Association and the East China Institute of Political Science and Law in 1958). In the symposium, the participants almost unanimously ruled out Lin Hsin's theory of bourgeois-socialist dichotomies. No matter how divergent their opinions were, they did not rule out the fact that a general international law does exist.[17]

Because general international law is unable to adjust the relations among socialist countries, Ho Wu-shuang and Ma Chun developed a theory of the bourgeois-socialist science of international law. They wrote:

> The law which at present adjusts the different relations between states with different types of social systems is a kind of general (recognized) international law.... As the law existing at the time is a general international law, does there also exist a general science of international? Our answer is negative.
> At present in the world, there exists two sciences of international law.... They ... serve the policies of different classes.[18]

The science of bourgeois international law is fabricated for serving the foreign policy of capitalism according to its needs in different stages of economic development.[19] The science of proletarian international law serves the socialist countries' foreign policy, defending the proletarian and all the laboring populations in the world.[20]

THE DEFINITION OF INTERNATIONAL LAW

Chinese writers rejected the traditional definition of international law and presented their own. They argued that there are more than 100 definitions of international law in accordance with the statistics collected by a Cuban scholar.[21] Among them, Oppenheim's definition has been used by most Western writers. Accordingly, international law is defined as "the name for the body of customary and conventional rules which are considered legally binding by civilized states in their intercourse with each other."[22] International law applying restrictively to the civilized states has been severely criticized by writers in the PRC.[23] Chu Ch'i-wu criticized the definition as

> possessing the prejudice of Western nations and tainted by imperialism and colonialism. It makes international law restrictively applying to the so-called Christian states only and excludes many old countries with long histories and excellent cultures. It discriminates against the countries of the Third World.... It creates the theoretical bases for the policies of aggression and the expansion of imperialism and colonialism.[24]

In addition to definitions of the Western scholars, a Soviet scholar gave the following definition. International law can be defined as:

> The aggregate of rules governing relations between States in the process of their conflict and cooperation, designed to safeguard their peaceful coexistence, ex-

pressing the will of the ruling classes of these States and defended in case of need by coercion applied by States individually or collectively.[25]

The definition of international law is an advance on Oppenheim's according to a Chinese writer's opinion, because it emphasizes that the aim of international law is to safeguard peaceful coexistence.[26]

However, the Chinese present their own definition. They revised Oppenheim's definition and argued that international law is the product of international relations among all states. Chu Ch'i-wu in the PRC wrote:

> International law is the aggregate of rules of states' behaviors, including principles and systems with legal binding force upon states in their international relations, expressed by the will of the ruling classes formed during the process of international intercourses, and generally recognized by all states.[27]

According to this definition, international law applies with binding force upon all states rather than just the so-called civilized ones.

NATIONAL SOVEREIGNTY

The PRC, like all other revolutionary countries, has always emphasized the sanctity of the doctrine of national sovereignty.[28] Chou Keng-sheng, a noted jurist in mainland China, wrote that sovereignty has been a concept of traditional international law for several hundred years; sovereignty even under the present international situation is still a very valuable attribute of states. The burden of modern states is how to safeguard sovereignty rather than limiting it or giving it up.[29]

In the period before the Sino-Indian boundary disputes, writers in the PRC launched an attack against the bourgeois theories of national sovereignty and the policy of imperialism.[30] Wu An-yu in his article entitled "Revealing the Nature of Reaction in Political Science Departments of Old Colleges" charged them with advocating bourgeois theory of limited sovereignty.[31] Another writer, Ying T'ao, declared: "Some capitalist states . . . use all means to undermine and uproot the sovereignty of other states."[32] Those writers pointed out that the following methods were often used by the imperialists for violating the sovereignty of the weak states:

1. Completely destroying the sovereignty of other states.[33]
2. Bearing down on weak and small states as vassal or protected states.[34]
3. Using armed aggression in occupying other's territory[35] and planting puppet regimes. For example, Japan set up "Manchukuo" in the Chinese Northeastern Three Provinces in 1931.[36]
4. Forcefully establishing leased territories on the territory of the weak and small states. Foreign powers had several leased territories in weak China.[37]

5. Plundering maritime customs and privileges, and establishing extraterritoriality.[38]
6. Preying on other economic interests, such as the rights of domestic river navigation, mining, and the building up of factories, etc.[39]
7. Interfering or controlling others' domestic and foreign policies under the name of economic aid[40] or based on either agreements or humanitarianism.[41] For example, the Committee of the Jurists of International Law supported by the "imperialists" interfered with China's policy in Tibet in 1959 and requested the United Nations and related countries to help the Tibetans for justice and freedom.[42]

Writers in the PRC accused bourgeois international law of serving the needs of the capitalistic big powers[43] and creating the concepts of fully sovereign states as well as states not fully sovereign, such as vassal states and protected states. Those states that are not fully sovereign cannot be full, perfect, and normal subjects of international law in the community of nations; their foreign affairs are managed completely by the capitalistic big powers.[44]

Furthermore, the writers and the PRC particularly criticized the theory of limited sovereignty which has been developing since World War II.[45] They thwarted the bourgeois concept of world order because it is built on the basis of transnational law or world law instead of traditional international law and because it uses world sovereignty to replace national sovereignty. They argued that the "imperialists" often used the United Nations as an instrument for aggression and intervention. For example, during the meeting of the General Assembly in 1962, the "imperialists" unjustly inserted the "Tibet question" into the agenda.[46]

The PRC also attacked the theory of limited sovereignty exercised by the Soviet Union. When the rift between the Soviet Union and the PRC was becoming wider in the mid–1960s,[47] the Soviets were employing more troops along the Sino-Soviet border, and after the Soviet troops marched into Czechoslovakia in 1968, China's fear of the Soviets' invasion grew tremendously.[48] In 1968, less than three months before the Sino-Soviet armed conflicts in Chenpao Island (Damansky in Russian) in the Amur River, *Hong-ch'i*, an official periodical, published an article entitled "Smash the New Tsar's Theory of 'Limited Sovereignty,' "[49] It compares the theory of limited sovereignty between the U.S. imperialist and the Soviet revisionist. The two "overlords" sing the same tune. "The Soviet revisionists have been riding roughshod over other countries in the 'community', violating their sovereignty at will, intervening in their internal affairs and destroying recognized elementary principles of states sovereignty lock, stock and barrel." So "the relationship between Soviet revisionism and the other member countries in this 'community' is one . . . between master and slave, a relationship between suzerain state and its colonies and dependencies." The theory of the limited sovereignty exercised by the Soviet revisionist social-imperialists allowed the Soviet revisionism to intrude into other socialist countries' territory and trample them underfoot.

Rejecting the concept of limited sovereignty does not mean supporting the theory of absolute sovereignty or unlimited sovereignty. Exercising absolute sovereignty by one nation would encroach upon the sovereignty of others. The theory of absolute sovereignty is merely suited for the policy of imperialist aggression.[50] The theory of absolute sovereignty is not only inconsistent with the principles of traditional international law, but also violates the Charter of the United Nations.[51]

The norm of the national sovereignty has been used by China to interpret international events that happened only after she had accepted Western international law. Events happening before that time have not been expounded either by Russia or by China, in terms of international law, even though the term "sovereignty" existed. Here is an example. The Soviet government in 1969 accused China of a policy of expansion in the seventeenth century:

> The Manchu-Chinese emperors . . . actively pursued a predatory, colonialist policy, adding to their possessions with piece after piece of land taken from other countries and peoples. The process of the formation of China's territory within its present borders was accompanied by the forced assimilation of oppressed nationalities and their physical annihilation.[52]

The Soviet government then asserted that during the seventeenth century, "China's state frontier on the north, for example, was marked for a distance of about 4,000 km, by the Great Wall of China, which, . . . is more than 1,000 km, southwest of the Amur and Ussuri Rivers."[53] For this charge, the PRC replied:

> The different sections of the Great Wall were constructed in the fourth century B.C., while the linking up of these sections by the Chin Dynasty took place in the third century B.C. But even then, the Great Wall did not form China's boundary. While discussing the Sino-Soviet boundary question, the Soviet Government referred to the Great Wall which was built more than 2,000 years ago and dwelt upon it with such great relish, we should then ask: And where was Russia's boundary at that time?[54]

In contrast to Soviet charges, China only charges tzarist Russia with expanding eastward in the sixteenth century.[55] Neither the Soviet nor the Chinese government raised the question of the sovereignty of the nationalities, which were in the process of forming states.[56]

The PRC, thus, emphasized the principle of mutual respect for national sovereignty. Mao Tse-tung announced on the day of the founding of the PRC in 1949 that China was desirous of establishing diplomatic relations with other states "on the basis of equality, mutual benefit, and mutual respect for sovereignty and territorial integrity."[57] This principle was repeated by Chou En-lai, premier of the PRC, in 1955: "We respect each other's sovereignty and territorial integrity. We shall adhere to this principle."[58]

China's official position was also stated in her relations with neighboring states. During the Sino-Indian boundary disputes in the late 1950s and early

1960s, the PRC repeatedly blamed India for infringing upon China's sovereignty and territorial integrity.[59] In 1960, "The Chinese Government, in line with its policy of being consistently opposed to foreign prerogatives and respecting the sovereignty of other countries, renounces China's right of participation in mining enterprises at Lufang of Burma as provided in the notes exchanged between the Chinese and British Governments on June 18, 1914."[60]

TERRITORIAL ACQUISITION

While China's past humiliation has caused the Chinese to resent the bourgeois theory of territorial acquisition, her policy of being friendly toward the Third World has aided the Chinese in presenting their own concept of the "changes of territory." The Chinese have argued that territory provides the material wealth a state needs. It is the foundation of states' survival and independence. To infringe upon other states' territories is violating their sovereignty and destroying their independence.[61]

Although at present the PRC has not been irredentist,[62] the writers in the PRC have vehemently rejected the theory of bourgeois models of territorial acquisition. According to Ying T'ao: "Occupation, cession, subjugation, accretion and prescription are methods imperialists use to seize territory from the weak, small and defeated states."[63] "Modern international law does not have such norms, nor can we find such international law documents," Shih Sung, Yu Ta-hsin, Lu Ying-liu, and Tsao K'o wrote.[64] "On the contrary, some important documents of modern international law express the principle of the inviolability of territory," they added.[65] They, then, cited Article 2, Paragraph 4, of the Charter of the United Nations to support their argument, which states that "all members shall refrain in their international relations from the threat or use of force against the territorial integrity or political independence of any state."[66]

According to Chinese writers, however, territory could be "adjusted" in world politics.[67] Adjustment differs from acquisition. First, it is not that the big powers take advantage of the weak and the small, but that colonial people have the political right of self-determination. Second, historical grievances should be rectified; a state has the perfect right to recover her sovereignty over her territory. This implies that a huge territory ceded to Russia under the unequal treaties should be recovered.[68] Third, neighboring states may make minor adjustments of their territories in accordance with the principle of international law. In fact, the PRC, in considering the historical data and actual conditions, traded the perpetually leased Namwan triangular area (Namwan Assigned Tract) by Burma in exchange for the territory of three villages.[69]

STATE EQUALITY

To achieve equal status in international society has always been a main goal of the Chinese revolutions. Dr. Sun Yat-sen, the founding father of the Republic in 1911, and Mao Tse-tung, the founder of the People's Republic in 1949, have expressed this goal clearly.[70] The Constitution of 1954 stipulates China's foreign policy on the principle of equality, mutual benefit, and mutual respect for other's sovereignty and territorial integrity.[71]

The Chinese emphasis on state equality as a core of foreign policy has resulted from her suffering semicolonial status during the late nineteenth century and early twentieth century. During that period of time, China was not treated fairly by the big powers in the international community. One writer, Ying T'ao has accused imperialistic international law with inappropriately classifying states as civilized and uncivilized.

> Among the existing states in the world, which are civilized states and which are uncivilized states? In accordance with the answer of the bourgeoise, only the states of Christian civilization could be called civilized states. All states different from Christian civilization, mainly states of the Orient are uncivilized states. As Oppenheim indicates, such states as China, Persia, Siam and Abyssinia were uncivilized states before World War One. Their civilization had not yet reached that condition necessary to enable their Governments and their population in every respect to understand and to carry out the rules of international law.[72]

Therefore, when the big powers had international intercourse with China, "China could only fulfill her obligations in accordance with agreements, and was not allowed to cite public law in her defense."[73]

The PRC believed that in the treaties of 1946 and 1965, the United States treated the Nationalist government unequally.[74] It is not difficult to understand why the PRC has been emphasizing the equality of states as a basic principle of foreign policy and placed it in the well-known Five Principles of Peaceful Coexistence.[75]

In addition, a Chinese writer argues that a nation which is struggling for independence, and which is in the process of forming a state, should be equally treated as a member in international society. Therefore, any intervention or war against such a nation should be prohibited by the principles of international law.[76] The principle of equality up to this point is beyond the goal of China's national revolution. It becomes an instrument of foreign policy to woo the Third World.

UTILITY OF INTERNATIONAL LAW

"All states attempt to utilize international law to cloak their foreign policy with the mantle of legality."[77] The PRC is no exception. Writers in the PRC spoke more frankly on this point than the Western scholars.[78] In this section we will study the theory of the utilization of international law and utilization-oriented education in international law.

As we have analyzed earlier in this chapter, the writers in the PRC dichotomized the bourgeois science of international law and the proletarian science of international law. "The science of bourgeois international law is an instrument for defending capitalist big powers' policies of aggressionism and colonialism, and with an effort for upholding capitalist world order (the antisocialist principle of law)."[79] "The main devoir of the proletarian science of international law is to scientifically discuss, prove and propagandize the system of international law for serving peace, democracy and progressive enterprise; and to make this democratic, progressive system and principle of international law a strong weapon for struggling international peace and security, defending national independence and national sovereignty among the peace loving countries as well as all peace loving peoples."[80] International law as a weapon in defense of national independence and national security is illustrated more thoroughly by Chu Li-lu:

> International law is one of the instruments of settling international problems. If this instrument is useful to our country, to socialist enterprise, or to the peace enterprise of the world, we will use it. However, if this instrument is disadvantageous to our country, to socialist enterprise or to peace enterprises of the people of the world, we will not use it and should create a new instrument to replace it.[81]

The purpose of international law education in political science and college law departments is to train incumbent political-legal cadres and teachers in the ways of Marxism-Leninism, concerning international law and the states.[82] "Under the leadership of the Party," Ho Wu-shuang and Ma Chun stated,

> We started learning, with the assistance of the Soviet specialists, the Soviet proletarian science of international law. We have primarily established a new Chinese science of international law and trained a first group of scientific cadres for research in international law.[83]

Based upon the philosophy of utility, we have found two corollaries: First, academic work and propaganda are combined. For example, the editor of the *Chen-fa yen-chiu* (Studies in Political Science and Law, hereafter cited as *CFYC*), the best known and most important journal of political science and law in the late 1950s and early 1960s published by the China Political Science and Law Association and Institute of Law of China Academy of Science reported: "It is almost impossible at present to publish academic research periodicals and general or propaganda periodicals separately."[84] The policies of the *CFYC* are primarily:[85]

1. To propagandize and expound the theory of nation and law as found in Marxism-Leninism and in the works of Mao Tse-tung.
2. To propagandize and expound our orientation and policies with regard to current domestic as well as important political events.
3. To criticize political science and the law of modern revisionism and capitalism, and appropriately select and introduce related materials of foreign countries.

Second, teaching, research, and practice are complementary. In the PRC, legal research must be conducted in accordance with, among other things, the principle of closely linking theory with practice.[86] Practice provides abundant materials for research and teaching. For example, Peking Political Science and Law College sent teachers and researchers to work with various governmental agencies conducting survey and research.[87]

The results of research provide information for teaching as well as for governmental practice. For example, Wei Liang wrote that a watershed could be used to delineate the Chinese-Indian international boundary line, if a watershed separates the two countries. However, if a watershed is within Chinese territory, it is wrong to use it as a Chinese-Indian boundary line. This opinion was written into an official Chinese note delivered to the Indian government in 1959 blaming the latter for using a watershed in Chinese territory as the Chinese-Indian international boundary line.[88] The relationship between research and practice can also, for example, be examined by studying the background of the members of the Editorial Committee of the *CFYC* and the contributors to that journal. All the members of the Editorial Committee of 1955 have their incumbent positions in various governmental agencies,[89] and most of the contributors were members of the China Political Science and Law Association.[90] The journal served personnel involved with legal research organizations and political-legal organs, and teachers, students, and researchers of the political-legal institute of higher learning.[91] From this fact, we can assert that teaching, research, and practice are closely related.

SUMMARY

The PRC believes that international law possesses a strong character of class. Bourgeois international law serves the interests of the bourgeoisie only. Thus, the PRC as a socialist country should develop a new science of international law to serve her own foreign policy, and refuse to accept certain norms of Western international law. She should only accept those theories which are generally recognized as basic and common in international intercourse and are helpful to her in attaining her basic foreign policy.[92]

The Chinese proposed a new definition of international law. They offered a new theory of territorial changes and put it into practice while concluding the Sino-Burmese Boundary Treaty. They suggested that nations in the process of forming states should be subjects of international law. Moreover, the PRC proposed the Five Principles of Peaceful Coexistence as a basic border policy, which will be studied in the next chapter.

NOTES

1. See Hungdah Chiu, "Hsi-fang 'kuo-chi-fa' hsu-ju chung-kuo ti chin-ko" (The Introduction of Western "International Law" to China), *Tung-fang cha-chih* (The Eastern

Miscellany) 1, no. 12 (June 1968): 28–34; also Immanuel C. Y. Hsu, *China's Entrance into the Family of Nations: The Diplomatic Phase 1858–1880* (Cambridge: Harvard University Press, 1960), Part 2.

2. Chiu, "The Introduction of Western "International Law";" Hsu, *China's Entrance into the Family of Nations*, Parts 1 & 3.

3. James C. Hsuing, *Law and Policy in China's Foreign Relations: A History of Attitude and Practice* (New York: Columbia University Press, 1972); Hungdah Chiu, "Communist China's Attitude Toward International Law," *American Journal of International Law* 60, no. 2 (April 1966): 245–67 (hereafter cited as *AJIL*).

4. Richard A. Falk, "Revolutionary Nations and the Quality of International Legal Order," in Morton A. Kaplan, ed., *The Revolution in World Politics* (New York: John Wiley and Sons, 1962), pp. 314–15.

5. See Mark Mancall, "The Persistence of Tradition in the Chinese Foreign Policy," *The Annals of the American Academy of Political and Social Science* (September 1963), 349: 15–26; also Albert Feuerwerker, "Chinese History and the Foreign Relations of Contemporary China," *The Annals of the American Academy of Political and Social Science* (July 1972), 402: 1–14.

6. Mao Tse-tung asserted that China was a semicolonial country under indirect imperialist rule and that the Communist revolution was the outcome of the Chinese peasants' struggle, see Committee of the Communist Party of China, ed., *Selected Works of Mao Tse-tung*, 5 vols. (Peking: Foreign Languages Press, 1951–1977), 1: 13, 65, 118, 123, 129, 259; 2: 121, 287, 312, 324; see also Feuerwerker, "Chinese History," p. 6.

7. Regarding the foreign powers' privileges in China, see Westel W. Willoughby, *Foreign Rights and Interests in China*, 2 vols. (New York: Paragon Book Gallery, 1966).

8. The founding father of the Republic of China, Dr. Sun Yat-sen's last testament in 1925 indicates that the object of the national revolution "is to raise China to a position of independence and equality [in international society]," *China Yearbook 1975* (Taipei: China Publishing Co., 1976), page facing the Foreword; regarding Communist China's demand for sovereignty and territorial integrity, see *Selected Works of Mao Tse-tung* 4: 401–2.

9. Chou Keng-sheng, *Hsien-dai ying-mei kuo-chi-fa shih-hsiang t'ung-hsian* (Trends in Thought of Modern Anglo-American International Law), (Peking: Ssu-chieh chih-shih ch'u-peng-se [World Knowledge Press], 1963), p. 66.

10. Ho Wu-shuang and Ma Chun, "P'i-p'an Ch'en T'i-ch'ien tsai ku-chi-fa-hsueh fang-meng ti fan-t'ung kuan-tien" (A Critique of Ch'en T'i-ch'ien's Reactionary Viewpoint on the Science of International Law), *Chen-fa-yen-chiu* (Studies in Political Science and Law), no. 6 (1957): 37 (hereafter cited as *CFYC*).

11. Ibid., p. 37.

12. Ibid., p. 35.

13. Ch'iu Jih-ch'ing, "Systems of International Law at the Present Stage," *Fa-hsueh* (Science of Law), no. 3 (1957):16–19, cited by Chiu, "Communist China's Attitude," pp. 252–53.

14. Lin Hsin, "A Discussion of the Post World War II Systems of International Law," *Chiao-hsueh yu yen-chiu* (Teaching and Research), no. 1 (1958): 34–38, cited by Chiu, "Communist China's Attitude," p. 253.

15. Chu Ch'i-wu, "Looking at the Class Character and Succession Character of Law from the Point of View of International Law," *Kuang Ming Jih-pao* (Kuang Ming Daily), May 13, 1957; Chou Tsu-ya, "The Question of the Nature of Modern International

Law—the Class, Specially Compulsion and Succession Character of International Law,'' *Hsueh-shu yueh-k'an* (Academic Monthly), no. 7 (1957): 67, 71–72. The above two citations in Chiu, "Communist China's Attitude," p. 255; Chu Ch'i-wu, "Tan-tan kuo-chi-fa ti ting-i wen-t'i" (Talking About the Question of the Definition of International Law), *Fa-hsueh yen-chiu* (Studies in the Science of Law), no. 3 (1981): 51–53.

16. Chu Li-lu, "Refute the Absurd Theory Concerning International Law by Ch'en T'i-ch'ien," *Jen-min-jih-pao* (People's Daily), September 18, 1957.

17. See a special issue of *Fa-hsueh* (Studies of Law), no. 3 (1958), with a heading of "A Discussion of the Question Concerning Contemporary Systems of International Law," cited by Chiu, "Communist China's Attitude," p. 256.

18. Ho and Ma, "A Critique of Ch'en T'i-ch'ien's Reactionary Viewpoint," pp. 35–36.

19. Ying T'ao, "Ts'ung chi-ko chi-pen k'ai-nien jeng-shih chih-ts'an chieh-chi kuo-chi-fa ti tseng-mine-mu" (Recognizing the True Face of Bourgeois International Law from Several Basic Concepts), *Kuo-chi wen-t'i yen-chou* (Studies in International Problems), no. 1 (1960): 51 (hereafter *KCWTYC*).

20. Ho and Ma, "A Critique of Ch'en T'i-ch'ien's Reactionary Viewpoint," pp. 36–37.

21. Ibid., p. 35.

22. L. Oppenheim, *International Law*, 7th ed. Revised by Hersch Lauterpacht. (London: Longmans, 1948), vol. 1, p. 4. However, the 8th edition omits the adjective "civilized" before states in the definition of international law, vol. 1, (London: Longmans, 1955), pp. 4–5.

23. See Ying, "Recognizing the True Face," p. 51; Chu, "Looking at the Class Character"; K'ung Meng, "Tui chih-ts'an chieh-chi kuo-chi-fa kuan-yu-kuo-chi-fa chu-t'i ho kuo-chia ch'en-jeng ti li-nun ti p'i-p'an" (A Critique of the Bourgeois International Law Regarding Subjects of International Law and Theories of Recognition of States), *KCWTYC*, no. 2 (1960): 44–53; Ch'ien Ssu, "P'i-p'an chih-ts'an chieh-chi kuo-chi-fa tsai chu-ming wen-t'i shang ti chu-chang" (A Critique of the Advocacy Regarding the Question of Residents in Bourgeois International Law), *KCWTYC*, no. 5 (1960): 40–49.

24. Chu, "Looking at the Class Character," p. 15.

25. F. I. Kozhevnikov, ed., *International Law: A Text Book for Use in Law Schools* (Moscow: Academy of Sciences of the U.S.S.R. Institute of State and Law, Foreign Languages Publishing House, 1957), Translated from the Russian by Dennis Ogden, 1961, p. 7.

26. Chu, "Looking at the Class Character," p. 52.

27. Ibid.

28. Falk, "Revolutionary Nations," p. 314; Ying, "Recognizing the True Face," p. 51; Yang Hsin and Ch'en Chien, "Hsieh-nu ho p'i-p'an ti-kuo-chu-i-tse kuan-yu kuo-chia chu-ch'uan wen-t'i ti miu nun" (Exposing and Criticizing the Absurd Theories Concerning the Question of National Sovereignty of Imperialism), *CFYC*, no. 4 (1964): 6–11.

29. Chou, *Trends in Thought*, p. 66.

30. Ibid.; also Yang and Ch'en, "Exposing and Criticizing"; Ying T'ao, "Tui chih-ts'an chieh-chi kuo-chi-fa kuan-yu kuo-chia chu-ch'uan wen-t'i ti p'i-p'an" (A Critique of Bourgeois International Law Concerning the Question of National Sovereignty), *CFYC*, no. 3 (1960): 47–52; K'ung, "A Critique of the Bourgeois International Law"; I Hsin,

"Chih-ts'an chieh-chi kuo-chi-fa tsan kan-se wen-t'i-shang shao-ming-liao sheng-mo" (What Did the Bourgeois International Law Say About the Question of Intervention?) *CFYC*, no. 4 (1960): 47–54.

31. Wu, An-yu, "Hsieh-lu chiu-ta-hsueh cheng-chih-hsi ti fan-t'ung pen-chih" (Revelling the Nature of Reaction in Political Science Departments of Old Colleges), *CFYC*, no. 6 (1957).

32. Ying, "A Critique of Bourgeois International Law," p. 48.

33. Ch'ien, "A Critique of the Advocacy," pp. 40–49; Yang, "A Critique of Bourgeois International Law," p. 48; Yang and Ch'en, "Exposing and Criticizing," p. 7.

34. Ying, "A Critique of the Bourgeois International Law," p. 48; Yang and Ch'en, "Exposing and Criticizing," p. 7; also K'ung, "A Critique of the Bourgeois International Law," p. 51.

35. Yang and Ch'en, "Exposing and Criticizing."

36. Ying, "A Critique of the Bourgeois International Law," p. 48.

37. Ibid.; also Ch'ien, "A Critique of the Advocacy," p. 43.

38. Ying, "A Critique of the Bourgeois International Law," p. 48; Ch'ien, "A Critique of the Advocacy," p. 46.

39. Ying, "A Critique of the Bourgeois International Law," p. 48.

40. Yang and Ch'en, "Exposing and Criticizing."

41. Ch'ien, "A Critique of the Advocacy," p. 42; I Hsin, "What Did the Bourgeois International Law Say," pp. 46–48; Chou Keng-sheng, *Trends in Thought*, pp. 39, 45–47, 64.

42. Ch'ien, "A Critique of the Advocacy," p. 42.

43. The term "big power" (*lieh-chiang*) has been used in all the Chinese literature instead of "great power" usually used in the Western writings. Because this study is wholly related to China, this author employs the Chinese usage of "big power" throughout this book.

44. Ying, "A Critique of Bourgeois International Law," pp. 48–49.

45. K'ung, "A Critique of Bourgeois International Law," pp. 44–45.

46. Chou, *Trends in Thought*, p. 45.

47. Regarding the Sino-Soviet rift, see William E. Griffith, *Sino-Soviet Relations 1964–1965* (Cambridge: The M.I.T. Press, 1967); G. F. Hidson, Richard Lowenthal, Roderick MacFarquhar, *The Sino-Soviet Dispute* (New York: Praeger, 1963); and Donald S. Zagoria, *The Sino-Soviet Conflict 1956–1961* (Princeton: Princeton University Press, 1962).

48. Harold C. Hinton, *The Bear at the Gate: Chinese Policy-Making under Soviet Pressure* (Washington, D.C.: American Enterprise Institute for Public Policy Research, 1971), pp. 9, 16–27.

49. Chi Hsiang-yang, "Smash the New Tsar's Theory of 'Limited Sovereignty'," *Hong-chi* (Red Flag), no. 5 (1969). English text in *Peking Review* 12, no. 21 (May 23, 1969): 20–22 (hereafter cited as *PR*).

50. Ying, "A Critique of the Bourgeois International Law," p. 49.

51. Chou, *Trends in Thought*, p. 66.

52. "Statement of the U.S.S.R. Government on March 29, 1969," *Pravda*, January 14. English text in the *Current Digest of Soviet Press* 12, no. 24 (July 9, 1969): 9–13.

53. Ibid.

54. "Refutation of the Soviet Government's Statement of June 13, 1969," *PR* 12, no. 41 (Oct. 10, 1969): 10.

55. Statement of the Government of the PRC May 24, 1969," *PR* 12, no. 22 (May 30, 1969): 3–9.

56. According to K'ung Meng's theory, nations which are in the process of forming states are subjects of international law and thus have sovereignty, see section titled State Equality in this chapter and note 75, *infra*.

57. *Handbook on People's China* (Peking: Foreign Languages Press, 1957), p. 9.

58. "Speech to the Political Committee of the Asian-African Conference on April 23, 1955," George McTurnan Kahin, *Asian-African Conference, Bandung, Indonesia, April, 1955* (Ithaca: Cornell University Press, 1955), p. 59.

59. For example, a Chinese note to the Indian Counsellor in Peking, 1959, indicated: "The Chinese Government must point out solemnly that . . . the brazen intrusion and occupation of Chinese territory by batches of Indian troops . . . constitute grave encroachments on China's sovereignty . . . ," *Notes, Memoranda and Letters Exchanged and Agreements Signed Between the Governments of India and China, White Paper* (New Delhi: Ministry of External Affairs, Government of India, 1954–1963) 1: 34 (hereafter cited as *White Paper*).

60. Article 3 of the Agreement Between the Government of the People's Republic of China and the Government of the Union of Burma on the Question of the Boundary Between the Two Countries, English text in *Important Documents on the Settlement of the Sino-Burmese Boundary Question* (Peking: Foreign Languages Press, 1960), pp. 33–37.

61. Hsin Wu, "Tui chih-ts'an chieh-chi kuan-yu kuo-chia lin-tu wen-t'i ti p'i-p'an" (A Critique of the Bourgeois International Law Concerning the Question of States Territory), *KCWTYC*, no. 7 (1960): 42.

62. See A. Doak Barnett, *Communist China and Asia: Challenge to American Policy* (New York: Harper, 1960), p. 78; Samuel S. Kim, *China, The United Nations, and World Order* (Princeton: Princeton University Press, 1979), p. 44; Harold C. Hinton, *The Bear at the Gate*, p. 11.

63. Ying, "Recognizing the True Face," p. 42.

64. Shih Sung, Yu Ta-hsin, Lu Ying-lui, and Tsao K'o, "An Initial Investigation into the Old Viewpoint in the Teaching of International Law," *Chiao-hsueh yu yen-chiu* (Teaching and Research), no. 4 (1958): 14. To the Western scholars, modern international law and international law are synonymous. To the Chinese writers, modern (*hsien-tai*) international law is opposed to bourgeois international law. For this terminology and dichotomy see K'ung, "A Critique of Bourgeois International Law," p. 53.

65. Shih Sung et al., "An Initial Investigation," p. 14.

66. Ibid.

67. Ibid.

68. For the discussion of equal treaties, see Chapter 5 of this book.

69. See "Report on the Question of the Boundary Line Between China and Burma by Chou En-lai, Premier and Foreign Minister, at the Fourth Session of the First National People's Congress, July 9, 1957," in *Important Documents*, pp. 16–27; and the Sino-Burmese Boundary Treaty of 1960, *PR* 3, no. 4 (October 4, 1960): 33–34. For an historical analysis of the Namwan Assigned Tract, see J.J.G. Syatauw, *Some Newly Established Asian States and the Development of International Law* (The Hague: Martinus Nijhoff, 1961), Ch. 3.

70. *China Yearbook 1975; Selected Works of Mao Tse-tung* 4: 401–2.

71. Preamble of the Constitution of the PRC, 1954. English text in Theodore H. E.

Chen, ed., *The Chinese Communist Regime, Documents and Commentary* (New York: Praeger, 1967), pp. 75–76.

72. Ying, "Recognizing the True Face," p. 44.

73. K'ung, "A Critique of the Bourgeois International Law," p. 45.

74. A noted jurist in the PRC, Keng-sheng Chou, criticized the Sino-American treaty of commerce in 1946 violating the principle of state equality in international law because it allowed the U.S. to exploit China economically, see his "Ts'ung kuo-chi-fa nun ho-p'ien kung-ch'u ti yuan-tse" (On the Principle of Peaceful Coexistence in International Law), in *CFYC*, no. 6 (1955): 41. The 1965 Sino-American Agreement on the status of United States Armed Forces in the Republic of China, which bestowed certain privileges on the U.S. armed forces in Taiwan, was severely criticized by Communist China as a treaty between the strong and the weak. Text of the treaty in *United States Treaties and Other International Agreements* (Washington, D.C.: Government Printing Office, 1967), vol. 17, p. 373; China's critique, for example, in "U.S.-Chiang Illegally Signed 'Status Agreement' Concerning U.S. Force of Aggression," *People's Daily*, September 13, 1965, p. 2; citations see Chiu Hungdah, "Comparison of the Nationalist and Communist Chinese view of Unequal Treaties," in Jerome A. Cohen, ed., *China's Practice of International Law: Some Case Studies* (Cambridge: Harvard University Press, 1972), p. 261, 93.

75. Regarding the Five Principles of Peaceful Coexistence as the Chinese basic border policy, see Chapter 3 of this book.

76. K'ung, "A Critique of the Bourgeois International Law," p. 49.

77. Barnard Ramundo, *Peaceful Coexistence* (Baltimore: Johns Hopkins University Press, 1967), p.23.

78. See Chiu's analysis in his "Communist China's Attitude," p. 267.

79. Ho and Ma, "A Critique of Ch'en T'i-ch'ien's" p. 36.

80. Ibid.

81. Chu Li-lu, "Refute the Absurd Theory."

82. Tao-tai Hsia, "Chinese Legal Publications: An Appraisal," in Jerome A. Cohen, ed., *Contemporary Chinese Law: Research Problems and Perspectives* (Cambridge: Harvard University Press, 1970), pp. 57, 60–63.

83. Ho and Ma, "A Critique of Ch'en T'i-ch'ien's" Reactionary Viewpoint, p. 37.

84. *CFYC*, no. 1 (1955): 66.

85. *CFYC*, no. 1 (1962): 49.

86. This is the official policy of the Institute of Law of China Academy of Sciences. It was declared by the Deputy Director, Chou Hsin-min, see Tao-tai Hsia, "Chinese Legal Publications," p. 51.

87. *CFYC*, no. 1 (1962): 48.

88. Wei Liang wrote: "Another reason of India's insisting on the so-called McMahon Line [as the ideal Sino-Indian boundary line] is that this line possesses its 'merits'; that is, it has been drawn along the watershed. This saying is also untenable. This watershed is within the Chinese territory.... If China relying upon the same reason requested the Indian Brahmaputra River as the [ideal] Sino-Indian boundary line, would India accept this request because of its 'merits'?" See his "Ts'ung kuo-chi-fa chueh-tu kan shu-wei McMahon hsien" (From the Angle of International Law to look at the So-called McMahon Line), *KCWTYC*, no. 6 (1959): 47–52 and 24. In 1959, China sent a note to India indicating that "it is particularly impermissible to use the watershed as a pretext for seeking a boundary line within the territory of another country." English text of the note

in *The Sino-Indian Boundary Question*, enlarged ed. (Peking: Foreign Languages Press, 1962), p. 68; also in *White Paper* 3: 66.

89. According to the Editorial Note in 1955, the members of the Editorial Committee had their incumbent positions in various government agencies. Total members including chairman and vice-chairman were 26. Two of them were employees of the Ministry of Foreign Affairs; three, of the China Political Science and Law Association; seven, of colleges or universities; three, of the State Council; two of the Supreme People's Procuracy; one each, of the National People's Congress, Chinese People's Political Consultative Conference, Chinese People's Institute of Foreign Affairs, Law Press, Ministry of Justice, the Supreme Court and Ministry of Public Security, see *CFYC*, no. 1 (1955): 66.

90. "Ch'ung-kuo cheng-chih fa-lu hsueh-hui kung-tso pao-kao" (Working Report of the China Political Science and Law Association), *CFYC*, no. 2 (1956): 2.

91. *CFYC*, no. 1 (1962): 49.

92. James L. Brierly observed that new states "are inclined to look at international law as an alien system which the Western nations, whose moral or intellectual leadership they no longer recognize, are trying to impose upon them, and in effect they have begun to claim the right to select from among its rules only those which suit their interests." See his *The Law of Nations*, 6th ed. (London: Oxford University Press, 1963), p. 43.

3

BORDER POLICY

INTRODUCTION

The traditional Chinese world order was hierarchical, not equalitarian. The relationship between the Chinese empires and their neighbors was in general based on a tribute system wherein China received payment protection from her neighbors when she was strong.[1] There were frontiers between China and her neighbors but no boundary lines, only the maintenance of the then-existing tribute system. Based on this relationship, it was unthinkable that China would sign a boundary treaty with a tributary (tribute payer) which would place them on equal terms.

The problem of precise boundaries first developed with a challenge by Russia in 1689 and later by some big powers in the nineteenth century. After the middle of the nineteenth century, a weak China continued to employ a border policy trying to deter the big powers from territorial expansion.

On the mainland, the Republic of China (1911–1949) faced a series of domestic and international problems. She was unable and had no time to form a general border policy. Even though the Political Program of the Nationalist government was promulgated for defining some of her uncertain boundaries, it was never implemented.[2]

After 1949, the PRC realized that undefined boundaries with several neighboring countries were giving rise to boundary disputes and "imperialists" engaging in subversive activities in China. She wanted above all to settle her boundary questions with all her neighbors. During the next two decades after the establishment of the PRC, a general border policy based upon the national interests and the reality of international politics was forced and put into practice.

This chapter analyzes the PRC's border situations which gave rise to the formation of a general border policy, its implementation, and its significance in international law.

THE SOUTHWESTERN BORDER

Chaos on the Borders: The Need for Border Policy

Sino-Burmese Border Situation. The Sino-Burmese border situation in the early 1950s was in chaos, caused by the intrusion of Nationalist troops, the influx of refugees into Burma, the Khamba revolt in eastern Tibet, and the movement of minorities across the border.

After the Nationalist government collapsed on the mainland in 1949, some defeated troops moved toward the southwestern provinces of China. A group of several thousand troops under General Li Mi entered Burma in mid-1950 where they built bases and launched an offensive into the Yunnan Province of China.[3] This province borders on the Shan and the Wu states of Burma and the boundary in this area had been disputed.

At the end of that year, Li flew to Taiwan.[4] This confirmed that Li's troops were supported by the Nationalist government in Taiwan, and Peking was afraid that Li would continue to cause troubles along the Sino-Burmese border. In 1953, Burma took the issue to the United Nations. Under the auspices of the United Nations, some 7,000 of Li's troops and their dependents were withdrawn to Taiwan in 1954. However, there were still some troops remaining in the vicinity of the border between Burma and Thailand.[5]

Following the withdrawal of the Nationalist government from the mainland, many Chinese refugees flowed from Yunnan into Burma. After 1949, the influx of refugees increased yearly, and the Burmese worried that their social order would be disturbed by the Chinese refugees. The Chinese were also concerned. From their point of view, the refugees could be organized and sent back to Yunnan for subversive activities by the Nationalists and the United States.[6]

The refugees and General Li's troops were not the only threats to the border security of the PRC. Since 1955, the Khamba revolt against Chinese authority in eastern Tibet added salt to the wound. The fighting was fierce and later on extended to other parts of Tibet. Peking seriously worried about possible aid to the Khambas from outside sources. The aid could pass through the northern part of the Sino-Burmese border, which was in dispute. It is the nearest access from outside to the area in which the fighting took place. In 1966, it was reported that Chinese troops had invaded Burma.[7] The Chinese might have suspected that the Khambas had used Burma as a shelter, but no result was announced.

The minorities living along the Sino-Burmese border—the Kachins and the Shans—were another threat to the security of China's border. In Yunnan, an autonomous area for minority peoples had been established in 1953. After that the Ministry of National Defense of the PRC (not the local government) began to woo the Kachins and the Shans on the Burmese side of the border. The Burmese took counteraction by calling a special conference with Kachin leaders in Kachin state.[8] The Chinese then feared that if the Kachins in Burma took a hostile position to China, the Kachins in China would cooperate with them.

China also suspected the United States of encouraging the minorities to commit subversive acts. Reports in 1950 pointed out that Chinese troops entered the Kachin states for a short time, ostensibly to see if the United States was building an air base there.[9] Chou En-lai, prime minister and foreign minister, remarked in 1957 that "in recent years the forces of imperialism have constantly used the boundary question between China and Burma to sow discord between the two countries in an attempt to create a tense situation."[10] Chou also pointed out that China wanted to settle outstanding questions with her neighbors through peaceful means.[11]

The Sino-Indian Border Situation. The Sino-Indian border situation in the 1950s and the early 1960s was even worse than that of the Sino-Burmese border. It was complicated by India's objection to the Chinese marching into Tibet, the Indian establishment of administrative centers in the Himalayas, the Khamba revolt, the moving of the Chinese and Indian military forces to the frontiers, and the Chinese construction of roads across the Aksai Chin Plateau. It soon became evident that the two countries could not avoid a large-scale armed clash in 1962.

The dispute began in 1950, when the Chinese People's Liberation Army was entering Tibet. The government of India accused China of action deplorable and contrary to the interests of peace.[12] Indian Prime Minister Nehru addressed the Indian Parliament on December 7, 1950, saying that "the last voice in regard to Tibet should be the voice of the people of Tibet and nobody else."[13] For the Indians, Tibet was an independent country[14] not a region of China.[15] They never recognized China's sovereignty in Tibet before 1954.[16]

For the Chinese, Tibet was always a part of China.[17] Thus, Peking was furious about India's policy. A note to New Delhi said: "Tibet is an integral part of Chinese territory and the problem of Tibet is entirely a domestic problem of China. The Chinese People's Liberation Army must enter Tibet, liberate the Tibetan people and defend the frontier of China."[18]

Moreover, the Indians asserted that they had inherited certain rights in Tibet from the British.[19] These rights included extraterritoriality and the stationing of troops. India continued the British policy toward Tibet—to make it a buffer zone between China and India, and to prevent China from exercising authority there. After independence, India retained the last British political representative, Hugh E. Richardson, in Lhasa. The British mission in Lhasa was turned into the Indian mission, the existing staff was retained in its entirety and the only change was that of the flag.[20]

As early as 1949, when China was fighting her civil war, the Tibetans expelled from Lhasa the Republic of China's Amban (representative of the Central government). It was suspected that the Indian representative in Lhasa had been behind this expulsion.[21] India, then seizing the opportunity of China's absence, delivered arms and ammunition to Tibet and sent high-ranking military officers to help the Tibetans build up their own military forces.[22] At the same time, the government of India also supplied small arms to the government of Burma.[23]

The Nehru government also set up administrative centers in the Himalayas.[24] In February 1951, the Northeastern Border Defense Committee was established. Later in 1953, the committee recommended the extension of administration in the North East Frontier Agency (NEFA).[25] That same year, an Indian official with an escort and several hundred porters moved into Tawang,[26] a place south of the Himalayan crest, which had been an important center of Tibetan administration. Although the Tibetans requested that New Delhi withdraw her forces immediately, the Indian government ignored the request.[27]

The border tension increased when the Khamba revolt began in 1955 in eastern Tibet. The revolt spread into central and southern Tibet and by early 1959 had become a much wider insurrection. In March 1959, fighting also broke out in Lhasa causing thousands of refugees to cross the border into India. The Dalai Lama, spiritual and political leader of Tibet, fled Lhasa and arrived in India, where he received an "impressive welcome" and held talks with Nehru.[28] In order to prevent the rebels from crossing the border for sanctuary, and to cut off the influx of refugees, China pushed her troops close to the border. The Indians responded, pushing their outposts right up to the McMahon Line, and in some places beyond it.[29]

Since both China and India sent troops to the frontier, conflict was inevitable. On August 25, 1959, Indian troops intruded south of Migyitun, a small village north of the McMahon Line, and fired on Chinese border guards. China's border guards fired back. Both China and India protested and accused the other side of firing first. India accused China of "deliberate aggression" in an attempt to occupy India's territory by force and warned that her forces on the Indian frontier posts had been ordered to "use force on the trespassers if necessary."[30] China accused Indian troops of violating Chinese territory and warned India to stop armed provocation, "otherwise the Indian side must be held responsible for all the serious consequences arising therefrom."[31]

The Khamba revolt jeopardized Chinese communication with Tibet from the east. The alternate way of approaching the west of Tibet is from Sinkiang Province across the Aksai Chin Plateau. In 1956 and 1957, China built roads linking Sinkiang and Tibet across the Aksai Chin Plateau, and area also claimed by India.[32]

After learning of the existence of the new roadways from a Chinese map published in July 1958, the government of India decided to set up border posts and sent forward patrolling forces there. A patrolling force of about 70 men came into contact with the Chinese at the Kongka Pass, which lies on the junction between Tibet, Sinkiang, and Ladakh. The Chinese regarded Kongka Pass as the boundary and had already established a post there. Three men of the Indian patrolling force were detained by the Chinese on October 20, 1959. On the next day, gun fire was exchanged. Nine of the Indian patrolling force were killed and ten were taken prisoners. The Chinese also suffered casualties.[33]

The border situation since 1959 went from bad to worse. India continually strengthened her military force in NEFA and, in the following year, began to build roads from Kashmir to Ladakh.[34] India also bought transport aircrafts and high altitude helicopters from the United States[35] and began to buy similar military equipment from the Soviet Union.[36] In the spring of 1961, Indian troops began to move forward in the Ladakh and the Aksai Chin areas. By the autumn of 1962, they had established a total of 43 posts on territory claimed by China.[37] In 1961, China warned India that if she continued her forward movements in Aksai Chin, China would attack south of the McMahon Line.[38]

During 1962, incidents continually increased. On June 6, India accused Chinese troops of intruding into Indian territory.[39] On July 10, the Indian government accused Chinese troops of surrounding an Indian outpost in Aksai Chin.[40] On July 21, Chinese troops fired on an Indian patrol for the first time since 1959.[41] On August 4, China accused Indian troops of crossing the McMahon Line.[42] On September 15, a fairly serious clash occurred near the western end of the McMahon Line.[43] During the next few weeks, other clashes also occurred there.[44]

On October 20, Chinese troops launched a major offensive at several points along the entire border. In the eastern sector, Chinese troops pushed forward to the south of the McMahon Line. This offensive lasted about four days but did not penetrate beyond the territory the Chinese claimed.[45] On October 24, China proposed a cease-fire, asking each side to withdraw 20 kilometers (approximately 12.4 miles) from the "line of actual control."[46] The "line of actual control" was later explained by China as the line controlled by both sides before November 1959; namely, India would stay south of the McMahon Line, and China would stay in the Aksai Chin Plateau. This proposal was rejected by India.[47]

On November 14, Indian troops attacked a commanding hill held by the Chinese.[48] On November 16, Chinese troops launched another major offensive. Fierce fighting followed,[49] and on November 20, there was no organized Indian military force left in the frontier area; the Chinese victory was complete.[50]

On November 21, China repeated her proposal of October 24, and announced unilaterally that her frontier guards would cease fire the next day and withdraw 20 kilometers behind the line controlled before November 1959.[51] The Chinese withdrawal began on December 1 and continued roughly on schedule.[52]

In the border clashes, the Chinese used three divisions of troops and three to four hundred men were killed. Indian forces numbered about 25 battalions, equivalent to just under three normal infantry divisions. The Defense Ministry of India in 1965 released figures showing the loss of more than 7,000 men: 1,383 had been killed; 1,696 missing; and 3,986 captured.[53]

The Border Situation and "Imperialist" Activities. The PRC believed that her regime had seriously suffered from "imperialist" hostility and that the United States had played a leading role. Washington in fact disliked the Communist regime in China and took an inimical attitude toward it. Thus, Peking believed that the United States was particularly using the chaos of her border situation to engage in subversive activities and create an anticommunist force.[54]

As early as 1950, when the Chinese Liberation Army was entering Tibet, China suspected the United States of urging India to protest.[55] The Ministry of Foreign Affairs therefore warned that China had "to prevent imperialism from invading even one inch of the territory of the fatherland, and to safeguard and build up the frontier regions of the country."[56] In the following year, the agreement between the Chinese Central People's government and the Tibetan government on the administration of Tibet emphasized that they would "unite and drive out the imperialist aggressive force" from Tibet.[57]

In 1955, a Chinese writer openly accused the United States of hostile acts: "It is the official policy of the United States to overthrow foreign governments which are not to its taste by espionage, sabotage, subversion, and other violent means."[58]

The suspicion that the United States was assisting the Tibetans against China was not her imagination. In Kalimpong (a small Indian town near Tibet), there circulated copies of a booklet on top-secret military briefings for U.S. troops in Tibet and plans for the escape of the Dalai Lama's brother, Takser Rimpoche, via India to the United States in July 1951.[59] Later on, more literature was published showing that the United States had supported and trained the Tibetans to resist the Chinese Liberation Army. Colonel Fletcher Prouty, who helped organize the U.S. Special Operations Force said:

> We knew the Chinese were eventually going to come to Tibet. So we started recruiting a resistance force among the natives. Up to 42,000 Tibetans were put under arms. We flew groups of tribesmen from Tibet to Spain and from there to the Rocky Mountains in Colorado where the atmosphere is similar to the Himalayas, for combat training. In six weeks they are [sic] back in Tibet, and a fairly good ground force was built up.[60]

Concerning U.S. logistic support, it was reported that

> Since 1949, the U.S. . . . has used Indian, Burmese, Laotian, Thai, Nepalese and Pakistani territory as staging areas for clandestine operations against China. . . .
> According to knowledgeable sources, the Central Intelligence Agency provided logistic support for the Dali Lama's escape from Tibet, using STOL (short takeoff and landing) aircraft based in India and it also supported tribal revolt in Tibet.[61]

When the Khamba rebellion was breaking out in 1955, Chinese uneasiness and distrust of the United States increased. Thousands of refugees fled to India to be trained by the "imperialists" and sent back to Tibet for "antirevolutionary" activities. China's worry was expressed in a 1961 publication of the Chinese Military Affairs Commission of the Central Authorities, which indicated:

In Kansu, Chinghai, Szechwan, Tibet, and Yunnan, and in some other places armed rebels ... have already been reduced to submission.... The counterrevolutionaries outside were still in communication with those inside, and there is in some places the danger of repeated uprising and new uprisings. In addition, rebels who had escaped abroad may return for further action....

Regarding bandits returning from abroad to fight, we must also strictly observe the principles contained in the Southwest Region Border Defense Regulations.[62]

It was reported that the United States indirectly delivered supplies by aircraft to the Khambas. Those airdrops were arranged by radio links between Taiwan and the Nationalist forces in Tibet. To enter Tibet, the aircraft usually flew over the northwest of Burma and the northeast of India. When India's Defense Minister Krishna Menon protested the flying of Chinese airplanes over the NEFA,[63] Chou En-lai told Nehru that the airplanes flying over the NEFA of India were American.[64] Chou publically declared that they "took off from Bangkok, passed over Burma or China and crossed the Chinese-Indian border or penetrate [sic] deep into China's interior where they parachuted weapons, supplies, and wireless sets to secret agents and then flew back to Bangkok."[65]

China also told the Burmese government that the aircraft belonged to the United States and that Burmese could shoot any unidentified aircraft down or force it to land. The Burmese did shoot down one airplane which proved to belong to the Nationalist government in Taiwan.[66]

Peking also complained about the U.S. use of Kalimpong as a base to carry out subversive and disruptive activities against China's Tibetan region. Chou En-lai personally complained to Nehru concerning this matter in 1953. He pointed out that Kalimpong had been used "as an international base by the United States and others to undermine Chinese influence in Tibet."[67] Later, on July 10, 1958, a note given by China to the Indian Counselor in Peking complained of the "imperialists' operations" in Kalimpong:

> Using Kalimpong as a base they are actively inciting and organizing a handful of reactionaries hidden in Tibet for an armed revolt there in order to attain the traitorous aim of separating the Tibet region from the People's Republic of China. . . . The Chinese Government regards the criminal activities of the above-said reactionaries and special agents as a direct threat to China's territorial integrity and sovereignty and yet another malicious scheme of United States imperialists to create tension in Asia and Africa.[68]

In spite of these protests, the Indian government denied that there had been any foreign activity in Kalimpong.[69]

The Formation and Practices of a Good Neighbor Policy

When forming a good neighbor policy, national security had to be China's primary consideration. Facing the hostility of the United States, Peking felt very unsafe, especially after the outbreak of the Korean War in 1950. Washington, using its military forces, not only threatened to invade Manchuria but also undertook operations along China's coast.[70] More important, as we have seen, the United States supported Chinese dissident forces engaging in internal subversive activities with the cooperation of China's neighboring countries. Worried about the spread of communism, neighboring countries were also hostile toward the Communist regime in China.

Reacting to the U.S. inimical actions, the PRC felt it important to woo neighboring countries. Cadres in the Ministry of Foreign Affairs must have been familiar with Mao's theory of united front tactics which "requires recruiting larger forces for the purposes of surrounding and annihilating the enemy."[71] In foreign relations, it would mean that a friendly or neutral neighbor would be helpful for stabilizing the border situation and for preventing the influence of "imperialism" along China's frontier. This idea was revealed by a Chinese document; Peking decided together with Lhasa that "there will be peaceful coexistence with neighboring countries and the establishment and development of fair commercial and trading relations with them on the basis of equality, mutual benefit, and mutual respect for territory and sovereignty."[72]

The good neighbor policy was first put into practice toward India. In September 1951, Chou En-lai, prime minister and foreign minister, suggested to the Indian ambassador in Peking that the question of the stabilization of the Tibetan frontier should be taken up as early as possible.[73] In July 1952, Chou formally proposed a settlement of "pending specific problems" arising from India's inherent rights in Tibet and a discussion of commercial intercourse, trade, and the treatment of India nationals.[74] India agreed, and in September 1953, the government of India approached Peking for negotiations regarding the outstanding questions concerning Tibet.[75]

The conference, held in Peking, commenced on December 31, 1953. Intended for the promotion of trade and pilgrimage, the conference preferred not to discuss the boundary question at that time.[76] After four months, an agreement on trade and intercourse between "the Tibet region of China" and India was signed.[77] India gave up all extraterritorial rights that the British government had exercised in Tibet since 1914 and handed over the Indian post and telegraph facilities to China. The Indian military escorts were withdrawn thereafter. The central provisions of the agreement dealt with the regulations of trade markets, routes, and procedures for traders and pilgrims. The preamble to the agreement contains the well-known Five Principles, which supposedly bound the two countries. They are:

1. mutual respect for each other's territorial integrity and sovereignty,
2. mutual nonaggression,
3. mutual noninterference in each other's internal affairs,
4. equality and mutual benefit, and
5. peaceful coexistence.

After the outbreak of the Khamba revolt in eastern Tibet in 1955 and its extension into central and western Tibet in 1957 and 1958, the Indians worried about the situations on the border. The Chinese too were concerned that the disputed uncontrolled nature of the Sino-Indian frontier seemed to offer an opportunity for assistance by other countries to the Tibetan insurgents.[78] China suggested settling the boundary question through negotiations.[79] However, India insisted that the Sino-Indian boundary was "well-known and fixed."[80] Since the two countries held quite different positions toward their boundary question, they had never agreed to sit at a negotiation table to settle the question.

Besides India, Burma was another important neighbor with which the PRC wanted to have good relations and a settled boundary. Peking's motive was made clear by Chou En-lai, when he said that a friendly Burma could prevent the United States from sowing seeds of disharmony between the Chinese and the Burmese.[81] For this reason, Chou, following the close of the Geneva Conference in June 1954, visited India and Burma, where he had talks with Nehru and Burmese Prime Minister U Nu. They issued joint communiques, emphasizing that relations between China and these two countries would be based on the Five Principles.[82]

After the outbreak of the Khamba revolt in eastern Tibet, China was more anxious to woo Burma and settle the boundary question with her. Chou took the initiative, putting forward a "fair and reasonable proposal."[83] He claimed to be in a "spirit of mutual understanding and mutual accommodation" for negotiating a boundary settlement with Burma.[84] In January 1960, they signed a treaty of friendship and mutual nonaggression;[85] in October, a boundary treaty was signed based on the spirit of the Five Principles.[86]

China's good neighbor policy toward Burma had two purposes. First, China wanted the stabilization of the Sino-Burmese border. After concluding the treaty of friendship and nonaggression, an editorial in the *People's Daily* pointed out that the purpose of this treaty was, inter alia, to prevent U.S. influence in southeastern Asia and to tranquilize the Chinese frontier.[87]

The second purpose was that China wanted to use the Sino-Burmese Boundary Treaty in a diplomatic campaign to press India to settle the Sino-Indian boundary question. After the exchanges of artillery between Chinese and Indian soldiers in 1959 in Lonju and on the Kongka Pass, China's need for settling her boundary with India became more perceptible. An editorial in the *People's Daily* noted that "the agreement concluded between China and Burma on the boundary question provides an excellent example for Asian countries seeking reasonable settlement of their boundary disputes." The editorial then asked, "Why can't things which have happened between China and Burma also take place between China and other Asian countries . . . ?"[88]

Indeed, for the first time in Chinese history, Peking wanted to define China's boundaries with all neighboring countries. To accomplish this goal, Chou En-lai insisted that China had no territorial ambitions and wanted only to maintain the status quo pending a joint settlement of all boundaries. He said:

We respect each other's sovereignty and territorial integrity. We will adhere to this principle.... As to respect for territorial integrity, it is stated that China will not and should not have any demand for territory. We have common borders with four [sic] countries. With some of these countries we have not yet finally fixed our border line and we are ready to do so....

But before doing so, we are willing to maintain the present situation by acknowledging that parts of our border are . . . undetermined. We are ready to restrain our government and people from crossing even one step across our border.[89]

Years later, Chinese boundary treaties proved Chou's sincerity. China did not demand any "lost territory" from neighbors. In one case, she even gave up sovereignty over the Namwan Assigned Tract to Burma in exchange for three small villages. The details of China's boundary negotiations with her neighbors will be analyzed in the next chapter of this book.

The Five Principles of Peaceful Coexistence, first proclaimed in 1954, became the essence of China's good neighbor policy. Peking successfully inserted them in most treaties with her neighboring countries and maintained good relations with them. For example, the following treaties, communiques, and joint statements between China and her neighbors all contain reference to the Five Principles of Peaceful Coexistence:

1. China and Afghanistan: Treaty of Friendship and Mutual Non-aggression, August 26, 1960;[90] Boundary Treaty, November 22, 1963.[91]
2. China and Burma: Joint Statement by the Prime Ministers of China and Burma, Mr. Chou En-lai and Mr. U Nu, June 20, 1954;[92] Treaty of Friendship and Mutual Non-Aggression, January 28, 1960;[93] Agreement on the Question of Boundary, January 28, 1960;[94] Joint Communique on April 19, 1960;[95] Boundary Treaty, October 1, 1960.[96]
3. China and Cambodia: Joint Statement signed by Premier Chou En-lai and Premier Prince Norodom Sihanouk, August 24, 1958;[97] Treaty of Friendship and Mutual Non-Aggression, December 19, 1960;[98] Joint Communique of Chairman Liu Shao-ch'i and Prince Norodom Sihanouk, February 27, 1963.[99]
4. China and India: Communique on Talks between Nehru and Chou En-lai, June 28, 1954.[100]
5. China and Nepal: Agreement on the Normalization of Diplomatic Relations, August 11, 1955;[101] Treaty between the PRC and the Kingdom of Nepal, September 20, 1956;[102] Agreement on Chinese Economic Assistance to Nepal, October 7, 1956;[103] Agreement on the Question of the Boundary, March 21, 1960;[104] Treaty of Peace and Friendship, April 28, 1960;[105] Boundary Treaty, October 5, 1961.[106]
6. China and Pakistan: Boundary Agreement, March 2, 1963;[107] This agreement contains the Ten Principles in the Final Communique of the Bandung Conference, 1955. These Ten Principles were enriched and suggested by Chou En-lai based on the Five Principles, and adopted by the Bandung Conference.[108]

Consequently, Peking saw any unfriendly action or conflict as a violation of the Five Principles of Peaceful Coexistence. An Indian incident illustrates this point. When Indian troops invaded the Chinese-claimed territories of Migyitun, Samgar, and Sanpo in 1959, Peking let India know on June 23, shortly after the incident, that such intrusions "constitute grave encroachment on China's sovereignty and flagrant interference in China's internal affairs and are completely against the Five Principles of Peaceful Coexistence jointly initiated by China and India."[109]

It appears that China's good neighbor policy toward her southwestern neighbors since 1951 was generally successful. Except for India, the PRC had successfully settled boundary questions with all neighbors and thereafter maintained good relations with them.

THE FIVE PRINCIPLES OF PEACEFUL COEXISTENCE AND INTERNATIONAL LAW

Treaties are an important source of international law[110] and the PRC has endeavored to insert the Five Principles of Peaceful Coexistence in treaties with her neighbors. To gear the Five Principles to international law, the Chinese jurists explored the legal basis of the Five Principles. They believed that the Five Principles provided "the basic condition for the maintenance and development of modern international law,"[111] and were therefore the essence of "modern international law."[112] One writer had more to say: "The Five Principles of Peaceful Coexistence have replaced many of the old corrupt concepts of international law which served the interests of imperialism; they have become new elements of international law."[113]

However, the Five Principles were also said to share much in common with international law. Thus, according to the same author, the Five Principles of Peaceful Coexistence were by no means new. "The Five Principles of Peaceful Coexistence are collections of all the existing principles of international law, regarding living together in peace."[114] For tracing the roots of the Five Principles in international law, a noted jurist, Chou Ken-sheng, published an authoritative article in 1955.[115] Coincidently, in the same year, an Indian professor, C. J. Chacko, also traced the sources of the Five Principles of Peaceful Coexistence.[116]

Both Chou and Chacko pointed out that the principle of respect for territorial integrity and the respect for sovereignty can also be found in Article 2 of the UN Charter, and that organization "is based on the principle of sovereign equality of all its members."[117] But Chou went even further. He pointed out that any country using armed force to obstruct the recovery or unification of another country's territory or using other means to promote the division of another's country's territory is in violation of that country's territorial integrity.[118] This statement implied that the United States was to blame for the PRC's failure to "liberate" Taiwan, and also for subversive acts on the Chinese mainland.

Concerning the principle of mutual nonaggression, Chou pointed out that aggression is not only against Article 39 of the Charter of the United Nations, but also violates the Paris Pact of 1928, and the resolution of the Pan-American Conference of 1928. The Nuremburg and Tokyo International Military Tribunals declared aggressive war on "international crime." The Charter of the United Nations, in addition to affirming the illegality of aggression, further provides for measures of sanction against aggression. However, the UN Charter does not give a definition of aggression. The definition, Chou noted, can be found elsewhere. The 1933 London Convention for the Definition of Aggression, the proposals of the Soviet Union regarding the definition of aggression to the UN General Assembly in 1950, and the proposals of the Soviet Union in 1953 to the UN Special Committee for the definition of aggression, all provide a definition of aggression.[119]

Professor Chacko pointed out that Article 33 of the UN Charter was the foundation of mutual nonaggression, the second principle of the *Pancha Shila* (peaceful coexistence in the Indian language). He wrote:

> This Article includes the Articles for the Pacific Settlement of International Disputes incorporated in the Hague Convention of 1899 and 1907 as well as the provisions of the Paris Pact of 1928 for the outlawry of war as an instrument of national policy. The second principle of the Pancha Shila, "non-aggression," appears to be inherent in these instruments for the pacific settlement of international disputes.[120]

Both Chou and Chacko agreed that the third principle of the Five Principles of Peaceful Coexistence, noninterference in each other's internal affairs, is also recognized by Article 2 of the UN Charter.[121]

The fourth principle, equality and mutual benefit, is an important condition for promoting internal peace. Chou pointed out that equality of states is not only a traditional principle of international law, but also a fundamental principle, stressed by Article 2 of the UN Charter.[122] Chacko held the same view.[123]

Regarding the fifth principle, peaceful coexistence, Chou wrote that as early as 1928, the Paris Pact obliged signatories not to use war as an instrument of national policy or as a means for settling international disputes. Moreover, the purpose and principle of the UN Charter was to eliminate international war.[124]

Chacko also pointed out that "the main objective of peaceful coexistence is not only to put an end to the 'cold war' of today, but also to save humanity from another war." He then cited the Preamble of the UN Charter to support his view.

> Peaceful coexistence implies the acceptance and observance of a policy of mutual tolerance, since without it, any scheme of "live and let live" cannot be realistic. This point is already enshrined in the Preamble of the UN Charter, which stipulates that its signatories are determined . . . to practice tolerance and live in peace with one another as good neighbors.[125]

The two scholars, Chou and Chacko, demonstrated that the Five Principles of Peaceful Coexistence derive not just from treaties and the Charter of the

United Nations, but also from customs and proposals. According to Chou, "The Five Principles of Peaceful Coexistence should be considered fully consistent with the principles of international law and with the development of modern international law."[126]

THE NORTHERN BORDER

The Situation on the Border

On the Chinese northern border, the Mongolian People's Republic, and North Korea, had no serious border problems with China, but the Soviets did. Territorial expansion toward the Far East had been a century-old policy with Russia.[127] Even after the establishment of a Communist regime in China, the Sino-Soviet border was far from quiet. On the border between China's Sinkiang Province and the Soviet Union, the Soviets agitated among the Chinese minorities for incorporation into the Soviet Union. The Chinese charged that: "In April and May 1962 the leaders of the CPSU used their . . . personnel in Sinkiang, China, to carry out large-scale subversive activities in the Ili region and . . . coerced several tens of thousands of Chinese citizens into going to the Soviet Union."[128]

In Sinkiang Province of China, there are approximately six million Uighurs, Kazakhs, Kirghiz, and other non-Han minorities who have ethnic ties with those living in the Soviet Union close to the Sino-Soviet border.[129] Some of these minorities openly expressed their sympathy with the Soviet people,[130] and some served in the Chinese People's Liberation Army while holding citizenship in the Soviet Union.[131] Later, in 1970, it was reported that a Free Turkestan Movement in open collaboration with Soviet authorities, calling for the "liberation" of Sinkiang, was set up in neighboring Kazakhstan. The PRC finally closed the Soviet consulates in three districts in Sinkiang's Ili Chou. In some areas, China sealed off the Sino-Soviet border.[132]

In China's Inner Mongolia, approximately three million Mongolians belong to the same stock living in the Mongolian People's Republic (Outer Mongolia).[133] In 1950, an allegedly Soviet-supported Inner Mongolia People's Revolutionary Party was reported to be active and gaining strength.[134] In May 1950, the People's government of the Inner Mongolian Autonomous Region of China had to be moved to Chang-chia-k'ou from Huhehot because of the aforementioned party's activities. In 1954, Peking finally outlawed that party, apparently because of its secret ties with the Soviets.[135]

The Soviet activities in Manchuria also increased Chinese anxiety. As early a July 1949, Moscow signed a trade agreement directly with the party leader in Manchuria, Kao Kang. This deal exposed Soviet ambitions in Manchuria. The Chinese cannot forget the Soviets tried to separate Sinkiang Province from China by signing a series of agreements with the Sinkiang government during the 1930s and the 1940s. Now, the Soviets again signed an agreement directly with Manchuria. To eliminate the "independent kingdom," Mao purged Kao Kang in

1954 along with the organization chief of the Chinese Communist Party, Jao Shu-shih.

On the other hand, the Soviets accused the Chinese of violating the Soviet border near Manchuria. They said: "Since 1960, Chinese servicemen and civilians have been systematically violating the Soviet border. In 1962 alone more than 5,000 violations were recorded. Attempts are even being made to arbitrarily "take over" some pieces of Soviet territory."[136] The border dispute in this area developed into a large-scale armed conflict in 1969 and caused hundreds of casualties on both sides.

Applying the Five Principles of Peaceful Coexistence to the Socialist States

China, after the proclamation of the Five Principles of Peaceful Coexistence in April 1954, attempted to apply them to her relations with the socialist states. Among them, the Soviet Union was China's main object. Peking hoped that those principles would help her stabilize the situations on the borders and prevent the Soviets' influence in Sinkiang, Inner Mongolia, and Manchuria. However, the Soviets did not accept China's suggestion. The Soviets insisted that the relationships among socialist states should be guided solely by proletarian internationalism.

Moscow implied that the Five Principles would apply to nonsocialist countries only. In Peking on October 11, 1954, in a joint declaration, Mao and Khrushchev proclaimed that the two countries "will continue to build their relations with countries in Asia and the Pacific, as well as with other countries on the basis of the Five Principles of Peaceful Coexistence."[137] Khrushchev in his report to the Twentieth Party Congress of the Communist Party of the Soviet Union in 1954 stated that the Five Principles were to apply only "between the two systems" but he did not mention the Five Principles adjusting the relations among socialist countries.[138]

In 1956, after the uprising in Hungary and Poland, Moscow issued "The Foundation of the Development and Further Strengthening of Friendship and Cooperation between the Soviet Union and other Socialist States," in which the Soviets implied that the Five Principles could be added to proletarian internationalism, but they did not use the exact terms of the Five Principles. The declaration said:

> United by the common ideals of building a socialist society and by the principles of proletarian internationalism, the countries of the great commonwealth of socialist nations can build their mutual relations only on the principles of complete equality, of respect for territorial integrity, state independence and sovereignty, and of noninterference in one another's internal affairs.[139]

Two days after the Soviet declaration was issued, Peking seized the opportunity to issue a declaration of its own, advocating that the Five Principles should be applied to the relations among socialist countries. The Chinese emphasized:

> The People's Republic of China believes that the Five Principles of mutual respect for sovereignty and territorial integrity, mutual non-aggression, mutual non-interference in internal affairs, equality and mutual benefit, and peaceful coexistence should be the standard for the establishment and development of mutual relations between all countries in the world. Socialist countries are all independent and sovereign countries.... For this reason, mutual relations between socialist countries should all the more be established on the basis of these Five Principles.[140]

In the same year, Chou En-lai issued a joint communique with North Vietnamese Premier Phan Van Dong in Hanoi, advocating that the Five Principles should be the guide for relations among the socialist countries. The communique stressed the two prime ministers' pledge "that in the relations between the two countries . . . the Five Principles should be strictly adhered to and the mistake of chauvinism could be firmly avoided."[141]

Peking's pressure on Moscow to expressly accept the Five Principles was obviously rejected by the latter. On December 23, 1956, the Soviet Party organ *Pravda* published an article entitled "Proletarian Internationalism," in which the author, in replying to the Polish political commentator Bibrovsky, said:

> In discussing the correct relationships among fraternal Parties, Bibrovsky places emphasis on the principle of peaceful coexistence. The way he raises this question cannot but give rise to aversion among the Communists.... If relationships among Communist Parties were to be set up according to the suggestions . . . then what we would have would no longer be an inbreakable front of revolutionary forces bound together by a consistent world outlook, by self-conscious discipline, by obligations they are mutually willing to shoulder, and by common aims and objectives.[142]

Soviet opposition can also be detected in the address of the postrevolution Hungarian Premier Kadar, a man installed by Moscow. In Peking in October 1957 he stated that proletarian internationalism expresses the common destiny of the socialist countries. It means the alliance and the unbreakable friendship among the brotherly peoples and goes deeper than the Five Principles of Peaceful Coexistence. Thus, he concluded that "the principle of non-interference and the other four principles . . . is insufficient" to adjust the relationship among the socialist countries.[143]

It seemed likely that the Chinese in the 1950s failed to convince the Soviet Union to accept the Five Principles as the basis of intrabloc relations. For unknown reasons, Chou En-lai visited the Soviet Union, Poland, and Hungary in early 1957. On January 19, 1957, a Sino-Soviet statement was issued. It reaffirmed proletarian internationalism as the basis of the relations among socialist countries:

> The socialist countries are bound together by the ideals and endeavors of Communism; and therefore, their mutual relationships are based on the doctrine of Marxism-Leninism and the principle of proletarian internationalism. . . . The Soviet Union and China regard it as the highest of their international obligations to strengthen and secure the solidarity of the socialist countries on the basis of the above-said principles.[144]

In the 1960s, as Sino-Soviet relations deteriorated, the Chinese unilaterally called for the application of the Five Principles to intrabloc relations. In 1963, an editorial of the *People's Daily* said that "socialist countries too must abide by the Five Principles in their mutual relations."[145] After the Soviet and the Chinese soldiers clashed on Chenpao Island, Peking's statements no longer mentioned proletarian internationalism. They insisted that Sino-Soviet relations be built on the basis of the Five Principles. In a statement issued on October 7, 1969, Peking insisted that "the Chinese Government has never covered up the fact that there exist [sic] irreconcilable differences of principle between China and the Soviet Union and that the struggle of principle [sic] between them will continue for a long period of time. But this should not prevent China and the Soviet Union from maintaining normal state relations on the basis of the Five Principles of Peaceful Coexistence."[146] "Such a relationship," one writer said, "is by no means that between a father and his son or between master and his servant. In short, it is not the relationship of one at the beck and call of the other."[147]

Peking did not give up her effort to make the Five Principles the basis of the relations among socialist countries. In 1970, Vice-Minister of Foreign Affairs Ch'iao Kuan-hua stated at a reception at the Yugoslav embassy in Peking that the Chinese government had always believed that relations between states should be guided by the Five Principles of Peaceful Coexistence. He said, "These principles should apply to all countries, whether they have the same or different social systems."[148]

It goes without saying that Communist China was unable to insert the Five Principles into her treaties, communiques, or joint statements with any socialist state, except the Chou-Phan Van Dong statement on November 22, 1956, in Hanoi. On the contrary, Chinese treaties with socialist states applied proletarian internationalism as a means to adjust their relations.[149]

SUMMARY

In the 1950s and 1960s, China's foreign policy sought to safeguard the newly established Communist regime and to protect her territorial integrity from the hostility of "imperialism." To achieve these goals, Peking took Mao's theory of the tactics of the United Front and applied it to international politics, so as to align more neighbors on her side. Therefore, the Five Principles of Peaceful Coexistence were proposed to woo noncommunist neighbors. Originally, the good neighbor policy toward noncommunist countries was intended to counteract "imperialism," especially that of the United States.

China was able to successfully apply the Five Principles of Peaceful Coexistence, the essence of the good neighbor policy, to neighbors on the southwestern border. The Five Principles, after 1954, were not only inserted in China's many treaties with neighbors, but also were interpreted by both Indian and Chinese jurists as being fully consistent with the existing principles and customs of international law. China had settled the century-old boundary questions with them and then stabilized her border situation, with the exception of India who still disputes with the PRC about the bordering territories.

On the northern border, China failed in applying the Five Principles as a part of border policy to the Soviet Union, who had been insisting that the relations among socialist countries should be adjusted by proletarian internationalism.

NOTES

1. See Mark Mancall, "The Persistence of Tradition in Chinese Foreign Policy," *The Annals of the American Academy of Political and Social Science* (September 1963) 349: 17–18.
2. The text of the Political Program was printed in *The Collected Laws of the Chinese Republic*, 11 vols. (Shanghai: 1936), 1: 10–14, cited by William L. Tung, *China and the Foreign Powers: The Impact of and Reaction to Unequal Treaties* (Dobbs Ferry, N.Y.: Oceana Publications, 1970), p. 303.
3. See *Survey of International Affairs* (London: Royal Institute of International Affairs, 1951), pp. 474–75.
4. Ibid., p. 475.
5. William C. Johnstone, *Burma's Foreign Policy: A Study in Neutralism* (Cambridge: Harvard University Press, 1963), pp. 225–33, cited by Harold C. Hinton, *Communist China in World Politics* (Boston: Houghton Mifflin, 1966), p. 313.
6. Hinton, *Communist China*, p. 314.
7. Ibid., p. 313.
8. *The Nation*, April 20 and 26, October 22, 1955, cited by Hinton, *Communist China*, p. 311.
9. *New York Times*, Feb. 1, 1951, p. 6.
10. "Report on the Question of the Boundary Line between China and Burma Delivered by Chou En-lai, Premier and Foreign Minister, at the Fourth Session of the First National People's Congress, July 9, 1957," *Important Documents on the Settlement of the Sino-Burmese Boundary Question* (Peking: Foreign Languages Press, 1960), p. 16.
11. Ibid., p. 11.
12. "Indian Note of October 26, 1950 to China," *Documents of International Affairs*, 1953, pp. 550–51 (hereafter cited as *DIA*).
13. *China's Betrayal of India* (New Delhi: Publication Division, Ministry of Infor-

mation and Broadcasting, Government of India, November 1962), cited by Sudhaker Bhat, *India and China* (New Delhi: Popular Book Services, 1967), p. 10.

14. *Report of the Officials of the Governments of India and the People's Republic of China on the Boundary Question* (New Delhi: Ministry of External Affairs, 1961), p. 246 (hereafter cited as *Report*). Nehru in his autobiography also stated that Tibet was independent, see Bhat, *India and China*, p. 30.

15. *Report*, p. 248.

16. *Report*, p. 249.

17. Li Tieh-tseng, "The Legal Status of Tibet," *The American Journal of International Law* 50 (1956): 394–404. For semiofficial statement, see Panchen Erdeni's speech at a meeting of the National Committee of the Chinese People's Political Consultative Conference in Peking on April 29, 1959, in *Peking Review* (hereafter *PR*) no. 18 (May 5, 1950): 12–18, in which Erdeni said that Tibet became a part of China during the thirteenth century.

18. "China's Note of November 19, 1950, to India," *DIA* (1953), pp. 554–56.

19. "Indian Note of October 31, 1950," *DIA* (1953), pp. 552–54.

20. Hugh E. Richardson, *Tibet and Its History* (London: Oxford University Press, 1962), p. 173, cited by Neville Maxwell, *India's China War* (New York: Doubleday, 1972), p. 60.

21. Li Tieh-tseng, *Tibet: Today and Yesterday* (New York: Bookman Association, 1960), p. 199, cited by Maxwell, *India's China War*, p. 60.

22. Richardson, *Tibet and Its History*, p. 178, cited by Maxwell, *India's China War*, pp. 60–61.

23. Karunakar Gupta, *The Hidden History of the Sino-Indian Frontier* (Calcutta: Minerva Associates, 1974), p. 39.

24. Ibid.

25. Ibid., pp. 9–10.

26. *Report*, p. CR–107. ("CR" precedes all page numbers in the section which contains the report of the official of the PRC.)

27. Maxwell, *India's China War*, p. 66.

28. "Chinese Ambassador's Statement of May 16, 1959," in *Notes, Memoranda and Letters Exchanged and Agreements Signed Between the Governments of India and China: White Paper* (New Delhi: Ministry of External Affairs, 1959–1963) 1: 73–76 (hereafter cited as *White Paper*).

29. The McMahon Line was produced by the exchange of notes between Britain and Tibet in 1914, and China has never recognized it. For detail, see Chapter 4 of this book.

30. "India Note of August 27, 1959, to China," *White Paper* 1: 44.

31. "China's Note August 27, 1959, to India," *White Paper* 1: 43.

32. India learned of the roadway later in 1958 from a Chinese magazine, *China Pictorial*, no. 95 (July 1958): pp. 20–21, see *White Paper* 1:46.

33. "Letter from the Prime Minister of India to the Prime Minister of China, 26 September 1959, *White Paper* 2: 34–52.

34. *New York Times*, August 2, 1960, p. 9.

35. Ibid., June 10, 1960, p. 1.

36. Ibid., Oct. 5, 1960, p. 1; Nov. 15, 1960, p. 5.

37. Hinton, *Communist China*, p. 294.

38. "China's Note of Nov. 30, 1961," *White Paper* 4: 4.

39. "Note Given by the Ministry of External Affairs to the Embassy of China in India, 17 May 1960," *White Paper* 6: 60.

40. "Note Given by the Ministry of External Affairs to the Embassy of China in India, 4 April 1960, *White Paper* 6: 81.

41. "Note Given by the Ministry of Foreign Affairs, Peking, to the Embassy of India in China, 23 July 1962," *White Paper* 7: 2.

42. "Note Given by the Ministry of Foreign Affairs, Peking, to the Embassy of India in China, 4 August 1962," *White Paper* 7: 14–18.

43. "Note Given by the Ministry of Foreign Affairs to the Embassy of India in China, 18 September 1962," *White Paper* 7: 138.

44. "Note Given by the Ministry of Foreign Affairs to the Embassy of India in China, 25 September 1962," *White Paper* 7: 88.

45. "Note Given by the Ministry of Foreign Affairs to the Embassy of India in China, 20 October 1962," *White Paper* 7: 123–27.

46. "Letter from Premier Chou En-lai to Prime Minister of India, 24 October 1962," *White Paper* 8: 1.

47. "Letter from the Prime Minister of India, to Premier Chou En-lai, 27 October 1962," *White Paper* 8: 4–5.

48. Maxwell, *India's China War*, p. 420.

49. Hinton, *Communist China*, pp. 301–2.

50. Maxwell, *India's China War*, p. 437.

51. "Statement Given by the Chinese Government, 21 November 1962," *White Paper* 8: 17–21.

52. *New York Times*, Dec. 15, 1962, p. 2.

53. Maxwell, *India's China War*, pp. 455–56.

54. *Important Documents*, p. 16.

55. "China's Note of October 30, 1950, to India," *DIA*, (1949–1950), pp. 551–52.

56. *Chinese News Agency*, October 25, 1950, cited by Shanti P. Varma, *Struggle for the Himalayas: A Study in Sino-Indian Relations* (New Delhi: Sterling Publishers, 1971), p. 18.

57. Text in *DIA*, (1951), pp. 577–79.

58. Li Ta-kuang, "U.S. Espionage and Subversion against China," *People's China*, no. 3 (February 1, 1955): 9.

59. See Varma, *Struggle for the Himalayas*, pp. 19–20.

60. Premen Addy, "New Delhi and the Bandung Spirit: A Reappraisal," *Frontier* 27 (Nov. 1971), cited by Mohan Ram, *Politics of Sino-Indian Confrontation* (New Delhi: Vidas, 1973), p. 69.

61. Ibid.

62. *Bulletin of Activities, Secret (Dispatched to Regimental Level)*, no. 7 (Published by the General Political Dept. of the China People's Liberation Army, Feb. 1, 1961), English translation in J. Chester Chen, ed., *The Politics of the Chinese Red Army* (Stanford: Stanford University Press, 1966), pp. 190–91.

63. *New York Times*, April 17, 1960, p. 6.

64. Ram, *Politics of Sino-Indian Confrontation*, p. 69.

65. *New China New Agency*, Sept. 7, 1960, quotation in Ram, *Politics of Sino-Indian Confrontation*, p. 70.

66. Allen Whiting, "What Nixon Must Do to Make Friends in Peking," *New York*

Review (October 9, 1971), quotation in Ram, *Politics of Sino-Indian Confrontation*, p. 70.

67. Karunakar Gupta, *India in World Politics: A Period of Transition* (Calcutta: Scientific Book Agency, 1966), p. 74.

68. "Note Given by the Foreign Office of China to the Counsellor of India, 10 July 1958," *White Paper* 1: 60–61.

69. "Note Sent by the Ministry of External Affairs to the Embassy of China in India, 2 August 1958," *White Paper* 1: 63–65.

70. See Kenneth T. Young, *Negotiating with the Chinese Communists: The United States Experience, 1953–1968* (New York: McGraw Hill, 1968), p. 4.

71. Committee for the Publication of the Selected Works of Mao Tse-tung, Central Committee of the Communist Party of China, ed., *Selected Works of Mao Tse-tung*, 5 vols. (Peking: Foreign Languages Press, 1951–1977) 1: 163.

72. Article 14 of the Agreement between the China Central People's Government and the Tibetan Government for Administering Tibet in 1951, text in *DIA* (1951), p. 578.

73. *Prime Minister on Sino-Indian Relations* (New Delhi: Government of India, 1961) 1: Part 1, pp. 184–85, quotation in Maxwell, *India's China War*, p. 69.

74. Maxwell, *India's China War*, p. 69.

75. Bhat, *India and China*, p. 15.

76. The argument between China and India about their purposes for concluding the trade agreement and the interpretations of the agreement will be analyzed in Chapter 6 of this book.

77. Text in *White Paper* 1: 98–107.

78. See "China's Note to India of July 10, 1958," *White Paper* 1: 60–62.

79. "Letter from the Prime Minister of China to the Prime Minister of India, 23 January 1959," *White Paper* 1: 52–54.

80. "Nehru's letter to Chou En-lai," *White Paper* 1: 48–56.

81. *Important Documents*, p. 16.

82. Peter Cheng, *A Chronology of the People's Republic of China: From October 1, 1949* (Totowa: Rowman and Littlefield, 1972), p. 34.

83. The joint communique stated that Burma would consider a "fair and reasonable proposal" made by China, see Chou En-lai's report to the National People's Congress on Sino-Burmese boundary question, in *A Victory for the Five Principles of Peaceful Coexistence* (Peking: Foreign Languages Press, 1960), pp. 6–7, cited by Hinton, *Communist China*, p. 314.

84. "Joint Communique of the Chinese and Burmese Government," *PR* 3, no. 40 (Oct. 4, 1960): 26.

85. Text in *DIA*, (1960), pp. 499; also *PR* 3, no. 5 (Feb. 2, 1960): 13.

86. Text in *PR* 3, no. 40 (Oct. 4, 1960): 33–34.

87. *PR* 3, no. 5 (Feb. 2, 1960): 9–10.

88. *PR* 3, no. 5 (Feb. 2, 1960): 11.

89. "Supplementary Speech by Premier Chou En-lai, April 19, 1955," George McTurnan Kahin, *The Asian-African Conference, Bandung, Indonesia, April 1955* (Ithaca: Cornell University Press, 1956), p. 57.

90. Text in *DIA*, (1960), p. 502.

91. In *PR* 4, no. 48 (Nov. 29, 1963): 7–8.

92. Text in *DIA*, (1954), p. 315.

93. Text in *DIA*, (1960), p. 499; also in *PR* 3, no. 5 (Feb. 2, 1960): 13.
94. Text in *PR* 3, no. 5 (Feb. 2, 1960): 14–15.
95. Text in *PR* 12, no. 17 (April 26, 1969): 42.
96. Text in *PR* 3, no. 40 (Oct. 4, 1960): 33–34.
97. Text in *PR* 1, no. 27 (Sept. 2, 1958): 14–15.
98. Text in *PR* 4, no. 18, (May 5, 1961): 10.
99. Text in *PR* 6, nos. 10 & 11 (March 15, 1963): 70–71.
100. Text in *DIA*, (1954), p. 313.
101. Text in *Chung-hua jen-min kung-ho-kuo tui-wai kuang-hsi wen-chien-chi 1954–1955* (Collection of Documents Relating to the Foreign Relations of the People's Republic of China), vol. 3 (1961), pp. 332–33 (hereafter cited as *WCC*).
102. Text in *DIA*, (1956), p. 740.
103. Text in *DIA*, (1956), p. 746.
104. Text in *PR* 3, no. 18 (May 3, 1960): 8–9.
105. Text in *DIA*, (1960), p. 5.
106. Text in *PR* 4, no. 42 (Oct. 20, 1961): 5–8.
107. Text in *PR* 6, nos. 10 & 11 (March 15, 1963): 67–70.
108. Kahin, *The Asian-African Conference*, pp. 56–62.
109. "Note Given by the Foreign Office of China to the Indian Counsellor in Peking, 23 June 1959," *White Paper* 1: 34.
110. Regarding this conclusion, see Wei Liang, "Lueh-nun ti-erh-ch'ih szu-chieh-ta-chan-hou ti kuo-chi tiao-yueh" (On the Post Second World War International Treaties), in *Kuo-chi tiao-yueh-chi 1953–1955* (International Treaty Series), (Peking: World Knowledge Press, 1961), p. 666.
111. Chou Keng-sheng, "Ts'ung kuo-chi-fa nun ho-p'ing kung-ch'u ti yuan-che" (On the Principle of Peaceful Coexistence in International Law), in *Chen-fa yen-chiu* (Studies in Political Science and Law), no. 6 (1955): 38 (hereafter *CFYC*).
112. Mao Tao, "Ya-fei fa-lu kung-tso-tse hui-i ti tsung-ta ch'eng-chiu (The Important Accomplishment of the Conference of Asian-African Jurists), *CFYC*, no. 2 (1958): 9.
113. Ibid., p. 5.
114. Ibid., p. 8.
115. Chou, "On the Principle of Peaceful Coexistence," p. 38.
116. C. J. Chacko, "Peaceful Coexistence As A Doctrine of Current International Affairs," *Indian Yearbook of International Affairs*, vol. 4 (1955), pp. 14–15.
117. Ibid., p. 39; Chou, "On the Principle of Peaceful Coexistence," p. 39.
118. Chou, "On the Principle of Peaceful Coexistence," p. 39.
119. Ibid., pp. 39–40.
120. Chacko, "Peaceful Coexistence," p. 40.
121. Chou, "On the Principle of Peaceful Coexistence," p. 40.
122. Ibid., p. 41.
123. Chacko, "Peaceful Coexistence," p. 39.
124. Chou, "On the Principle of Peaceful Coexistence," p. 38.
125. Chacko, "Peaceful Coexistence," p. 39.
126. Chou, "On the Principle of Peaceful Coexistence," p. 36.
127. David J. Dallin, *Soviet Russia and the Far East* (New Haven: Yale University Press, 1948).
128. Peter Berton, ed., "Documents," *Studies in Comparative Communism*, vol. 2, Nos. 3 & 4 (July/Oct. 1969), p. 132.

129. Brian Hook, ed., *The Cambridge Encyclopedia of China* (London: Cambridge University Press, 1982), p. 98.

130. Usman Mametov, "I Cannot Be Silent!" letter to the editors of *Kazakhstanskaya Pravda* (Sept. 23, 1963), *Current Digest of Soviet Press* 15, no. 38 (Oct. 16, 1963): 17 (hereafter *CDSP*).

131. *New York Times*, Oct. 2, 1963, p. 13.

132. George Moseley, *A Sino-Soviet Cultural Frontier: The Ili Kazakh Autonomous Chou* (Cambridge: Harvard University Press, 1966), p. 110; see also Tai-sung An, *The Sino-Soviet Territorial Dispute* (Philadelphia: The Westminster Press, 1973), p. 85.

133. Hook, *The Cambridge Encyclopedia of China*, p. 98.

134. *Jen-min jih-pao* (People's Daily), May 7, 1950, quotation in James C. Hsiung, *Law and Policy in China's Foreign Relations* (New York: Columbia University Press, 1972), p. 55.

135. *Jen-min jih-pao*, Feb. 28, 1954, cited in Hsiung, *Law and Policy*, p. 55.

136. Berton, "Documents," p. 132.

137. Text in *DIA*, (1954), p. 323.

138. Text in the *CDSP*, vol. 8, no. 4 (March 7, 1956), pp. 10–11.

139. *Pravda and Izvestia*, Oct. 31, 1956, English text printed in the *CDSP*, vol. 8 no. 40 (Nov. 4, 1956), p. 10.

140. *WCC, 1956–1957*, vol. 4 (1958), pp. 148–50.

141. *Jen-min jih-pao*, Nov. 23, 1956, cited by Chin Szu-k'ai, *Communist China's Relations with the Soviet Union 1949–1957*, (Kowloon, Hong Kong: Union Research Institute, 1961), p. 96.

142. The Chinese version published in *Jen-min jih-pao*, Nov. 23, 1956, cited by Chin, *Communist China's Relations*, pp. 94–95.

143. *Jen-min jih-pao*, Oct. 4, 1957, quotation in Chin, *Communist China's Relations*, p. 95.

144. *Jen-min jih-pao*, Jan 20, 1957, quotation in Chin, *Communist China's Relations*, p. 98.

145. "Peaceful Coexistence—Two Diametrically Opposed Policies," *Jen-min jih-pao* (Dec. 12, 1963), pp. 1–4, English text printed in *PR* 6, no. 51 (Dec. 20, 1963): 13.

146. *PR* 12, no. 41 (Oct. 10, 1969): 3.

147. Wang Jinqing, "Why the Sino-Soviet Strains?" *PR* 27, no. 28 (July 9, 1984): 32.

148. "Yugoslav Ambassador to China Gives National Day Reception," *PR* 13, no. 49 (Dec. 4, 1970): 23.

149. For example, the Preamble of the Treaty of Friendship and Mutual Assistance between the PRC and the Mongolian People's Republic stipulated that the treaty was signed "on the basis of the principles of proletarian internationalism," text in *PR* 3, no. 23 (June 7, 1960): 10.

4

BOUNDARY DISPUTES AND SETTLEMENTS

INTRODUCTION

China has more than 20,000 kilometers (12,414 miles) of frontier land[1] shared with 12 countries. Except for Vietnam and Laos, all of the countries have had boundary disputes with China. During the 1960s, China negotiated boundary treaties with seven adjacent countries. In this chapter, we shall study the frontier disputes, the controversy over international law, China's proposed principles, and her attitudes toward boundary settlements. As China's boundary questions differ with each of her neighbors, we shall study each country separately.

THE SOVIET UNION

The Formation of Today's Sino-Soviet Boundaries

The Sino-Soviet boundaries, about 6,678 kilometers (4,150 miles), are comprised of two unconnected sections.[2] The boundary of the western section in Central Asia extends from the Altai Mountains in the north of China westward for 3,000 kilometers (1,850 miles) to the Pamir Mountains west of China. The eastern section is 3,700 kilometers (2,300 miles), and extends from the uplands of Transbaikulia to the Sea of Japan.[3] Between these two sections lies the Mongolian People's Republic. (See Map 1.)

The eastern section was delimited and in some areas demarcated by treaties concluded between the Ch'ing dynasty of China and tzarist Russia from the seventeenth through the nineteenth centuries. However, the Chinese have always

Map 1
The Sino-Soviet Disputed Boundaries

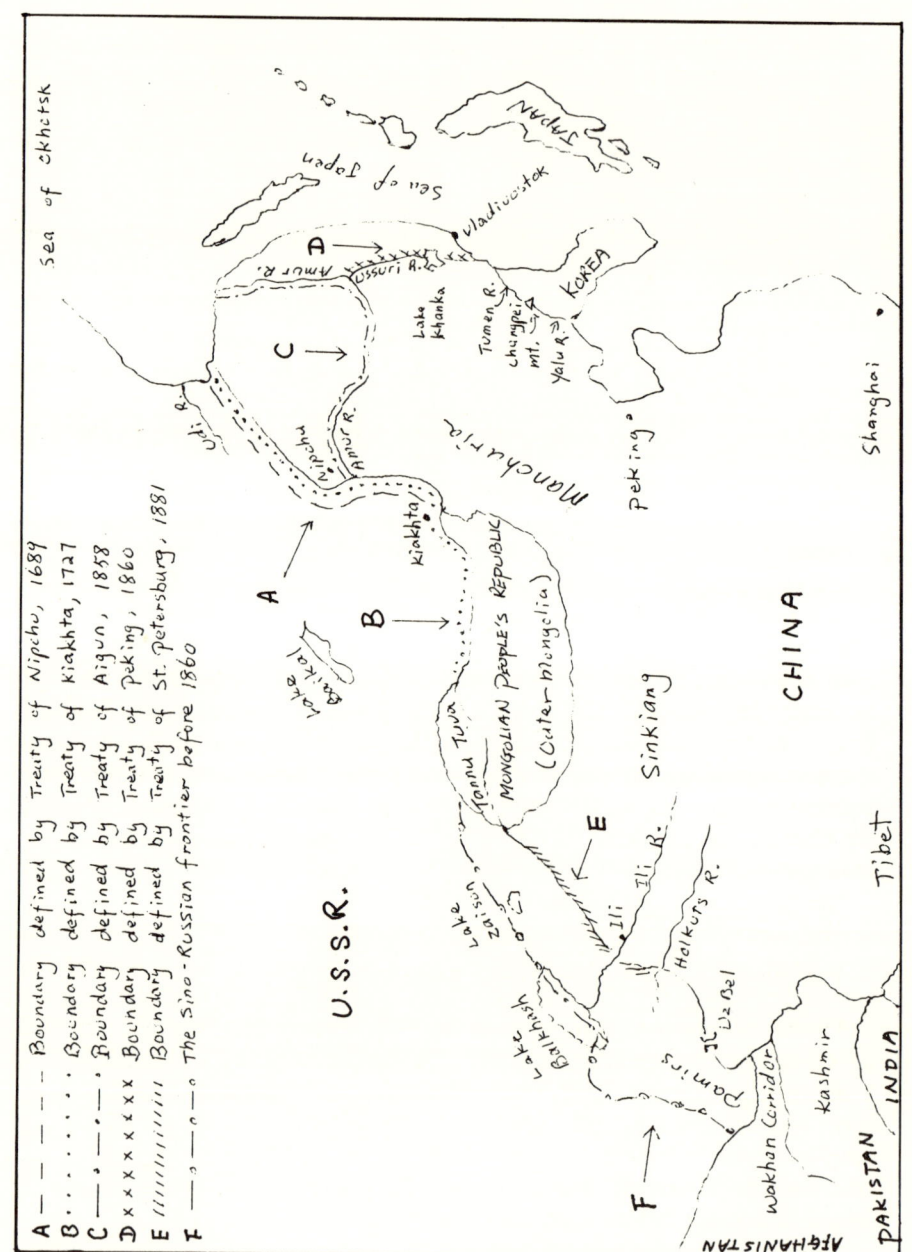

thought that those boundary treaties, except for two, are inequitable and were imposed by an expanding Russia on a weakening China. The two acceptable treaties are the Treaty of Nipchu and The Treaty of Kiakhta.

The Treaty of Nipchu (Nerchinsk). From the sixteenth century on, Russia has gradually penetrated into Siberia as did the Chinese. During the seventeenth century, China's forces reached the Sea of Okhotsk and controlled the Amur basin. In the eighteenth century, Russia and China clashed west of the Amur River (Heilungkiang), where the city of Nipchu (Nerchinsk) was located. In 1689, the Treaty of Nipchu was concluded.[4] This was the first Chinese boundary treaty and the Chinese have accepted its legitimacy even though they ceded about 240,870 square kilometers (93,000 square miles) of territory to tzarist Russia.[5] According to the original treaty, the boundary line was defined along the Aigun River, continuing along the Amur River to the south of Kerbechi, thence along the Kerbechi northward to the Stanovoy Mountains, and thence eastward along the crests of the mountains to the sound of the Udi (Ud) River. The valley of the Udi, lying between the northern and southern branches of the Stanovoy Mountains, remained undefined. The Russo-Chinese Agreement in Peking in April, 1727, reaffirmed the status of this undefined area.[6]

The Treaty of Kiakhta (Kyakhta). On August 30, 1727, the two empires signed a preliminary treaty, the Treaty of Bur, which set principles for delimiting the boundary between the present Mongolia and upper Aigun. On October 31, the Treaty of Kiakhta was signed and ratified the following year.[7] This treaty delimited the boundary between Mongolia and Siberia from the Saian (Sayan) Mountains and Sapintabakha (Shaban-Dabey) in the west to the Aigun River in the east. The valley of Udi remained undefined. Although by this treaty, China lost about 103,600 square kilometers (nearly 40,000 square miles) of territory to tzarist Russia,[8] the PRC recognized its legitimacy. However, the Sino-Russian boundaries were redefined by other treaties in the nineteenth century; treaties the Chinese see as "unequal."[9] These treaties were negotiated under the following circumstances.

The Treaty of Aigun. In the 1850s, Count Nikolas Muraviev of Russia led several expeditions into the Amur region. By the end of 1856, "the Russians were entrenched along the whole course of the Amur, with a series of well-chosen posts on the left bank. The Amur had virtually become a Russian river, and it was only necessary to obtain the nomial sanction of the *fait accompli* from the Chinese."[10] In 1857, Muraviev readied 16,000 infantrymen, 5,000 cavalry, 1,000 artillerymen with 40 pieces, and a reserve of 1,000 men and kept them at the rear on the frontier of Manchuria and Mongolia.[11] China was at that time deeply involved in suppressing the Tai-p'ing rebellion and had little energy to deal with the Russians. Under Russia's threat and demand, China signed the Treaty of Aigun in May 1858.[12]

According to Article 6, "the left bank of the Amur River, beginning at the Aigun River to the mouth of the Amur, will belong to the Russian Empire, and its right bank, down to the Ussuri River, will belong to the Chinese Empire, the territories and locations situated between the Ussuri and the sea will, as they are presently, be commonly owned by the Chinese Empire and the Russian Empire until the boundary between the two states is settled." According to the estimate of the PRC, Russia annexed more than 600,000 square kilometers (231,660 square miles) of Chinese territory by this treaty.[13]

The Treaty of Peking. A few years later, when China was busy dealing with the big powers, the Russian envoy at Peking under General Nicholas Ignatiev, played fast and loose with China. On the one hand, he advised the Anglo-French allies to menace Peking and, on the other hand, offered arms and ammunition to the Ch'ing government. When the Anglo-French joint forces were occupying Peking, Ignatiev requested the cession of the Trans-Ussuri territory. Prince Kung, then in charge of the Ch'ing government, was compelled to submit to this demand from the "honest broker." As a result, the Treaty of Peking was signed in November 1860.[14] The PRC has estimated that by the Treaty of Peking and its protocols, Russia annexed more than 444,000 square kilometers (171,428 square miles) of Chinese territory.[15]

According to Article 1 of this treaty, the commonly held territory between the Ussuri and the Sea of Japan was ceded to Russia. The boundary between Russia and China was to follow the Ussuri south to, and along its tributary, the Sungatcha, then across Lake Khanka to the Korean frontier. Delegates were to be appointed by the two governments to survey and map the frontier from Lake Khanka to the Tumen River (Article 3).

The western section of the Sino-Russian boundary was also defined by this treaty. The boundary line runs from Chabindabaga (Shaban-Dabey) southward along the mountains south of Issyk Kul (Ala Tau) to the limits of Kokand. A detailed delimitation of this area remained for a joint boundary commission to demarcate.

The treaty also stated that the Sino-Russian boundary line in this area should be based on the existing line of the Chinese pickets. There were two kinds of pickets: the permanent pickets which were close to the cities and towns, and the moveable pickets which were far from the cities and intended to prevent others from pasturing in Chinese territory. During the negotiations of the Tarbagatai Protocol, and under Russian pressure, China agreed to the boundary line followed along the permanent pickets and signed the Tarbagatai Protocol.[16]

The Treaty of Livadia. This boundary from Shaban-Dabey to Kokand was later adjusted by the Treaty of Ili in 1881. In 1871, when the Moslems were rebelling against the Chinese in Sinkiang, Russian troops, under the guise of maintaining law and order, occupied the upper Ili River valley. Russia promised to withdraw as soon as the Ch'ing government was able to govern Sinkiang effectively. By 1878, the Moslem rebellions were put down and the Ch'ing government reestablished effective administration over Sinkiang, but they refused to leave. In order to get the Russians out of the Ili valley, the Treaty of Livadia was proposed in 1879. By this treaty, China agreed to cede about 30 percent of the territory of the Ili valley to Russia in exchange for the Russians' departure.[17]

But the treaty aroused a strong protest among the Chinese people, and the Ch'ing government refused to ratify it.

The Treaty of Ili. In February 1881, the Treaty of Ili was signed to replace the Treaty of Livadia.[18] By the Treaty of Ili, Russia annexed only two small areas of Chinese territory: the Lake Zaisan territory eastward along the Cherny Irtysh, about 38,850 square kilometers (15,000 square miles), and a small area west of Holkuts River. The boundary lines east of Lake Zaisan and west of Kashgar, as determined by the Tarbagatai Protocol of 1884, were to be demarcated again.

After the conclusion of the Treaty of Ili, additional protocols were signed between 1882 and 1893 to complete the boundary lines:[19]

1. The protocol signed at Ili in August 1882
2. The protocol signed at Goulimtou in October 1882
3. The protocol signed at Kashgar in November 1882
4. The protocol signed at Tarbagatai in September 1883
5. The protocol signed at Novi-Margelian in May 1884
6. The protocol signed at Tarbagatai in December 1883

The Treaty of Ili and these additional boundary protocols delimited the boundary between Russia and Chinese Sinkiang as far south as Kizil Jik Dawan (Pass), located 38°40' North and 73°50' East. The PRC has estimated that by these instruments, China lost more than 70,000 square kilometers (about 27,027 square miles) of territory to tzarist Russia.[20]

Territorial Disputes and Border Violations

The main territorial dispute in the western section is in the area from the Uz Bel Pass down to Afghanistan's narrow Wakhan Corridor. The Chinese established their control of this area during the T'ang dyansty (A.D. 618–907). After an interval in which they lost control, the Chinese reestablished it in the eighteenth century. In the nineteenth century, Russia conquered Kokand and thereafter sent several expeditions exploring most of the Pamirs. In 1879, the Chinese army entered the eastern Pamirs and, in 1883, discovered that Russian troops were stationed there. When the Chinese queried the Russians as to why they had entered Chinese territory without first notifying the Chinese local government they received an unsatisfactory response.

In 1884, a second protocol on the Sino-Russian boundary in the Kashgar region was signed.[21] According to the preamble of the protocol, its purpose was to define the boundary between Russia's Semirechensk Province and China's Kashgar region along T'ien Shan range, and between Russia's Fergana Province and the western boundary of China's Kashgar region from the Tuinn Sonick Mountains to Uz Bel. Article 3 stipulates clearly that the boundary of the two countries terminates at the Uz Bel Mountains. However, the language is vague, stating that from this mountain "the Russian boundary turns to the southwest; the Chinese boundary runs straight south." (See Map 2.)

In 1892, a strong Russian armed forces was sent into the Pamirs and occupied the west of Sarikol range, which is in the east of the line running from Uz Bel straight south. The Russian troops remained there. At the present, this area is still held by the Soviet Union. According to a PRC statement, this area, about 20,000 square kilometers (7,720 square miles), is Chinese territory.[22]

The Soviet Union has denied the PRC's claim, saying that it is not Chinese territory because the Sino-Russian Boundary Protocol of 1884 "bears no relation whatever to the Pamir region." A statement of the Soviet Union in 1969 added:

> The demarcation in the Pamirs was accomplished by means of an exchange of notes in 1894; at that time, the two sides agreed "not to go beyond the limits of the positions they now occupy" in the Pamirs along the Sarikol Range. This line and no other exists up to the present.[23]

Answering the Soviet Union, the PRC pointed out that the notes in 1894 were only a proposal to "maintain temporarily the respective positions of the troops of the two sides pending a final settlement of the Pamir question."[24] The PRC explained that the Ch'ing government made an explicit reservation to the note of 1894. The reservation of the Ch'ing government is that:

> In adopting the above-mentioned measure, the Chinese government does not at all mean to abandon the rights China possesses over the territories of the Pamirs which are situated beyond the possessions occupied by the Chinese troops at present. It considers that it should maintain the rights based on the 1884 protocol until a satisfactory understanding is reached.[25]

In the eastern section of the Sino-Soviet boundary, as we can see, border conflicts and violations have intermittently been occurring since the seventeenth century. Things worsened in the 1960s when the two countries became involved in an ideological dispute. In 1963, the Soviets accused the Chinese of violating her border: "Since 1960, Chinese servicemen and civilians have been systematically violating the Soviet frontier. In the one year of 1952, more than 5,000 violations of the Soviet frontier from the Chinese side have been recorded."[26]

On the Chinese side, in 1966 Minister of Foreign Affairs Ch'en Yi accused the Soviet Union of provoking over 5,000 incidents between July 1960 and the end of 1965.[27] In the following years, China repeatedly accused the Soviets of violating her border. For example, in August 1969, the PRC charged that "from June 1 through July 31, the Soviet Government created as many as 429 incidents of provocation along the border."[28] The PRC accused the Soviets of intruding into Chinese territories; Nuyatung Island, Fuyuantachiahsintzu Island,[29] and Pa-cha Island[30] on the border river (Hielungkiang). The most significant violation

Map 2
The Sino-Soviet Disputed Area in the Pamirs

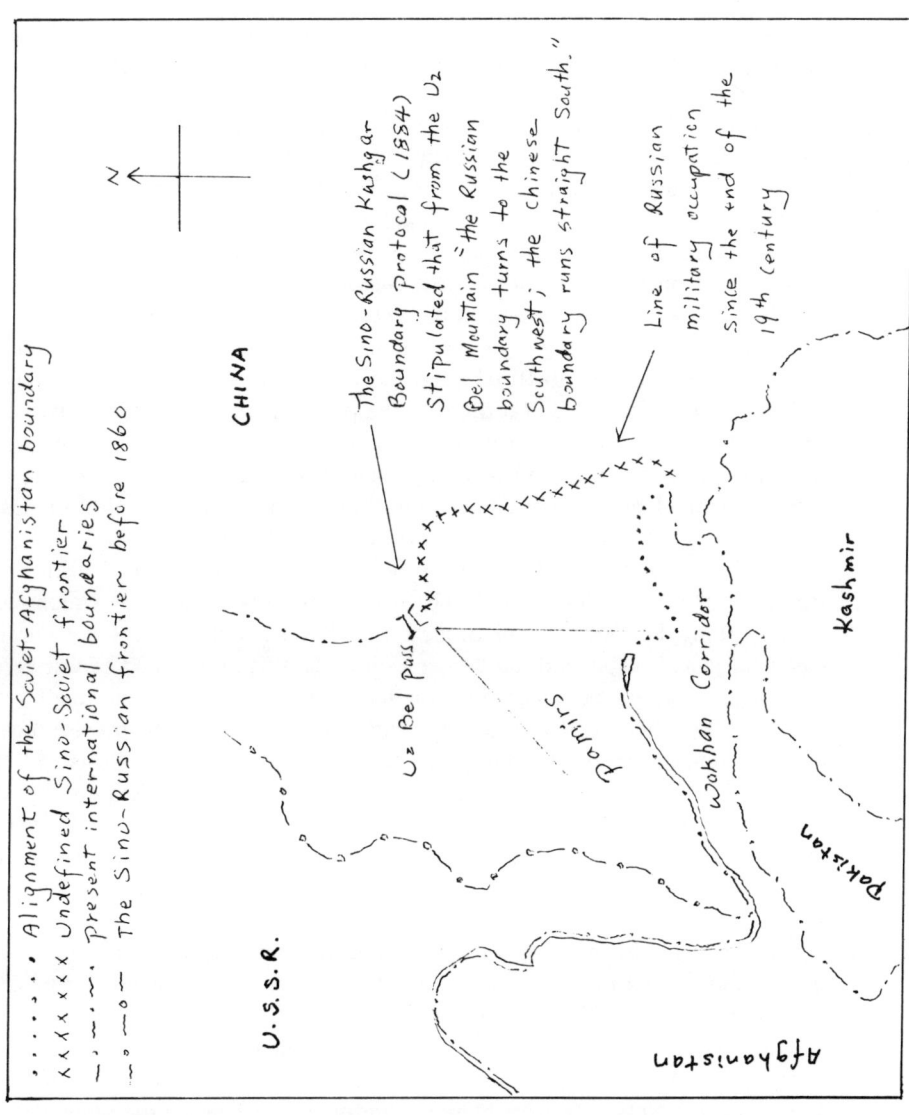

of the disputed river island was the dispute over Chenpao Island and Bear Island. (See Map 3.)

On the two boundary rivers between China and the Soviet Union, Amur and Ussuri (Wusuli), there are hundreds of small islands; many of them are accessible only in winter when the river is frozen. In spring, when the ice melts, the river rampages, floods its low-lying banks, and changes its channel. As a result, many islands change their locations and some new ones emerge, causing disputes over ownership.

Chenpao (Damansky in Russian) is a lozenge-shaped island in the Ussuri, approximately two miles long and a half mile wide. From the island to the Soviet shore, it is about 400 meters (122 feet); from the island to the Chinese bank, it is about 100 meters (30 feet). It is uninhabited because when the river floods, it is submerged. Both China and the Soviet Union claimed ownership of the island based on international law and custom. Based on international law, the Chinese claimed that according to the 1860 Treaty of Peking, the Sino-Russian boundary line "runs along the Ussuri and Sungacha Rivers. The land lying east of these rivers belongs to Russia and the land west of these rivers belongs to China." They added that according to the principle of international law, in the case of navigable boundary rivers, the central line of the main channel should form the boundary line and determine the ownership of islands. Chenpao is situated on the Chinese side of the central line of the main channel of the Ussuri River. Thus, they asserted that Chenpao Island belongs to China.[31]

The Soviets claimed ownership by referring to a map attached to the Sino-Russian Treaty of Peking (1860). The map shows a boundary line which passes directly along the Chinese bank of the Ussuri River and thus, the Soviets argued, Chenpao Island belongs to the Soviet Union. To this point, the Chinese replied that there is a red boundary line on the map but the scale is smaller than 1:1,000,000. This line does not, and cannot possibly, show the precise location of the boundary line in the rivers, not to say the ownership of the island. This happened because in 1861 the two countries surveyed and marked only the land boundary south of Hsingkai Lake not the river boundary on the Ussuri and Heilung rivers. Furthermore, the Chinese added, the boundary line on the map was drawn unilaterally by Russia before the survey in 1861; it was not drawn by the countries as the result of the survey.[32]

The Chinese also pointed out that during the boundary negotiations in 1964, the Soviets agreed that the central line of the main channel should be taken for determining the boundary line in rivers and for ownership of islands.[33]

The Soviets argued that over many years, the Chinese had applied to the competent Soviet authorities for permission to use certain Soviet islands on the Ussuri and the Amur rivers for economic purposes, such as hay-mowing, logging, etc. This application and permission to the Soviet authorities proved that these islands, including Chenpao, belong to the Soviet Union as a matter of custom.[34] However, the Chinese argued that Chenpao "has always been under China's jurisdiction and patrolled by Chinese frontier guards since long ago."[35]

Map 3
The Locations of the Sino-Soviet Disputed Chenpao/Damansky Island and Hei-hsia-tzu/Bear Island

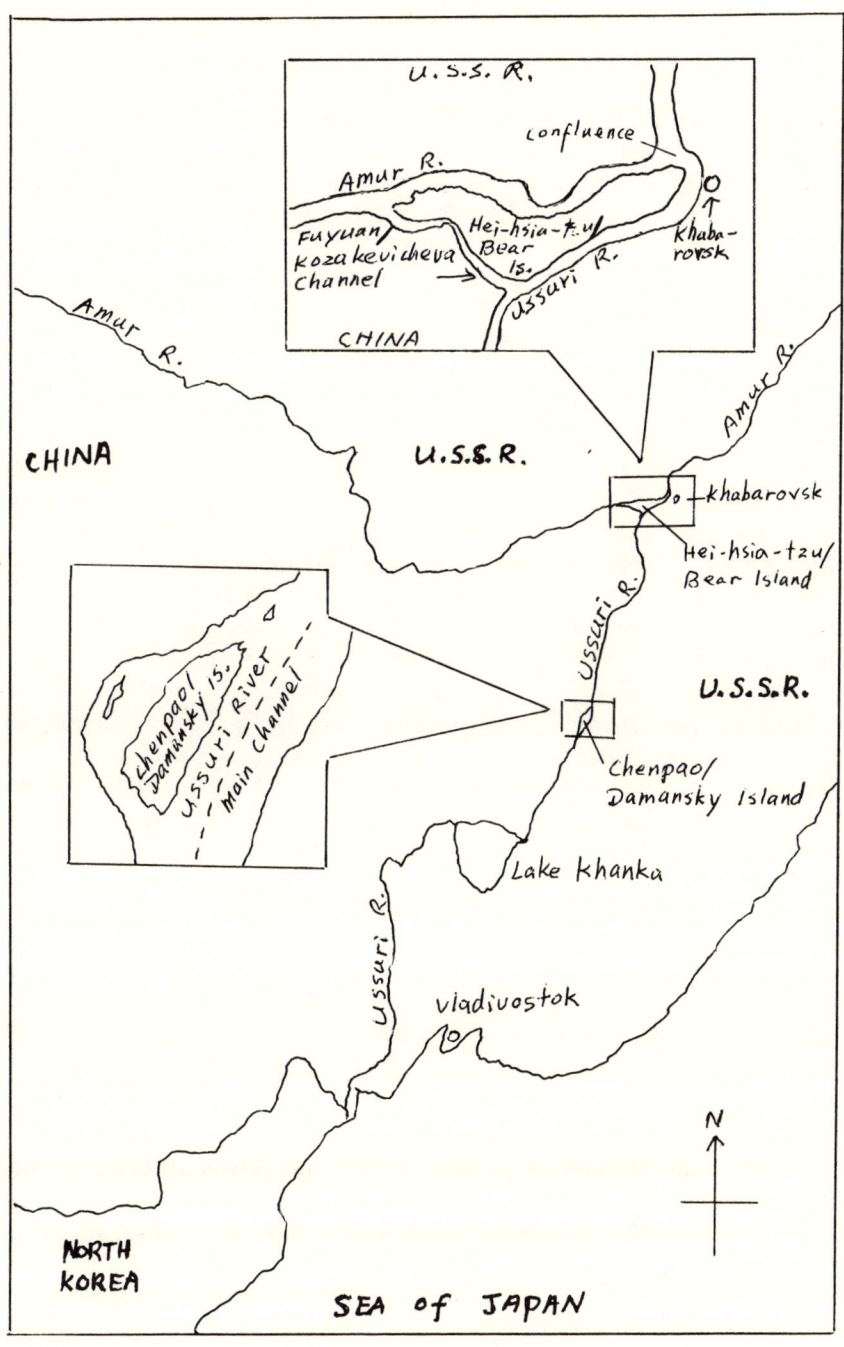

Bear Island (*Hei-hsia-tzu* in Chinese) is a delta of about 300 square kilometers (115 square miles) located at the confluence of the Amur and the Ussuri (see Map 3).[36] China has always maintained persistently that the island is Chinese territory. Across the confluence from the island is the important Russian city, Khabarovsk. At one side of the island is a channel (Fuyuan or Kozakevicheva) that connects the rivers upstream. Normally, the Chinese riverboats navigate down the Amur to the confluence, turning there to go back up the Ussuri. In 1967, a Chinese boat was stopped by Soviet gunboats some 40 kilometers (25 miles) upstream from the confluence, boarded, detained, and finally sent back.[37] Thus, the Soviet Union denied China the right to navigate from the Amur to the Ussuri through the confluence. The blockade forced the Chinese boats wishing to travel from the Amur to the Ussuri to use the interconnecting channel (Fuyuan or Kozakevicheva).

Legal arguments were presented by both sides. The Soviet Union, relying on maps exchanged between the two countries in 1861, claimed that the boundary line runs along the interconnecting channel, above the confluence of the Amur and the Ussuri rivers.[38] Therefore, the confluence, the rivers, and all the islands in the rivers belong to the Soviet Union. In reply, Peking pointed out that the Treaty of Peking (1860) only stipulated rivers as the boundary line; the treaty did not place the boundary line along the bank of the Chinese side. China's right to use the international waterways and ownership of the islands in the rivers, China argued, should be decided by the established principle of international law which places the boundary in the middle of the deepest part of the main channel of rivers (the *thalweg*).[39]

In May 1974, Moscow made a conditional offer to lift the blockade. Chinese vessels could navigate through the confluence and then go back to the upstream of the Ussuri, if China acknowledged that in doing so they were using Soviet national waterways with Soviet permission. Peking rejected this notion of Soviet sovereignty over the rivers, the confluence, and all the river islands, including Bear Island, and asserted her right of navigation in the main channel of the two rivers through the confluence as inalienable.[40]

In 1977, by the efforts of the Sino-Soviet Commission on river navigation, an agreement was reached and the blockade was lifted. Chinese vessels in the daytime could again navigate through the confluence, but they would first give the Soviet traffic authorities notice.[41]

The Principle for Settlement

Since the Chinese complained that all the Sino-Soviet boundaries are the result of tzarist expansion, defined by unequal treaties, they wanted a new boundary treaty with the Soviet Union on an equal basis and insisted that the Soviets recognize the inequality of all the previously signed treaties. The Chinese government, they said, "is ready to take these unequal treaties as the basis for determining the entire alignment of the boundary line between the two countries."[42]

But China's principle of acceptance of the fait accompli and repudiation of the unequal treaties was not acceptable to the Soviets. The Soviet Union would only make adjustments based on the existing boundary treaties.[43]

MONGOLIAN PEOPLE'S REPUBLIC

Fact

China exercised sovereignty over Outer Mongolia until January 1946, when the Nationalist government recognized Outer Mongolia as an independent state. The PRC also recognized Mongolian independence in 1950. However, the entire Chinese-Mongolian frontier was not delimited until 1962.

Settlement

In the autumn of 1962, Sino-Mongolian boundary talks began, and in December, China's Premier Chou En-lai invited Premier Tsedenbal of the Mongolian People's Republic to Peking. Tsedenbal arrived in Peking on December 25, 1962, and on the following day the Sino-Mongolian Boundary Treaty was signed.[44] It laid down the delimitation of the Sino-Mongolian boundary and set up a joint commission for demarcation which was to begin meeting in June 1963. However, the demarcation was never accomplished because relations between the two communist countries began to deteriorate. It was reported that the Mongols were not satisfied with the treaty, believing it favored the Chinese.[45] Border disputes were soon reported along the border region.[46]

NORTH KOREA

There is also controversy between the Chinese and Koreans concerning their boundary. Both of them know in general that their boundary follows the course of the Yalu River, which flows westward into the Yellow Sea, and the Tumen River, which flows eastward into the Sea of Japan. However, according to the Chinese map, their territory includes the vicinity of Chang-pei (Everwhite) Mountain, which is the Yalu-Tumen watershed. According to the Korean map, the boundary follows the watershed principle, with the line running through the summit.[47]

There are currently no boundary negotiations between Peking and Pyongyang. Both sides do not appear to take things seriously and are in no hurry to settle this minor discrepancy.

VIETNAM AND LAOS

Indochina, an area of about 460,450 square kilometers (255,000 square miles), bordering south China, had been under Chinese domination for centuries up until the end of the nineteenth century, when the French detached it from the Chinese.

In 1954, by the Geneva Convention, Indochina was divided into four states: North Vietnam, South Vietnam, Laos, and Cambodia. South Vietnam and Cambodia share no frontiers with China. In 1975, South Vietnam was united by the communists without affecting the Chinese boundary.

The Sino-Vietnamese and the Sino-Laotian boundaries were defined in the nineteenth century. In 1887, a French-Chinese agreement on the Tonkin boundary defined a line from the Gulf of Tonkin to the Black River. In 1895, this line was slightly modified and extended westward to the Mekong after the French annexed Laos.

It seems that China has accepted the 1887–1895 boundary line because no official claims of "lost territories" in Indochina have been made.[48] China's map, showing the boundaries in this region, do not differ from those of Vietnam or Laos.[49] Although China and Vietnam have had military conflicts along their borders, the conflicts are based on ideological differences and are not boundary disputes.

BURMA

Boundaries

China and Burma came into contact with each other early in the third century. For centuries, the Burmese had intermittent tributary relations with the Chinese empire. However, they did not have an exact boundary line or treaty. Only after the British in the late nineteenth century destroyed the old Burmese kingdom, which had been a vassal of the Ch'ing dynasty of China, did the boundary question surface. Subsequent British military expansions in the early twentieth century caused more territorial disputes with China.[50] After Burma became an independent state, she inherited all the historical unsolved boundary problems from Britain along her Chinese frontier of about 100 kilometers (620 miles).

For convenience of discussion, we can divide the Sino-Burmese border into four sectors. (See Map 4.)

1. The extreme northern border runs from the Diphu Pass, which is located at the junction of China, India, and Burma, southeastward to Isuraz Pass. This line is the eastern part of the so-called McMahon Line, which China never accepted.

2. The second sector runs from the Isuraz Pass southward to the High Conical Peak (approximate 25°35′N parallel). This line runs generally along the Irrawaddy-Salween watershed. In accordance with the two boundary treaties, this

Map 4
The Sino-Burmese Disputed Boundary

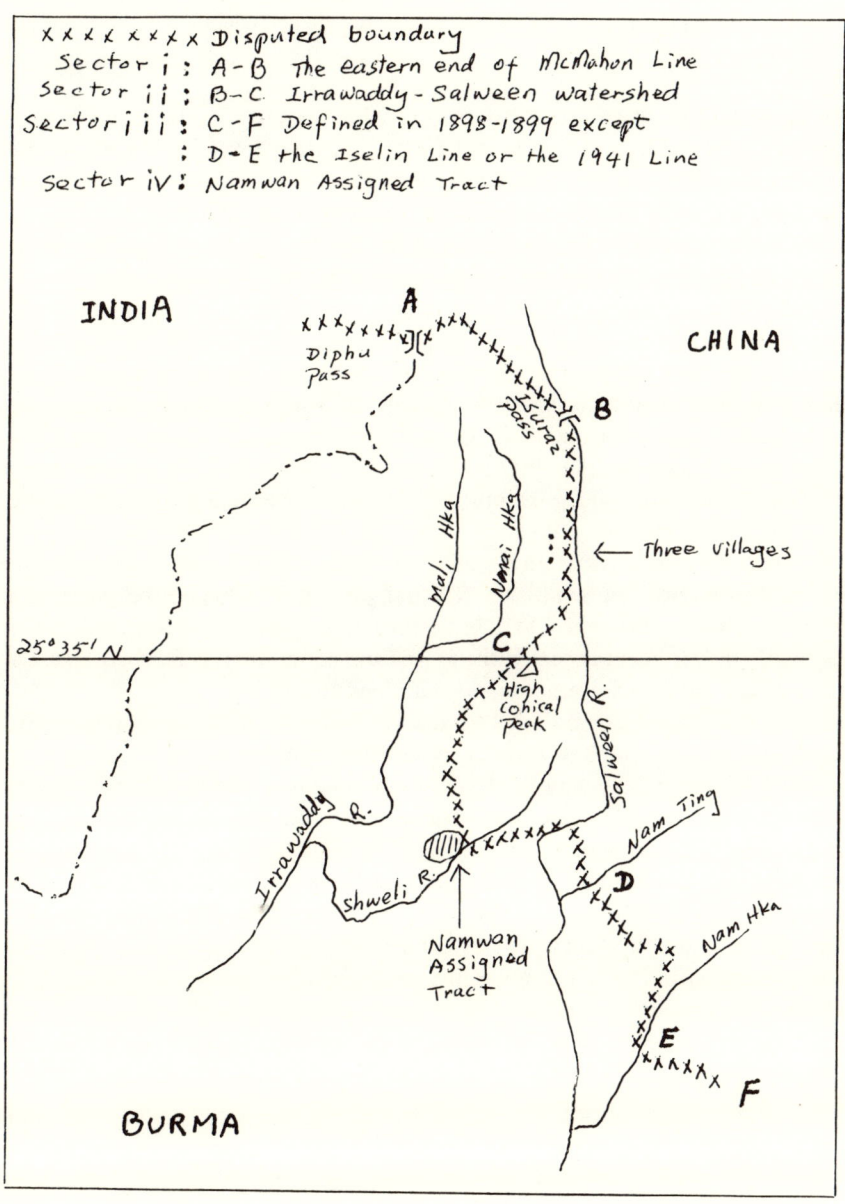

frontier was not defined. According to the convention between Great Britain and China of March 1, 1894, Article 4:

> It is agreed that the settlement and the delimitation of the portion of the frontier which lies to the north of latitude 25°35′ shall be reserved for a future understanding between the high Contracting Parties when the feature and condition of the country are more accurately know.[51]

The agreement between Great Britain and China modifying the Convention of March 1, 1894, relative to Burma and Tibet, signed on February 4, 1897, carried the same stipulation as that of Article 4 of the 1894 Convention; namely, the boundary line north of 25°35′N parallel remained undefined.[52]

3. The third sector is the line south of the 25°35′N parallel. This sector was defined in the 1894 Convention and demarcated in the 1897 Agreement with the exception of an approximate 200-mile strip in the Kawa area, separating the Wu state of Burma from Yunnan Province of China. In 1934, the British troops occupied this area against the resistance of the local tribes (the Panchung incident).[53] In 1935, a commission of the League of Nations under Colonel Frederic Iselin, a Swiss, surveyed and demarcated a line in this area. It is generally known as the Iselin Line, but the PRC refers to it as the 1941 Line because it was accepted by the Nationalist government in 1941 by the exchange of notes between the United Kingdom and China.

However, the Nationalist government of China was not happy about this line and tried to reopen negotiations a few months later.[54] Due to the outbreak of the Pacific War in October 1941, her efforts failed. The PRC declared that the Nationalist government accepted the 1941 Line under duress. Furthermore, they claimed that markers were never erected along this line.[55]

4. The Namwan Assigned Tract (or the Meng-Mao Triangular area) comprised a 260-square kilometer (100-square mile) area situated at the junction of the Namwan River and the Shweli River in the southern Kachin state of Burma. According to the 1897 Agreement between Britain and China, this area was assigned to Britain in "perpetual lease" for an annual payment of 1,000 rupees,[56] but China kept sovereignty. In 1948, the Nationalist government refused to accept the annual rent from Burma, and later, the PRC also refused this rent.[57] In 1957, Chou En-lai announced that "this is Chinese territory, a fact which Britain had also recognized in explicit terms in the treaty."[58]

The boundary problem became even worse after 1949 as described in chapter 3 of this book. Both China and Burma were anxious to settle their boundary question.

Settlement

Since both China and Burma wanted a settlement, the Sino-Burmese boundary negotiations started in 1956. On October 2, 1956, Prime Minister Ba Swe of Burma declared at a press conference that the negotiations had reached a stage where the "Chinese Government had accepted in principle the withdrawal of the troops from the boundary line established in 1941."[59] He added that the Chinese troops which had crossed the northern frontier had left Burma already.[60]

On October 24, 1956, Chairman U Nu of the Burmese Anti-Fascist People's Freedom League held talks with Chou En-lai in Peking. A joint communique which resulted from the talks stated that the Chinese had put forward a "fair and reasonable proposal" to which the Burmese government promised to give consideration.[61] The two governments agreed that by the end of November 1956, Chinese troops would be withdrawn from the area to the west of the 1941 Line; and Burmese troops would be withdrawn from the villages of Hipmaw, Kangfang, and Gawlum. The withdrawal would be completed before the end of 1956. It was later reported that the withdrawal of Chinese troops had been completed on December 12, 1956. It is believed that Burmese troops had also been withdrawn.[62]

On December 10, 1956, Chou arrived in Burma for a ten-day visit and had talks with U Nu. A communique was issued, which stated that the two premiers had "discussed in a spirit of cordial and mutual understanding the question of the settlement of the Sino-Burmese boundary line."[63] These discussions led to further classification of the problems and moved both heads of state nearer to a solution satisfactory to both sides.

On July 9, 1957, Chou delivered a "Report on the Question of the Boundary Line between China and Burma" to the National People's Congress. He revealed the Chinese proposal for settling the boundary problems. China was willing to accept the de facto boundary line drawn up by the British-Burmese government. The extreme northern boundary which runs from Diphu Pass to the Isuraz Pass Chou referred to as the "customary boundary line." The sector from the Isuraz Pass to the High Conical Peak can be determined along the watershed, excluding three villages: Hpimaw, Kangfang and Gawlum. Concerning the 1941 Line, Chou said: "It was the opinion of our government that on the question of boundary lines, demands made on the basis of formal treaties should be respected according to general international practice."[64] In other words, the PRC was ready to accept the 1941 Line and no longer claimed that it was signed under duress. Concerning the Namwan Assigned Tract, China expressed its readiness to negotiate with the Burmese government.

In January 1960, General We Wen of Burma went to Peking and signed a preliminary border agreement.[65] China gave up the claim of Namwan Assigned Tract in exchange for the three villages.

In October 1960, U Nu, who had resumed the premiership of Burma in July, went to Peking and signed the final boundary treaty[66] which was identical in substance with the preliminary one. Transfers of the border territories were completed in June 1961.[67]

Observation

The Sino-Burmese boundary questions were the product of complex historical developments. From the Ch'ing dynasty through the Republic and the People's

Republic of China, troop-crossings of borders had occurred, complaints of signing under duress were lodged, and rent for leased territory was refused. But eventually it was settled. Both China and Burma have expressed their satisfaction with the settlement.

On the Chinese side, the conclusion of the boundary treaty was a result of China's attitude toward the boundary negotiations. Chou, according U Nu's report, "had made it in a just and conciliatory spirit."[68] The mass media of the PRC credited the conclusion of the boundary treaty to the victory of the Five Principles of Peaceful Coexistence.[69]

Scrutinizing the negotiations and the contents of the treaty, the author has discovered that China virtually accepted all the previous boundary treaties with Burma, and gave up all territorial claims, except the claim for the three villages. As a result, the PRC received 340 square kilometers (131 square miles), and Burma received 220 square kilometers (85 square miles) of the disputed areas.[70]

INDIA

Frontiers

China shares a long frontier with India. For the convenience of study, the frontier will be divided into three sections: the western, the middle, and the eastern section. Between the middle and the eastern sections lie the three small Himalaya states: Nepal, Sikkim, and Bhutan. (See Map 5.)

The Western Section. The main conflict in this section is the frontier running from the Karakoram Pass in the extreme west to the Changchenmo valley in the south. It is a frontier between the Ladakh region of Kashmir state on the Indian side and Sinkiang and Tibet on the Chinese side. The area is called Aksai Chin, a bleak uninhabited plateau which in the past was visited only by the inhabitants of adjacent territories in quest of salt and by occasional hunters. India claims that the boundary runs from the Karakoram Pass to the Changchenmo Valley along the Kuen Lun Mountain range,[71] while China claims that the boundary line runs along the Karakoram Mountain range, southwest of the Kuen Lun Mountains.[72] (See Map 6.)

From Changchenmo Valley to the Spiti region, there have been a number of minor disputes such as those involving Chushul and Demchok; the border which Tibet shares with the Indian East Punjab.[73] The whole disputed frontier of this section is over 1,610 kilometers (1,000 miles) long. More than 38,850 square kilometers (15,000 square miles) of territory have been involved in disputes, and most of it under China's control.[74]

The Middle Section. The middle section in dispute, the Ari area, is a frontier approximately 640 kilometers (400 miles) long, from the Spiti region to the junction of the Tibet, India, and Nepal border. There have been several disputed points in Spiti, at Bara Hoti, in the Nilang region and near the Shipki Pass (see

Map 5
The Locations of the Sino-Indian Disputed Boundaries

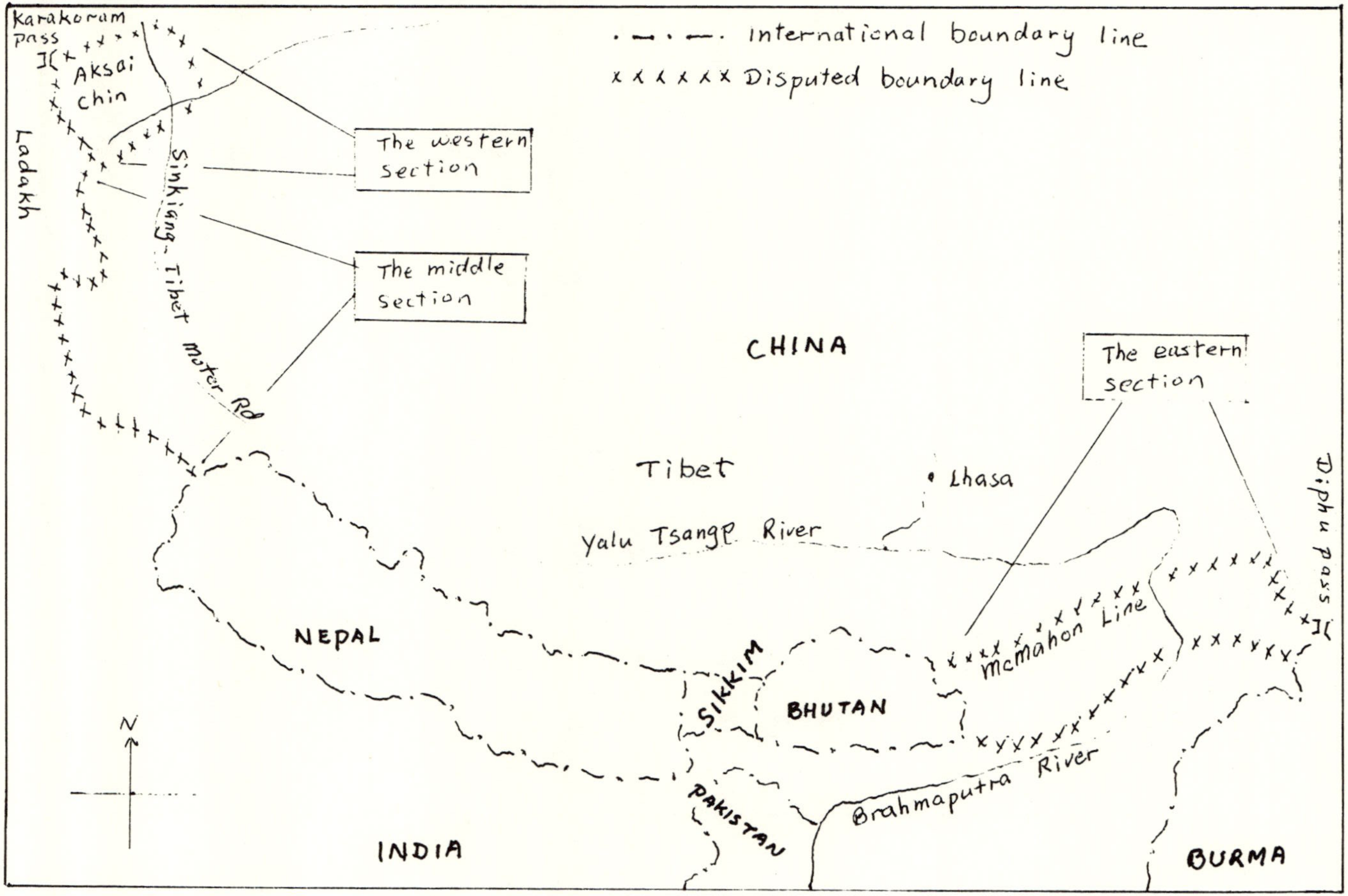

Map 6
The Sino-Indian Disputed Boundaries: Western and Middle Sections

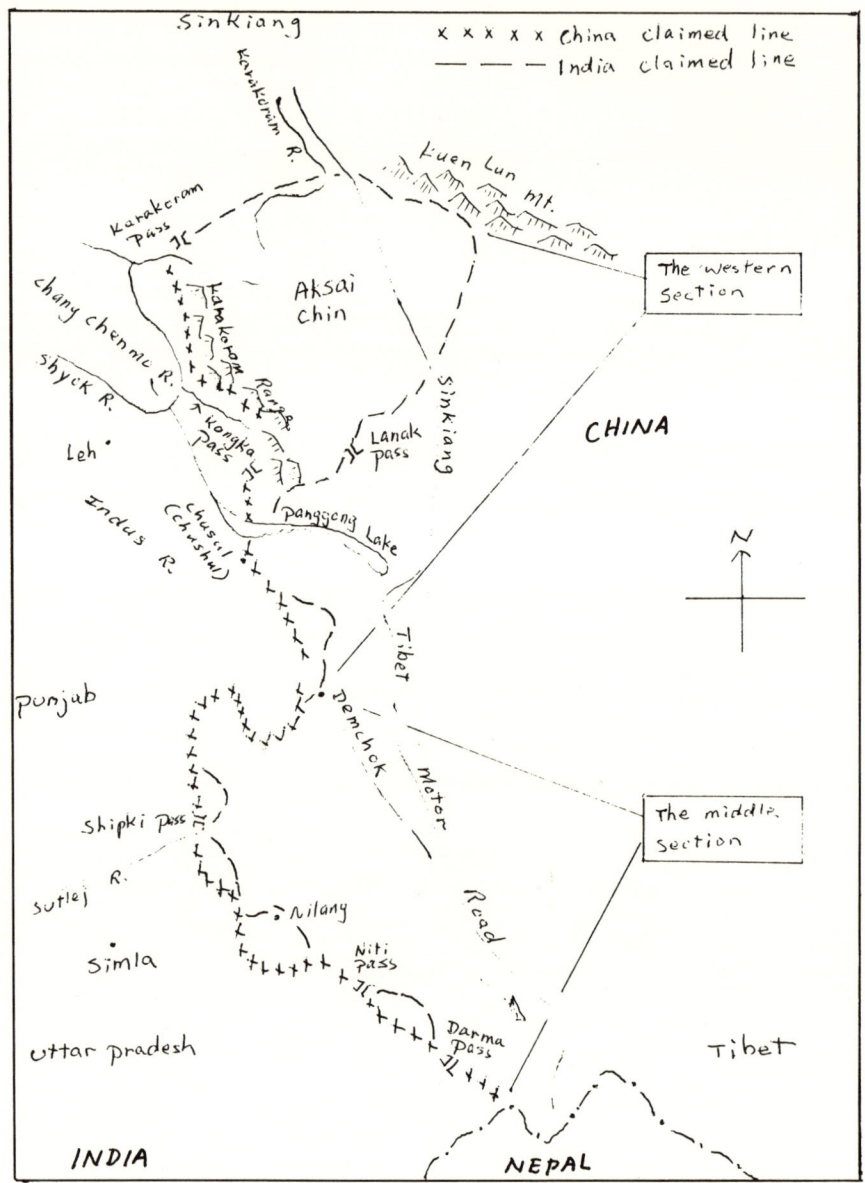

Map 6), altogether perhaps less than 500 square meters (200 square miles). These disputes have persisted for years and never been settled.[75]

The Eastern Section. The frontier in this section is an area of approximately 1,100 kilometers (700 miles) long, from Bhutan in the west to the Chinese-Burmese border in the east. India claims that the boundary line runs along the crest of the Himalayas;[76] south of the crest belongs to India. This line is the so-called McMahon Line, which we will study later in this chapter. China calls the McMahon Line illegal and instead claims a boundary line running along the foot of the Himalayan range.[77] The area between the two lines is approximately 82,900 square meters (32,000 square miles).[78] (See Map 7.)

Disputes

The main dispute between China and India concerning their boundary is whether or not there is a Sino-Indian boundary question. The Indians claim that there is no boundary question at all because all the Sino-Indian boundary lines were delimited either by treaties or custom and some areas were even officially demarcated. According to China, "China and India have never concluded any treaty to delimit the boundary, nor any treaty to confirm the boundary."[79] The focus of their controversy, logically, has been on the legality and the existence of boundary treaties.

Concerning the western section, India claims that the boundary between Ladakh and Tibet was defined by valid treaties. China claims that the boundary line between Ladakh and Tibet was never defined and needed not to be because Ladakh was a part of Tibet. The controversies can be summarized as follows:

1. India claims that between 1681 and 1683, a mixed force of Mongols and Tibetans invaded Ladakh. In 1684, a peace treaty between Ladakh and Tibet was concluded, which reads: "The boundaries fixed in the beginning, when Skyid-Ida-Ngeemagon gave a kingdom to each of his three sons, should still be maintained."[80] Skyid-Ida-Ngeemagon was then a Tibetan prince, who had conferred the Meryal (Ladakh) fief on his oldest son in the tenth century.

The PRC questions the existence of any such "treaty." Moreover, according to historical records, the fact that "Skyid-Ida-Ngeemagon conferred fiefs on each of his three sons only reflected a change in the ownership of manorial estates among the feudal lords of Tibet at that time. The three sons of the prince each took his share of fiefs from the united Skyid-Ida-Ngeemagon dominions, and Meryal at that time was a small state not an independent kingdom."[81] Peking concludes: "Therefore, the question of delimiting the boundary between Ladakh and Tibet as between two countries does not at all arise."[82]

2. The Indians also assert that in 1842 a peace treaty was signed by Kashmir and Ladakh, on the one hand, and Tibet and China, on the other. The treaty was in the form of an exchange of notes. The Indian government argued: "The notes exchanged . . . stated explicitly that the boundary between Ladakh and Tibet was well-known and that this boundary was being confirmed."[83]

Map 7
The Sino-Indian Disputed Boundary: Eastern Section

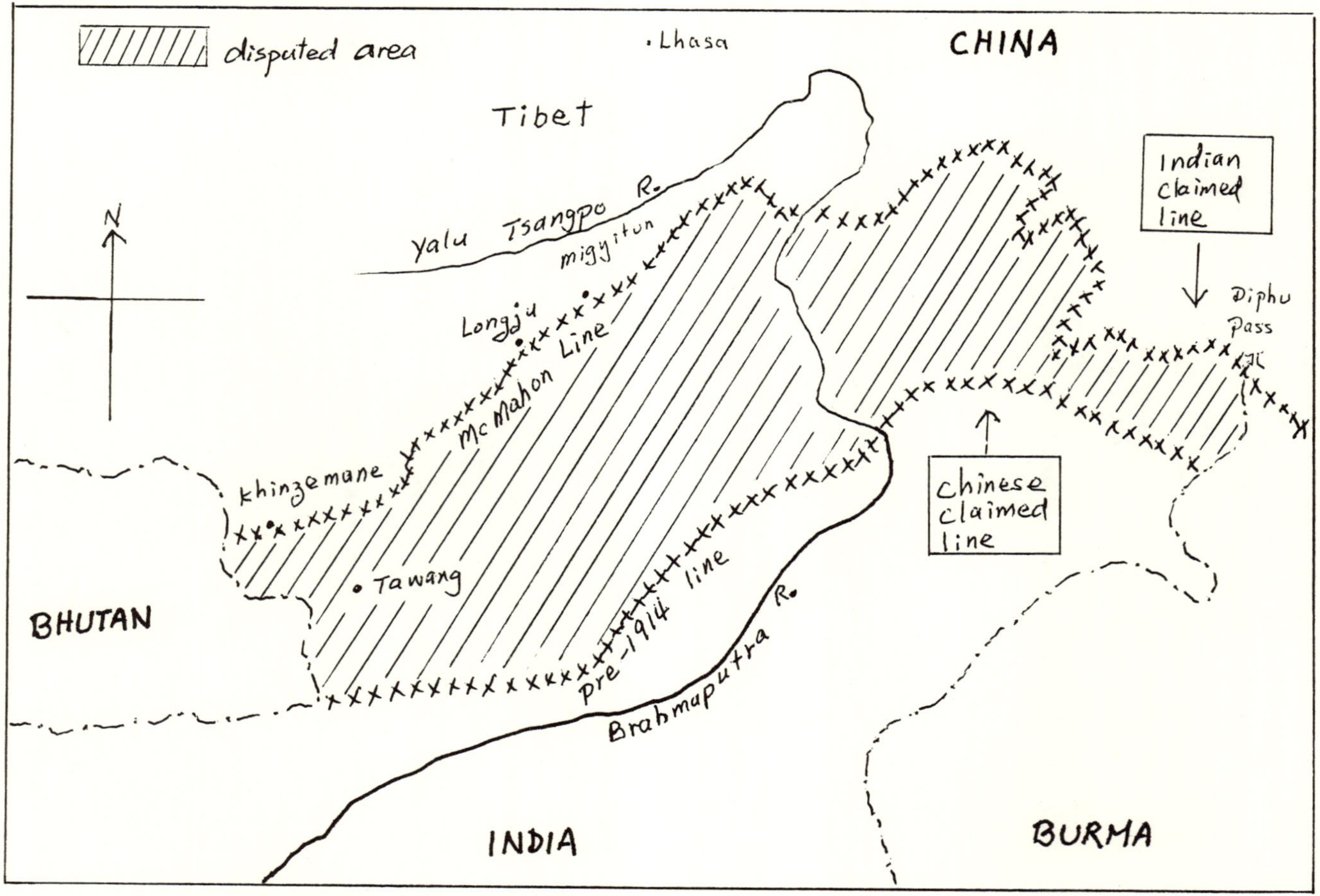

The Chinese government says that "this treaty was only an exchange of notes between the two sides after a war to ensure mutual non-aggression. It did not make any provision whatever of the specific location of the boundary."[84]

3. India argued that an agreement in 1852 between Ladakh and Tibet indicated that the boundary was defined. The agreement reads: "The boundary between Ladakh and Tibet remains the same as before."[85] The PRC says that "this agreement only referred to the maintenance of the old boundary by the two sides of Ladakh and Tibet, and provided that Ladakh should pay 'annual tribute' to Tibet but made no provision whatever about the boundary between Tibet and Ladakh."[86]

4. In 1847, a British official sent a proposal to the Chinese viceroy of Kwangtung and Kwangsi provinces for delimiting the boundary between Ladakh and Tibet. He replied: "The borders of the territories have been sufficiently and distinctly fixed."[87] The Indians adhere to this correspondence and assert too that the boundary was fixed. The PRC argues that China never accepted the proposal. It rejected the British proposal because China feared that the British would later take advantage of a weakened China to obtain even more Chinese territory.

5. In 1899, the British Minister to China, Sir Claude MacDonald, again proposed to the Chinese government a demarcation of the boundary between Sinkiang and Tibet on China's side and Ladakh on India's side, but China did not accept.[88] The PRC asserts that "the submitting of these proposals was in itself said to show that the boundary had not been delimited."[89] As a matter of fact, the proposal suggested a line from the Karakoram Pass eastward, different from any current Indian or British map; the suggested line defined more than half of China's present claims in the Aksai Chin as Chinese territory.

Regarding the middle section, India argues that six passes in the area had been defined as the boundary line by the Sino-Indian Trade Agreement of 1954.[90] China asserts that the 1954 Trade Agreement had nothing to do with the boundary line at all.[91] New Delhi also argues that Chuva and Chuje, in accordance with the aforementioned 1684 and 1842 treaties, belong to India.[92] Peking replies that the 1684 and 1842 treaties cannot constitute a legal basis for claiming Chinese territory on the western section, as Peking had stated already.[93]

Another area, Wuje, which was the first contested area between the two countries in 1954, was confirmed by the correspondence between 1889 and 1890 and 1914, in accordance with India's argument.[94] China says that the boundary was never formally negotiated.[95]

There are two kinds of disputes on the eastern section. One centers on the legality of the so-called McMahon Line along the crest of the Himalayas. India claims the McMahon Line as valid whereas China calls it "illegal."

The McMahon Line is the product of the exchange of notes between Great Britain and Tibet in 1914. Many books and articles on the background of the Simla Conference and the legality of the McMahon Line have been published.[96] Publications and arguments often serve to confuse and lead to different conclusions, drawn from the different points of view. However, a very objective and concise description of the conference is found in Alastair Lamb's work. He wrote that in August 1912, the British put pressure on China to determine the Chinese status in Tibet. The British acted as mediators and hosts to Tibetan and Chinese delegations at Simla in October 1913. On April 27, 1914, the Chinese delegate, Chen I-fan, initiated a text of a tripartite convention which defined the Outer Tibet and Inner Tibet boundary, but the Chinese Central government promptly repudiated the agreement. However, the British representative, Sir Henry McMahon, and the chief Tibetan delegate, the Lonchen Shatra, exchanged notes at Delhi on March 24–25, 1914. By these notes, the Tibetans accepted a boundary line along the crest of the Assam Himalaya. These notes and the attached map did not reveal to the Chinese delegation. As a matter of fact, the McMahon Line (named such by Alastair Lamb) was never discussed at the Simla Conference. Both Nationalist and Communist China mentioned that the McMahon Line was the creation of a British trick and the Chinese never accepted it.[97]

The Indians insist that the McMahon Line was produced by the Simla Conference and is a valid international boundary line between India and Tibet. There reasons are as follows:

First, The Simla Conference of 1914 was a tripartite conference among China, Tibet, and Britain. The Tibetan delegation was on an equal footing with the other two delegations for negotiations. India says that formerly China had recognized Tibet's right to conduct foreign affairs on her own and to deal with matters concerning her boundaries before the Simla Conference. For example, the Nepalese-Tibetan Treaty in 1856 was signed by Nepal and Tibet, and the treaty was recognized by China.[98]

Second, the McMahon Line was discussed in the Simla Conference and decided by the exchange of letters between Tibet and Britain. The nonadherence of the Chinese government to the convention was irrelevant as far as the governments of Tibet and India were concerned.[99]

However, Chinese governments deny the legitimacy of the exchange of letters between Tibet and Britain. The PRC presents the following reasons:

First, China was forced to attend the Simla Conference and did not sign the convention. Even when her delegate, under pressure, initialled the convention, the Chinese Central government promptly and formally repudiated the act.[100]

Second, the Simla Conference only discussed the boundary between Outer Tibet and Inner Tibet. The Indian-Tibetan boundary was produced by the exchange of letters between Britain and Tibetan local governments behind the back of the Chinese Central government.[101]

Third, the Chinese emphasize that China exercised full sovereignty over Tibet at that time.[102] Thus, Tibet had no right to decide her boundary with foreign countries. The exchange of letters between Tibet and Britain therefore had no binding force upon China. Regarding the Tibetan right to sign the 1856 Nepalese-Tibetan Treaty, the Chinese point out that it was dealt with by the Amban (representative of the Central government) in Tibet under authorization.[103]

Because the exchange of letters between Tibet and Britain was done "under the Threat and enticement of Britain,"[104] the Tibetans were not satisfied with it, and disputes about the legality of the McMahon Line occurred. In the 1930s, the Tibetans were still administrating and taxing the Tawang area south of the McMahon Line. In 1947, the Tibetans formally demanded that India return the Tibetan territories, "such as Sayul and Walong and in [the] direction of Pemakoe, Lonag, Lopa, Mon, Bhutan, Sikkim, Darjeeling and others on this side of [the] River Ganges and Lowo, Ladakh[,] etc. upto [the] boundary of Yarkhim."[105] The Indian government replied: "The Government of India would be glad to have an assurance that it is the intention of the Tibetan Government to continue relations on the existing basis until new agreements are reached on matters which either party may wish to take up."[106] During that time, China was deeply involved in civil wars and it was impossible for her to negotiate an agreement on the boundary with India.

The dispute is further complicated by disagreement over exactly where the McMahon Line runs. The Chinese say that the Indians had established a number of posts north of the McMahon Line, while the Indians insist that those posts are in Indian territory.[107] The Chinese see the western end of the McMahon Line at 27°44.6'N, 91°39.7'E, but the Indians see it at 27°48'N, 91°40'E.[108]

Principle for Settlement

Since the Sino-Indian frontiers have never been defined by treaty, China insists that they have to be defined formally by the two countries. Chinese governments have denied the legality of the Simla Convention and called the McMahon Line illegal. However, since India has established checkposts in some areas south of the line, the PRC is willing to take the actual situation as the basis for settlement of the boundary. Thus, the Chinese are willing to accept what they regard as a fait accompli. As early as 1956, when Chou En-lai was visiting India, he raised the question of the McMahon Line. In Nehru's account of the Chou-Nehru conversation, Chou told him that China had accepted the McMahon Line as the boundary with Burma because, although "this line, established by the British imperialists, was not fair... it was an accomplished fact and because of the friendly relations which existed between China and the countries concerned, India and Burma, the Chinese Government were of the opinion that they should give recognition to this McMahon Line."[109]

This principle was also expressed in a note dated January 23, 1959, that said the PRC would "take a more or less realistic attitude towards the McMahon Line."[110] China believed too that "a friendly settlement can eventually be found for this section of the boundary line."[111]

After the Longju incident and the Kongka Pass incident in 1959, Chou sent a letter to Nehru stating that "the Chinese Government proposes that the armed forces of China and India each withdraw 20 kilometers (12.4 miles) at once from the so-called McMahon Line in the east, and from the line to which each side exercises actual control in the west."[112] Chou's proposal implies that the Indians would keep the area south of the McMahon Line, and the PRC the greater part of Aksai Chin, pending the final settlement.

On December 26, 1959, China sent India notice that she has consistently held that "an overall settlement of the boundary question between the two countries should be sought by the Chinese and Indian sides, taking into account the historical background and present actual situation."[113] According to an Indian newspaper, when Chou visited India in April 1960 he told Nehru that China proposed a "reciprocal acceptance of present actualities in both sectors and constitution of a boundary commission."[114] This statement suggested that the Chinese would accept the McMahon Line in the eastern section in exchange for India's acceptance of China's position in the western section. This proposal was confirmed by Chou himself when he told the press in New Delhi:

> We have asked the Indian Government to adopt an attitude towards this western area similar to the attitude of the Chinese Government towards the area of the eastern sector; that is, it may keep its own stand, while agreeing to conduct negotiations and not to cross the line of China's administrative jurisdiction as shown on Chinese maps.[115]

However, China's suggestion was not accepted by the Indian government and the boundary between the two countries has remained a pending question.

THE THREE SMALL HIMALAYA STATES

Bhutan's boundary with China runs from the Sino-Sikkim-Bhutan trijunction in the west to the Sino-Indian-Bhutan trijunction in the east. The total length is from 300 to 500 kilometers (200 to 300 miles) long, depending upon what shared territory claimed by India and China is taken into consideration. (See Map 5.)

Bhutan has been India's protectorate. In 1958 and 1959 India, on Bhutan's behalf, made protests against Chinese troops intruding into Bhutan's territory. India accused the Chinese troops of occupying eight of Bhutan's villages. These villages, according to Indian governmental statement, had been under the jurisdiction of Bhutan for more than 300 years.[116] However, China refused to discuss the matter with India even though she had sometimes recognized Bhutan as a protectorate of India.[117] China acknowledged that there is "a certain discrepancy between the delineation on the maps of the two sides in the sector south of the so-called McMahon Line."[118]

Official negotiations have made no further progress but it was reported that the Sino-Bhutan boundary had been defined by a secret treaty between the two countries in 1961. That method was chosen because both countries wanted to avoid India's involvement.[119]

Sikkim has a border with China approximately 160 kilometers (100 miles) long between the Chinese-Nepalese boundary and the Chinese-Bhutan boundary. The boundary between Sikkim and the Tibet region of China "was defined in the Anglo-Chinese Convention in 1890 and jointly demarcated on the ground in 1895."[120] On December 26, 1959, China again confirmed that "the boundary between China and Sikkim has long been formally delineated and there is neither any discrepancy between the maps nor any dispute in practice."[121]

China and Nepal are separated by high mountains; the length of their common boundary is not available. However, the discrepancy between the two countries' versions concerning their border was neither large nor very controversial. The main dispute was the exact location of the boundary line passing through Mount Everest, the world's highest peak.

Taking the initiative, Chou En-lai visited Nepal in March 1960 and signed a preliminary boundary agreement with Prime Minister B. P. Koirala of Nepal.[122] The agreement put forth guidelines for delineation and demarcation of the Nepalese-Chinese boundary line "on the basis of the existing traditional customary line" (Article 1). A joint committee was established to discuss and solve the concrete problems, conduct surveys, erect markers, and draft a Nepalese-Chinese boundary treaty (Article 3).

The final boundary treaty was signed by King Mahmdra of Nepal and Chou En-lai of China on October 3, 1961, in Peking.[123] The treaty left details of the specific location to be delineated by the joint committee. According to a report published in the *Peking Review* in November 1962, "the joint erecting by China and Nepal of permanent boundary markers has been completed on schedule."[124] A final protocol was signed in January 1963 confirming the location of the markers.[125] However, many writers doubt that markers were ever erected on the summit of Mount Everest.[126]

Based on the treaty and demarcation, "the Chinese acceded to the Nepalese claims over as much as about 2,400 square kilometers (900 square miles) of the territory in dispute and obtained exclusive possession for themselves of only about 56 square miles."[127]

PAKISTAN

Boundary

The Chinese and Pakistani boundary problem centers around Pakistan's alleged entitlement to Kashmir. If Pakistan has sovereignty over the whole or even part of Kashmir, then she shares a boundary with China. If she does not, there is no common border.

The total length of the border line between China and Pakistan-controlled Kashmir in the west of the Indian-Pakistani cease-fire line is approximately 500 kilometers (300 miles). On the Chinese side, it comprises Sinkiang Province; on the Pakistani side, Hunza, Nagar, and Balistan districts.

Settlement

In 1961 Pakistan contacted Peking with the intention of concluding a boundary treaty. In May 1962, China announced that the two countries had agreed to negotiate the boundary question and sign a provisional agreement.[128] Talks began in Peking on October 12, 1962. On December 28, 1962, it was announced that "an agreement in principle has been reached on the location and alignment of the boundary actually existing between the two countries."[129] On March 2, 1963, the formal boundary agreement was signed in Peking.[130] "The two countries have fixed the alignment of the boundary line between China's Sinkiang and the contiguous areas the defence of which is under the actual control of Pakistan" (Article 2). "The two Parties have agreed that the settlement of the Kashmir dispute between Pakistan and India, the sovereign authority concerned will reopen negotiations with the Government of the People's Republic of China on the boundary . . . so as to sign a formal boundary treaty to replace the present agreement, provided that, in the event of that sovereign authority being Pakistan, the provisions of the present Agreement will be maintained in the formal Boundary Treaty to be signed between the People's Republic of China and Pakistan" (Article 6).

With the final boundary protocol of March 26, 1965,[131] about 3,496 square kilometers (1,350 square miles) of the disputed territory were transferred to Pakistan, including 1,942 square kilometers (750 square miles) of the territory which had actually been in China's possession, while China obtained 5,309 square kilometers (2,050 square miles).[132]

AFGHANISTAN

Boundary

The entire length of the China and Afghanistan border line depends on the following considerations: the delineation of the Sino-Soviet boundary line in the Pamirs, and whether or not China recognizes the Wakhan Corridor, a strip of Afghan territory created as a buffer in the late nineteenth century by Britain and Russia to separate the frontier of the two countries in South and Central Asia. The Wakhan Corridor is an area of about 12,950 square kilometers (5,000 square miles). The Nationalist government of the Republic of China has never recognized it. From the point of view of the Nationalist government, the Sino-Afghan border line approximates 675 kilometers (420 miles).[133] On the other hand, the PRC virtually recognized the Wakhan Corridor. The Chinese-Pakistani Boundary Agreement stipulates their boundary starting "from the northwestern extremity at height 5,830 meters (19,127 feet) [a peak, the reference co-ordinates of which are approximately longitude 74'34"E and latitude 37'03"N]."[134] This peak is located at the eastern end of the Wakhan Corridor. The PRC's maps have conceded the existence of this corridor since the mid–1950s.[135] Accordingly, if the Chinese-Soviet boundary lies from Uz Bel Pass due south rather than due southwest, it makes the Sino-Afghan border approximately 180 kilometers (102 miles).[136] However, the protocol on the Sino-Russian boundary in Kashgar region (1884) stipulated that the Soviet boundary from Uz Bel Pass turns southwest, as we have seen earlier in this chapter. Implied in the PRC map is the fact that territory on the right side of this line belongs to China. If that is the case, the China and Afghanistan border line extends to approximately 420 kilometers (140 miles).[137] (See Map 2.)

Settlement

It is conceivable that Afghanistan was very much concerned about her border with China, especially since the Sino-Indian boundary disputes of the 1950s. China's maps marked the Sino-Afghan boundary as undelimited. In March 1963, on the day of the signing of the Sino-Pakistani provisional boundary agreement, the Chinese Foreign Ministry issued a communique, stating that "China and Afghanistan had agreed to conduct negotiations for the purpose of formally delimiting the boundary existing between the two countries."[138]

The final boundary treaty was signed on November 22, 1963.[139] The treaty went into effect on the day of the signature (Article 5). It marked China's formal recognition of the existence of the Wakhan Corridor (Article 1). After the survey and demarcation by the Joint Boundary Demarcation Committee, the final protocol was signed on March 24, 1965.[140]

SUMMARY

The following observations may be drawn from this chapter:

First, China has had boundary disputes with all her neighbors except Vietnam and Laos. During the 1960s, she achieved an historical feat, concluding boundary treaties involving approximately 25,900 square kilometers (10,000 square miles) of territory with seven neighbors: Mongolian People's Republic, Burma, Bhutan, Sikkim, Nepal, Pakistan, and Afghanistan.

During these disputes, the PRC did not behave in an irredentist fashion, demanding the recovery of her "lost territories."[141] Instead, the PRC applied the well-established principles of international law, such as the *thalweg*, etc., to defend her boundary interests.[142]

In the course of the settlements, the PRC respected the equality of states, negotiated in a just and conciliatory spirit, and set forth reasonable proposals (especially the Sino-Burmese boundary settlement). Although boundary treaties signed in the past were questioned at the outset, virtually all were eventually accepted. Even the Wakhan Corridor created by Britain and Russia was formally recognized.

Second, the Chinese-Soviet frontiers, comprising approximately 1,100,000 square kilometers (424,710 square miles), seem unlikely to be completely settled in the near future. China is willing to conclude a new boundary treaty with the Soviet Union taking the unequal treaties as a basis, but she insists that the Soviets must admit the fact that all the Sino-Soviet boundary treaties of the past were unequal. The Soviets, however, are not willing to accept the past treaties as unequal, but they promise to "consult" with the Chinese and make some minor adjustments of their boundaries, based on the existing boundary treaties.

Third, the Chinese-Indian dispute is over a frontier area of approximately 149,500 square kilometers (50,000 square miles). China insists that the Sino-Indian boundary has never been delimited by any treaty. The Indians insist, however, that the boundary lines have been fixed either by valid treaties and/or by custom. The PRC has hinted that she may be ready to recognize India's claims and let her have the area south of the so-called McMahon Line; China in turn would keep the Aksai Chin Plateau. However, India to date has refused this offer.

NOTES

1. Frederica M. Burge and Rinn-Sup Shinn, ed., *China, A Country Study,* 3d ed. (Washington, D.C.: U.S. Government Printing Office, 1981), p. 47.

2. Ibid.; also Tai-sung An, *The Sino-Soviet Territorial Dispute* (Philadelphia: The Westminister Press, 1973), p. 13.

3. An, *The Sino-Soviet Dispute,* p. 13.

4. English text of the treaty in ibid., pp. 168–71.

5. Ibid., p. 30.

6. International Boundary Study, no. 64, Feb. 14, 1966, China-USSR Boundary (Washington, D.C.: Geographer, Office of Research in Economics and Science, Bureau of Intelligence and Research, United States Department of State), p. 8, cited by An, *The Sino-Soviet Dispute,* pp. 32 & 218, n. 16.

7. English text in An, *The Sino-Soviet Dispute,* pp. 178–82.

8. Ibid., p. 32.

9. "Unequal" treaty will be discussed in detail in Chapter 5 of this book.

10. Ivan P. Barsukov, *Graf Nokalai Nikolaevich Maraviev Amurskii Po Ego Pis'mam, Dokumentam, Rasskazam Sovremenikov i Pechatanym Ictochnikam* (Count Muraviev Amuskii According to His Letters, Documents, Tales of Contemporaries and Printed Sources), vol. 1 (Moscow: 1891), cited by Peter S. H. Tang, *Russia and Soviet Policy in Manchuria and Outer Mongolia: 1911–1931* (Durham, North Carolina: Duke University, 1959), p. 29.

11. Ernest G. Ravenstein, *The Russians on Amur* (London: Trubner and Co., 1861), pp. 253–54, cited by An, *The Sino-Soviet Dispute,* p. 36.

12. English text of that treaty in An, *The Sino-Soviet Dispute,* pp. 183–85.

13. "Statement of the Government of the People's Republic of China on May 24, 1969," in *Peking Review* 12, no. 22 (May 30, 1969): 4 (hereafter cited as *PR*).

14. English text of the treaty in An, *The Sino-Soviet Dispute,* pp. 185–89.
15. *PR* 12, no. 22 (May 30, 1969): 4.
16. English text of the protocol in An, *The Sino-Soviet Dispute,* pp. 190–98.
17. Tien-fong Cheng, *A History of Sino-Russian Relations* (Washington, D.C.: Public Affairs Press, 1957), pp. 46–47.
18. English text in An, *The Sino-Soviet Dispute,* pp. 198–202.
19. Ibid., p. 43.
20. *PR* 12, no. 22 (May 30, 1969): 4.
21. The text of this protocol is in Yuan Tung-li, *Russo-Chinese Treaties and Agreements Relating to Sinkiang 1851–1949,* Sinkiang Colletanea, no. 4 (Hong Kong: 1963), p. 71, cited by John W. Garver, "The Sino-Soviet Territorial Dispute in the Pamir Mountains Region," *The China Quarterly,* no. 85 (March 1981): 111.
22. *PR* 12, no. 22 (May 30, 1969): 5.
23. "Statement of the U.S.S.R. Government of June 13, 1969," *The Current Digest of the Soviet Press* 21, no. 24 (July 9, 1969): 11 (hereafter *CDSP*).
24. *PR* 12, no. 41 (Oct. 10,1969): 14.
25. Ibid.
26. "Soviet Government Statement of September 20, 1963," English text in John Gettings, *Survey of the Sino-Soviet Dispute: A Commentary and Extracts from the Recent Polemics* (London: Oxford University Press, 1968), p. 162; also in Dennis J. Doolin, *Territorial Claims in the Sino-Soviet Conflict: Documents and Analysis* (Stanford: Hoover Institute on War, Revolution, and Peace, 1965), p. 32 with some verbal changes.
27. Gettings, *Survey,* p. 160.
28. "Chinese Government Lodges Strong Protest with Soviet Government," *PR* 12, no. 24 (August 22, 1969): 4.
29. "The Chinese Government Lodges Strong Protest with Soviet Government, Chinese Foreign Ministry's June 6 Note," *PR* 12, no. 24 (June 13, 1969): 4–5.
30. "The Chinese Government Lodges Strong Protest with the Soviet Government," *PR* 12, no. 28 (July 11, 1969): 6.
31. "Chenpao Island Has Always Been Chinese Territory," *PR* 12, no. 11 (March 14, 1969): 14–15.
32. "Statement of the People's Republic of China on May 4, 1969," *PR* 12, no. 22 (May 30, 1969): 3.
33. *PR* 12, no. 22 (May 30, 1969): 4.
34. "Soviet Statement of March 29, 1969, to the CPR," English text in Peter Berton, "Background to the Territorial Issue," *Studies in Comparative Communism* 2, nos. 3 & 4 (July/October 1969): 184; also in *New York Times,* March 31, 1969, p. 16.
35. Berton, "Background to the Issue," p. 162.
36. The source of the Sino-Soviet conflict on Bear Island, see Neville Maxwell, "Why the Russians Lifted the Blockade at the Bear Island," *Foreign Affairs* 57, no. 1 (Fall 1978): 138–45, illustrative map in p. 139.
37. Ibid., p. 141.
38. Ibid.
39. Ibid., p. 142.
40. Ibid., p. 143.
41. Ibid., p. 142.
42. *PR* 12, no. 22 (May 30, 1969): 14.

43. "Statement of the U.S.S.R. Government of June 13, 1969," *CDSP* 21, no. 24 (July 9, 1969): 12.

44. Chinese text of the treaty in *Jen-min jih-pao* (People's Daily), March 26, 1963.

45. Harold C. Hinton, *Communist China in World Politics* (Boston: Houghton Mifflin, 1966), p. 330.

46. George Po-chung Chen, "Some Legal Aspects of the Sino-Soviet Border Dispute," (Ph.D. diss., Southern Illinois University, Dec. 1974), p. 138.

47. Hinton, *Communist China,* p. 329.

48. Alastair Lamb, *Asian Frontiers: Studies in a Continuing Problem* (New York: Praeger, 1968), p. 175.

49. Chen, "Some Legal Aspects," p. 104.

50. "Report on the Question of the Boundary Line Between China and Burma Delivered by Chou En-lai, Premier and Foreign Minister, at the Fourth Session of the First National People's Congress on July 9, 1957," *Important Documents on the Settlement of the Sino-Burmese Boundary Question* (Peking: Foreign Languages Press, 1960), pp. 19–20.

51. Citation in J.J.G. Syatauw, *Some Newly Established Asian States and the Development of International Law* (The Hague: Martinus Nijhoff, 1961), p. 123.

52. Ibid., pp. 123–24.

53. *Important Document,* p. 19.

54. Syatauw, *Some Newly Established Asian States,* p. 125; Hinton, *Communist China,* pp. 307 & 310.

55. Chen, "Some Legal Aspects," p. 19.

56. Syatauw, *Some Newly Established Asian States,* p. 124.

57. Hinton, *Communist China,* p. 330.

58. *Important Documents,* p. 20, the "terms" Chou referred to are in Article II of the Convention of 1897, which stipulated: "Great Britain engages to recognize as belong to China the tract to the south of the Namwan River," citation in Syatauw, *Some Newly-Established Asian States,* p. 124.

59. *The Times,* Oct. 3, 1956, quotation in Hinton, *Communist China,* p. 90.

60. Hinton, *Communist China,* p. 90.

61. *New China News Agency,* Nov. 12, 1956, quotation in Hinton, *Communist China,* p. 90.

62. Hinton, *Communist China,* p. 93.

63. *The Nation* (Rangoon), Nov. 11, 1956, quotation in Hinton, *Communist China,* p. 92.

64. *Important Documents,* p. 19.

65. English text of the agreement in ibid., pp. 33–37.

66. English text of the treaty in *PR* 3, no. 40 (Oct. 4, 1960): 33–34.

67. *PR* 4, no. 23 (Jan. 9, 1961): 10.

68. "The Burma-Chinese Frontier Dispute," *The World Today* (London) 13, no. 12 (Feb. 1957): 91.

69. See, for example, Editorial of the *People's Daily* on Oct. 2, 1960, "Warm Greetings to the Signing of the Sino-Burmese Boundary Treaty," English text in *PR* 3, no. 40 (Oct. 4, 1960): 37–39.

70. Chen, "Some Legal Aspects," p. 143.

71. See *Report of the Officials of the Governments of India and the People's Republic*

of China on the Boundary Question (New Delhi: Ministry of External Affairs, Government of India, 1961), p. 1 (hereafter cited as *Report*).

72. *Report*, p. CR–1. ("CR" precedes all page numbers of the section which contains the report of the PRC officials.)

73. *Report*, pp. 1–2, and CR–1–2.

74. Alastair Lamb, *The China-India Border: The Origins of the Disputed Boundaries* (London: Oxford University Press, 1964), p. 7.

75. Ibid., pp. 7–8.

76. *Report*, p. 2.

77. Ibid., pp. CR–2–3.

78. Lamb, *The China-India Border*, p. 9.

79. *Report*, p. CR–28.

80. Quotation in *Report*, p. 51.

81. *Report*, pp. CR–13–14.

82. Ibid., p. CR–14.

83. Ibid., p. 53.

84. Ibid., p. CR–14.

85. Ibid., p. 54.

86. Ibid., p. CR–15.

87. Ibid., p. 54.

88. Full text of Sir Claude MacDonald's note (14 March, 1899) in Lamb, *China-Indian Border*, pp. 180–82.

89. *Report*, p. 55.

90. Ibid., pp. 85–87.

91. Ibid., pp. CR–18–19.

92. Ibid., pp. 71–73.

93. Ibid., p. CR–17.

94. Ibid., pp. 77–83.

95. Ibid., p. CR–18.

96. For examples, Alastair Lamb, *The McMahon Line: A Study in the Relations Between India, China and Tibet, 1904 to 1914* (London: Routledge and Kegan, two volumes, 1966); Wei Liang, "Ts'ung kuo-chi-fa chueh-tu kán shu-wei McMahon Hsien (From the Angle of International Law to Look at the So-called McMahon Line)," *Kuo-chi wen-t'i yen-chiu* (Studies in International Problems), 1959 (no. 6), pp. 47–52.

97. Lamb, *China-India Border*, pp. 142–45.

98. *Report*, pp. 110–15.

99. Ibid.

100. Ibid., pp. CR–19–23.

101. Ibid., pp. CR–23–25.

102. Ibid., p. CR–26. The draft of the Simla Conference (Art. 2) also stipulated: "The Governments of Great Britain and China recognizing that Tibet is under the suzerainty of China," text in Lamb, *The McMahon Line*, vol. 2, p. 621.

103. *Report*, p. CR–25.

104. Ibid., p. CR–28.

105. *Notes, Memoranda and Letters Exchanged and Agreements Signed Between the Governments of India and China: White Paper* (New Delhi: Ministry of External Affairs, 1959–1963) 2: 39 (hereafter cited as *White Paper*).

106. *White Paper* 2: 39.

107. Ibid., 2: 3–10.
108. Ibid., 8: 9. An enlarged map of the western end of the McMahon Line is printed in *Sino-Indian Boundary Question* (Peking: Foreign Languages Press, 1962).
109. "Nehru in Rajya Sabba on Oct. 9, 1959," *Prime Minister on Sino-Indian Relations* 2: 137, quotation in Neville Maxwell, *India's China War,* (New York: Doubleday, 1972), p. 88.
110. *White Paper* 1: 53.
111. Ibid.
112. Ibid., 3: 44–45.
113. Ibid, 3: 71.
114. *Times,* April 21, 1960, quotation in Maxwell, *India's China War,* p. 161.
115. *PR* 3, no. 18 (May 3, 1960): 20.
116. *White Paper,* 1: 46 and 96.
117. Ibid., 2: 30.
118. Ibid., 3: 77.
119. George N. Patterson, "Recent Chinese Policies in Tibet and Towards the Himalayan Border States," *The China Quarterly,* no. 12 (Oct. 1962): 199.
120. *White Paper,* 1: 55.
121. Ibid., 3: 77.
122. English text of the treaty in *PR* 3, no. 13 (March 29, 1960): 8–9.
123. English text of the treaty in *PR* 4, no. 42 (Oct. 20, 1961),: 5–8; also in Arthur Lall, *How Communist China Negotiates* (New York: Columbia University Press, 1968), pp. 262–68.
124. *PR* 5, no. 45 (Nov. 2, 1962): 24.
125. Hinton, *Communist China,* p. 322.
126. Ibid., pp. 321–22; also Lamb, *China-India Border,* p. 132, footnote.
127. Lall, *How Communist China Negotiates,* p. 200.
128. *PR* 5, no. 19 (May 11, 1962): 10.
129. *PR* 5, no. 52 (Dec. 28, 1962): 8.
130. English text of the agreement in *PR* 6, nos. 10–11 (March 15, 1963): 67–70.
131. *PR* 8, no. 14 (April 2, 1965): 5.
132. A. O. Cukwurah, *The Settlement of Boundary Disputes in International Law* (New York: Oceana Publications, 1967), p. 146; also Hinton, *Communist China,* p. 319.
133. Garver, "The Sino-Soviet Territorial Dispute," pp. 116–17.
134. English text of the agreement in *PR* 6, nos. 10–11 (March 15, 1963): 67–70.
135. Hinton, *Communist China,* p. 320.
136. Garver, "The Sino-Soviet Territorial Dispute," p. 117.
137. Ibid.
138. *PR* 6, nos. 10–11 (March 15, 1963): 5.
139. English text of the treaty in *PR* 6, no. 48 (Nov. 29, 1963): 7–9.
140. *PR* 8, no. 14 (April 2, 1965): 4.
141. Concerning the "lost territories," see Chapter 5 of this book.
142. The PRC's applying the principles of international law to dispute with neighboring states and defend her boundary interests will be examined in greater detail in Chapter 6 of this book.

5
UNEQUAL BOUNDARY TREATIES

INTRODUCTION

After the middle of the nineteenth century, China "lost" huge territories to the big powers. Some were ceded to them under unequal treaties, and some were occupied and annexed by force. Some proclaimed themselves independent states under the influence of the big powers. These "lost territories," according to Dr. Sun Yat-sen's view, included Taiwan, the Penhu Archipelago (the Pescadores), Burma, Annam (Vietnam), the Amur and Ussuri river basins, and the areas north of Ili, Kholand, as well as such tributary areas as the Ryukyu (Okinawa), Thailand, Borneo, the Sulu Archipelago, Java, Ceylon, Nepal, and Bhutan.[1] Chiang Kai-shek, the late president of the Republic of China, agreed with Dr. Sun.[2] Mao Tse-tung in 1939 also listed the Chinese territories ceded or leased to the imperialists after the Opium War.[3] In 1954, a map in a history textbook, published in Shanghai, lists in detail the "lost territories."[4]

A Chinese wished that some day they could recover these "lost territories." Chiang Kai-shek declared that, "the peoples as a whole must regard this [losing territory] as a national humiliation, and not until all lost territories have been recovered can we relax our efforts to wipe out this humiliation and save ourselves from destruction."[5] Mao held a similar view. He said to Edgar Snow in 1936 that: "It is the immediate task of China to regain all our lost territories."[6]

The Chinese have been trying to legally recover some of the "lost territories" which were ceded or leased to the big powers under the unequal treaties. They also have been trying legally to redefine their boundaries since the Nationalist revolution in 1911. This chapter analyzes: (1) The concept of the unequal treaty,

(2) the unequal boundary treaties, and (3) the efforts to solve the unequal boundary treaty question.

THE CONCEPT OF THE UNEQUAL TREATY

Although the concept of the unequal treaty was discussed by classical Western writers, such as Hugo Grotius, Emerich De Vattel, H. W. Halleck, and Harris Taylor, the Chinese concept had its origin in China,[7] because the big powers, after the Opium War of 1840, not only seized China's territories violating her administrative integrity, but also controlled her economy through these unequal treaties. Ch'ien T'ai gave the definition of the unequal treaty:

> Generally, treaties between states are based on mutual benefit and equality; if only one party undertakes an obligation and the other party does not have a corresponding obligation, the inequality is obvious. For instance, China allowed other states to enjoy consular jurisdiction in China... but other states did not allow China to enjoy the same right in their territories.[8]

Ch'ien's basic theory is built on "mutual benefit and equality" between states. Any treaty violating these principles is an unequal treaty. A similar view was expressed by two noted scholars, Wang Shih-chieh and Hu Ching-yu. They wrote that modern states all insist on mutual benefit and the equality. "If between the contracting states only one party undertakes obligations and the other party enjoys rights, the treaty providing such a relationship is naturally an unequal treaty."[9]

Ch'ien, Wang, and Hu did not reveal the source for equality among the states. Chou Keng-sheng did so. He pointed out that the equality of states is a traditional principle of international law and expressed by Section 1, Article 2 of the United Nations Charter.[10] The Chinese governmental interpretation of treaty is also based on this notion; that is, unequal treaties violated the equality of states.[11]

Writers in the PRC have claimed that unequal treaties are void. The purpose of the unequal treaties, they asserted, was not to benefit the contracting parties but to serve the interests of the imperialists. Mao Tao, for example, had this to say:

> Old international law virtually denied the principles of equality and mutual benefit. The most obvious point is that it openly recognized the validity of unequal treaties. It provided a "legal" basis for the ugly behavior of the imperialists.[12]

Unequal treaties, it is argued, have no binding force because they were imposed on weak states. For example, Japan forced the Ch'ing dynasty of China to cede Taiwan and Penhu Archipelago through the unequal Treaty of Shimonoseki after the Sino-Japanese War of 1895. Hsin Wu wrote: "This is tantamount to saying it is legal for a robber to rob valuables by brandishing a dirk before an owner, threatening his life and forcing him to put his fingerprint on a document expressing his consent."[13]

However, whether unequal treaties are ipso facto void from the beginning or a certain procedure is needed to invalidate them is a question. Writers have held different views. Wang Yao-t'ien wrote: "Progressive mankind takes fundamentally different attitudes towards different kinds of treaties. Equal treaties *should be strictly observed*. Unequal treaties are in violation of international law and *without legal validity*" (emphasis added).[14]

According to his advocacy, states do not have to observe the unequal treaty because it is without legal validity from the beginning. Four other cowriters held a different view. They wrote:

> Treaties can be classified into equal treaties and unequal treaties and the latter undermine the most fundamental principles of international law—such as the principle of sovereignty; therefore they are illegal and void, and *states have the right to abrogate* this type of treaty at any time [emphasis added].[15]

The same view was expressed by the law workers (*Fa-lu kung-tso-tse*)[16] from Asian and African countries in a conference held in Damascus, Syria, in 1957. According to the report of China's delegate, Mao Tao, the conference "condemned unequal treaties.... It declared that *states which were imposed upon to sign the unequal treaties have the right to be liberated*" (emphasis added).[17]

Accordingly, if a state does not use her right, the unequal treaty has binding force upon her. That is to say, a procedure of abrogation is needed in order to invalidate an unequal treaty.

When the United Nations International Law Commission codified the law of treaties in 1966, the PRC did not attend these meetings. The Nationalist government in Taiwan did, but it had no intention of promoting the concept of the unequal treaty.[18] At the 1968 and 1969 Vienna Conference on the Law of Treaties, the delegate of the Nationalist government did not participate vigorously.[19] The Chinese concept of the unequal treaty therefore has not been incorporated into the annals of international law.

THE UNEQUAL BOUNDARY TREATIES

We will now examine which boundary treaties are regarded by the Chinese as being unequal.

Sino-Russian Boundary Treaties

In 1943, when Generalissimo Chiang Kai-shek described the Sino-Soviet boundary, he only said that "the frontier problems between China and the Soviet Union have not yet been satisfactorily settled,"[20] without specifically pointing out any boundary treaty. The question of Sino-Russian boundary treaties was obviously not systematically examined by the Nationalist government.

In 1939, the Chinese Communist leader Mao Tse-tung also blamed the "imperialists" for the inequitable treaties that cost China land. He wrote:

> The imperialist powers have waged many wars of aggression against China, for instance, the Opium War launched by Britain in 1840, the war launched by the Anglo-French allied forces in 1857, the Sino-French War of 1884, the Sino-Japanese War of 1894, and the war launched by the allied forces of the eight powers in 1900. After defeating China in war, they not only occupied many neighboring countries formally under her protection, but seized or "leased" parts of her territory.[21]

He was not specific concerning the Sino-Soviet boundary treaties. That was probably because the Chinese Communists needed the support of the Soviet Union in the 1930s and the 1940s. When conflict arose and Soviet support ceased, the problem of the unequal boundary treaties emerged.

The Sino-Soviet boundary question was triggered in 1962 when Khrushchev sarcastically referred to Peking's attitude toward Hong Kong and Macao.[22] Peking responded in a letter dated March 8, 1963, addressed to the Communist Party of the U.S.A., but unmistakably meant for Khrushchev:

> In the hundred years or so prior to the victory of the Chinese revolution, the imperialist and colonial powers—the United States, Britain, France, Czarist Russia, Germany, Japan, Italy, Austria, Belgium, the Netherlands, Spain, and Portugal—carried out unbridled aggression against China. They compelled the government of old China to sign a large number of unequal treaties—the Treaty of Nanking of 1842, the Treaty of Aigun of 1858, the Treaty of Tientsin of 1858, the Treaty of Peking of 1860, the Treaty of Ili of 1881, the Protocol of Lisbon of 1887, the Treaty of Shimonoseki of 1895, the Convention for the extension of Hong Kong of 1898, the International Protocol of 1901, etc. By virtue of these unequal treaties, they annexed Chinese territories.[23]

In this letter, Peking mentioned four unequal treaties relating to the Sino-Russian boundaries—the Treaty of Aigun of 1858, the Treaty of Tientsin of 1858, the Treaty of Peking of 1860, and the Treaty of Ili of 1881. The following year, Mao made a more comprehensive statement to the Japanese Socialist delegation in Peking: "About a hundred years ago, the area to the east of Lake Baikal became Russian territory, since then Vladivostok, Khaborovsk, Kamchatka, and other areas have been Soviet territory. We have not year presented our account for this list."[24] This statement is tantamount to saying that the Chinese boundary was at the east of Lake Baikal as defined by the treaties of Nipchu and Burinsky.

The PRC statement of May 24, 1969, also supported Mao's position:

> In 1689, China and Russia concluded their first boundary treaty, the "Treaty of Nipchu," which defined the eastern sector of the Sino-Russian boundary. In 1927,

China and Russia concluded the "Burinsky Treaty," which defined the middle sector of the Sino-Russian boundary (the large part of this sector of the boundary has now become Mongolian-Soviet boundary). As for the western frontier of China, it was then at the Balkash Lake....

After the Opium War of 1840... tsarist Russia forced China to sign a series of unequal treaties by which it annexed more than 1.5 million square kilometers of Chinese territory.[25]

For evidence in support of the statement, the PRC pointed to the Sino-Russian Treaty of Aigun in 1858, the Sino-Russian Treaty of Peking in 1860, the Tahcheng Protocol on the Delimitation of Sino-Russian Boundary in 1864, and the Sino-Russian Ili Treaty in 1881. The PRC concluded that "the treaties relating to the present Sino-Soviet boundary are all unequal treaties, that they should all be annulled."[26]

The PRC declared that "the treaties relating to the present Sino-Soviet boundaries are *all* unequal treaties imposed on China by tsarist Russian imperialism" (emphasis added).[27] In contrast, the PRC recognized the validity of the protocol on the Sino-Russian boundary in the Kashgar region in 1884. The Chinese Foreign Ministry pointed out:

Although the Sino-Russian Kashgar Boundary Treaty (1884) was signed by the Chinese Qing [Ch'ing] Government under tsarist Russian duress, the treaty remains *the only valid boundary treaty* determining the alignment of the Chinese and Soviet frontiers in the Pamirs [emphasis added].[28]

We do not know why the PRC called the 1884 Protocol the only valid boundary treaty. Nevertheless, the Nationalist government takes a different point of view. Maps being published by the Nationalist government show that China once claimed a huge territory beyond the line the 1884 Treaty laid down.[29] Obviously, the Nationalists treat the 1884 Protocol as an unequal treaty.

Outer Mongolian-Soviet Boundary Treaties

An analysis of China's unequal boundary treaties should include study of the treaties concerning the Outer Mongolian region and Russia.

The Mongols ruled China proper as the Yuen dynasty (A.D. 1279–1368). They were driven out during the Ming dynasty (A.D. 1368–1644), and forced back to the steppe. In the middle of the seventeenth century, the Manchus overthrew the Ming dynasty (A.D. 1644) and conquered China proper and later Mongolia (both Inner and Outer Mongolia), making it a part of China.

In 1911, during the Nationalist Revolution in China, the Russians sent arms to the Mongols and thus helped the establishment of the Empire of Mongolia. Facing the situation created by the Russians, China held long negotiations with Russia. On November 5, 1913, China and Russia issued a joint declaration wherein China recognized the autonomy of Outer Mongolia. In 1921, the People's Revolutionary government at Urga was established. In 1924, the Mongolian People's Republic was proclaimed. During this period, the Soviets gradually took dominion over Outer Mongolia.

In 1945, the United States, Great Britain, and the Soviet Union signed a secret agreement at Yalta. The United States and Great Britain accepted Stalin's demand for the preservation of "the status quo in Outer Mongolia," namely, the preservation of the Mongolian People's Republic.

The Nationalist government, under pressure from Washington, signed the Sino-Soviet Treaty of Friendship and Alliance on August 14, 1945. There in the Nationalist government declared that it was prepared to "recognize the independence of Outer Mongolia," if "a plebiscite of the people of Outer Mongolia confirmed that they desire" it.[30]

The plebiscite was held on October 20 of the same year, in which 98.4 percent of the Mongols voted in favor of the separation from China.[31] In January 1946, China declared Outer Mongolia an independent state.

At the northwestern corner of Outer Mongolia there was a thinly populated region of approximately 165,760 square kilometers (64,000 square miles), Tannu Urianghai (or Tannu Tuva). The 1864 Sino-Russian Protocol of Chuguchak defined Tannu Urianghai as being within Chinese domain.[32] It had been under the jurisdiction of the Chinese military governor at Uliassutai until 1911.

In 1914, the tzar made Tannu Urianghai a Russian protectorate. In 1925, the Soviets drew up a treaty of friendship between the Mongolian People's Republic and the People's Republic of Tannu Tuva. The Soviets instructed the two governments to sign this Soviet-drawn treaty, which they did in 1926. In it, each recognized the other's independence and agreed to enter into diplomatic relations.[33] The Soviets did not discuss this matter with China even though at that time Outer Mongolia was still nominally a part of China. In 1944, the Soviets formally incorporated Tannu Tuva into the Soviet Union as an autonomous region.[34]

All these treaties relating to the status of Outer Mongolia and Tannu Urianghai were imposed on China by the Soviets. However, the PRC has never officially mentioned any of them as an unequal treaty.

Sino-Burmese Boundary Treaties

Concerning the Sino-Burmese boundary, Chou En-lai reported to the National Congress in 1957 that "the question of the boundary line between China and Burma is the result of the policy of aggression carried on over the years by the imperialists."[35] Chou thus named two treaties as unequal: The Convention of 1897 by which the Namwan Assigned Tract was assigned to Britain in perpetual lease for an annual payment of 1,000 rupees, and the exchange of notes between Great Britain and China concerning the Burma-Yunnan boundary in 1941, which created the "1941 Line."

In 1948, the Nationalist government refused to receive the annual payment of 1,000 rupees from Burma. The PRC also refused to accept the annual payment. She did so because she held that the Convention of 1897 was "inconsistent with the relations of equality . . . between China and Burma."[36] Regarding the 1941 exchange of notes, both governments rejected it because it was drawn up at a time when China was deeply involved in a war against Japan.[37]

EFFORTS TO REVISE OR ABROGATE THE UNEQUAL BOUNDARY TREATIES

Sino-Russian Boundary Treaties

To revise or abrogate the unequal treaties was one of the main goals of the Nationalist revolution in 1911. To accomplish this goal, the Nationalist government abandoned the view that unequal treaties are ipso facto invalid from the beginning. Instead, it invoked the principle of *rebus sic stantibus* and used negotiations to abrogate them. For example, the Nationalist government, on May 4, 1931, promulgated an act entitled "Regulations Concerning the Exercise of Jurisdiction over Foreign Nations in China."[38] This act abrogated the big powers' consular jurisdiction (extraterritoriality) in China. The National People's Representative Conference, on May 12, 1931, passed a resolution supporting this act. The resolution invoked the norm of *rebus sic stantibus* and Article 19 of the Convention of the League of Nations concerning the reconsideration of treaties that have become inapplicable.[39]

However, the efforts to abrogate the Sino-Russian unequal boundary treaties were initiated by the Soviets. On July 25, 1919, the Soviet government "proclaimed that all the secret treaties concluded with Japan, China, and the former Allies were annulled," and "the Soviet Government has renounced the conquests made by the Tsarist Government which deprived China of Manchuria and other areas."[40] On September 27, 1920, a Soviet-Chinese agreement was proposed by the Soviet government. Article 1 stipulated: "The Government of Russian Socialist Federated Soviet Republics declares as void all the treaties concluded by the former Government of Russia with China, renounces all the annexation of Chinese territory, all the Concessions in China."[41]

On May 31, 1924, the Agreement on General Principles for the Settlement of the Questions Between the Republic of China and the Union of Soviet Socialist Republics was signed at Peking.[42] It affirmed that the two governments agreed to "annul . . . all Conventions, Treaties, Agreements, Protocols, Contracts, etc., . . . concluded between the Government of China and the Tsarist Government and to replace them with new treaties, agreements, etc., on the basis of equality, reciprocity, and justice" (Article 3). The two parties also agreed "to redemarcate their natural boundaries" (Article 7). However, the Soviet delegation shortly thereafter disappeared from the negotiating table for unknown reasons.

The PRC wanted her boundary questions to be settled peacefully. In theory, she took a stronger position, as Shih Sung et al. advocated, that states have the right to abrogate unequal treaties. A statement issued by the PRC in 1969 said that "the treaties relating to the present Sino-Soviet boundary are *all* unequal treaties, . . . *they should all be annulled*" (emphasis added).[43] Actually, the PRC did not unilaterally annul any boundary treaty, including the Sino-Russia boundary treaty, because Peking said that "the Chinese Government has never demanded the return of the territory tsarist Russia had annexed by means of the unequal treaties."[44]

The Soviets asserted that the Sino-Soviet boundary was not arbitrarily decided by unequal treaties, but came about as a natural result of historical developments confirmed by treaties. A Soviet governmental statement said:

> The border between the Soviet Union and China, which came about many generations ago, reflected and continues to reflect the actual settlement of the land by the peoples of these two states along natural mountain and river frontiers. Along its entire length, this border has been given definite and clear legal formulation by treaties, protocols and maps.[45]

Moscow then listed the Treaty of Aigun (1858), the Treaty of Tientsin (1858), the Treaty of Peking (1860), and the 1861 protocol as examples.[46] She concluded that to "the Soviet peoples who have lived and worked on this land for several generations and consider it their homeland, the present border has developed historically and was fixed by life itself."[47]

Moreover, Soviet historians and jurists accused the Chinese of encroaching upon Russian territories through unequal treaties. For example, one writer, V. M. Khvostov, argued that the Treaty of Nerchinsk of 1689 (China recognized its legality) was signed by Russia under threat from superior Ch'ing Chinese forces, and the Treaty of Aigun of 1858 (China calls it unequal) was unequal in the sense that it favored China because Russia in that treaty recovered only a part of the territory she had lost to China through the Nerchinsk Treaty.[48]

The Soviets, in the Declarations of 1919 and 1920 and in the Sino-Soviet Agreement of 1924, declared the Sino-Russian unequal treaties void, but in 1969 they argued that the boundary treaties were not included in those unequal treaties. A governmental statement said:

> Neither the 1919 appeal nor the 1924 agreement between the Soviet Union and the Chinese Republic contained any indication—nor could they have contained any—to the effect that the treaties defining the location of the present Soviet-Chinese border were included among the unequal or secret treaties. Naturally, there was also no discussion of their abrogation or revision."[49]

However, Article 7 of the 1924 Agreement stipulated that the two countries had agreed to redemarcating their boundaries. To this point, a Soviet writer explained that "under the 1924 Agreement, the understanding was that the frontiers would not be 'redefined' but 'checked'."[50]

Up to the present, efforts of both the Nationalist and People's governments of China to revise or abrogate the Sino-Russia unequal boundary treaties have failed because the Soviets have never sincerely wished to alter them, and have even gone as far as to deny their inequality.

The Frontier of Mongolia

The PRC quietly began to negotiate over the Mongolian frontier boundary with the Soviets. Here, Peking tried a low-key diplomacy, but apparently without success. In October 1954, the leaders of the PRC raised the question of Outer Mongolia with Khrushchev and the other Soviet leaders at Peking. However, Khrushchev refused to discuss the matter,[51] and Peking could do nothing about it. But the Chinese did not forget the matter. After ten years, in 1964, Mao told the Japanese Socialist Party delegation in Peking: "There are too many places occupied by the Soviet Union. . . . The Soviet Union, under the pretext of assuring the independence of Mongolia, actually placed the country under its domination."[52] Obviously, the Chinese believed that the treaties relating to the status of Outer Mongolia were imposed on them by Russia and are thus unequal.

The Sino-Burmese Boundary Treaties

The Nationalist government before moving into Taiwan also made an effort to study the Sino-Burmese boundary treaties. As early as 1929, the political program of the Nationalist government during the Period of Political Tutelage was proclaimed. The program obliged the executive branch, inter alia, to establish a committee for examining boundary treaties and to define the uncertain boundaries with Burma.[53] By the Sino-British exchange of notes of April 19, 1935, a Yunnan-Burma Commission was established in order to define the boundary between Burma and China's Yunnan Province.[54] However, the war against Japan prevented China from completing that task. Therefore, the Chinese-Burmese boundary question remained an issue until the formation of the People's Republic.

The PRC inherited the problem and took a diplomatic approach to settle the Sino-Burmese boundary question. Chou En-lai emphasized this in his report to the National Congress in 1957. He said: "Our government has consistently held that a fair and reasonable settlement of all outstanding questions between China and other countries should be sought through peaceful negotiation."[55]

According to Chou, two of the Sino-Burmese treaties were unequal: The Convention of 1897 (the British leased the Namwan Assigned Tract) and the 1941 Agreement (delimitation between the Nam Ting and the Nam Hka rivers). The Chinese complained that they approved these treaties under duress. According to principles of international law, duress cannot be claimed if the representatives of the contracting parties are not intimidated or coerced. Peking might have realized this because during negotiations with Burma, she did not insist that these treaties were necessarily void.

In 1956, U Nu, chairman of the Burmese Anti-Facist People's Freedom

League, held talks with the leaders of the PRC in Peking. Their joint communique stated that Burma would consider a "fair and reasonable proposal" made by the PRC.[56] The general principle of this proposal was revealed by Chou, when in a speech he delivered on the border issue to the National People's Congress he said: "It was the opinion of our government that on the question of boundary lines, demands made on the basis of formal treaties should be respected according to general international practice."[57]

Peking, in the 1960 Sino-Burmese Boundary Treaty, virtually recognized all the boundary treaties signed in the past. China gave up the claim of the Namwan Assigned Tract and accepted the "1941 Line." Peking used two kinds of data for determining the boundary line with Burma; data "which can be used as a legal and reasonable basis" and data "which have only reference value."[58] It indicates that treaties formally signed and ratified have legal basis without mentioning the question of equality.

SUMMARY

The concept of unequal treaties arose from the Chinese national experience. All writers have the same view that unequal treaties violate the fundamental principle of equality in international law. The writers differ only in that some believe that to invalidate these treaties, a certain procedure—abrogation—is needed, while others imply that unequal treaties in themselves are void from the beginning.

The Chinese and the Soviets have disagreed over the characteristics of their boundary treaties. The Chinese have insisted that all the Sino-Russian boundary treaties are unequal; the Soviets have denied the inequality of those treaties. In China, there are also internal disagreements as to which treaties are and are not equitable.

The Chinese government took a diplomatic approach in negotiating with her neighbors to abolish or revise the unequal boundary treaties. Because the Soviets have refused to admit the inequality of the Sino-Russian boundary treaties, they have rejected any Chinese proposals to abrogate the unequal boundary treaties and to form new treaties based on the actual border conditions. They are only willing to make minor adjustments based on the existing boundary treaties. With Burma, the PRC signed a new boundary treaty without preconditions. The new boundary alignments varied very little from the treaties of the past.

NOTES

1. Dennis J. Doolin, *Territorial Claims in the Sino-Soviet Conflict: Documents and Analysis* (Stanford: Hoover Institute on War, Revolution and Peace, Stanford University Press, 1965), p. 15, note 3.
2. Ibid.
3. Mao Tse-tung, "The Chinese Revolution and the Chinese Communist Party," in

Committee for the Publication of the Selected Works of Mao Tse-tung, Central Committee of the Communist Party of China, ed., *Selected Works of Mao Tse-tung*, 5 vols. (Peking: Foreign Languages Press, 1951–1977), 2: 311.

4. The map in Chinese was reprinted with English illustration in Doolin, *Territorial Claims*, pp. 16–17; also in Samuel S. Kim, *China, the United Nations, and World Order* (Princeton: Princeton University Press, 1979), p. 44.

5. Chiang Kai-shek, *China's Destiny*, English ed. (New York: Roy Publishers, 1947), p. 34.

6. Edgar Snow, *Red Star Over China* (New York: Grove Press, 1973), p. 110.

7. See Hungdah Chiu, "Comparision of the Nationalist and Communist View of Unequal Treaties," in Jerome A. Cohen, ed., *China's Practice of International Law* (Cambridge: Harvard University Press, 1972), pp. 239–48.

8. Ch'ien T'ai, *Ch'ung-kuo pu-p'ing-teng t'iao-yueh chih yuan-ch'i chi ch'i fei-ch'u chih ching-kuo* (The Origin and the Process of Abrogation of China's Unequal Treaties), quotation in Chiu, "Comparison," p. 249.

9. Wang Shih-chieh and Hu Ching-yu, *Ch'ung-kuo pu-p'ing-teng t'iao-yueh chih fei-ch'u* (The Abrogation of China's Unequal Treaties), p. 45, quotation in Chiu, "Comparison," p. 249. However, one writer, Wang Yao-t'ien, credited the classification of equal and unequal treaties to Marxism-Leninism. He wrote: "In accordance with Marxism-Leninism, there are equal treaties and unequal treaties," in his *Kuo-chi mao-i t'iao-yueh ho hsieh-ting* (International Trade Treaties and Agreements), (Peking: Ts'ai-cheng ching-chi Press, 1958), p. 10, quotation in Chiu, "Comparison," pp. 258–59.

10. Chou Keng-sheng, "Ts'ung kuo-chi-fa nun ho-p'ing kung-ch'u ti yuen-che" (On the Principle of Peaceful Coexistence in International Law), *Chen-fa yen-chiu* (Studies in Political Science and Law), no. 6 (1955): 41 (hereafter cited as *CFYC*).

11. See "Statement of the Government of the People's Republic of China," in *Peking Review* 12, no. 22 (May 30, 1969): 3–8 (hereafter cited as *PR*).

12. Mao Tao, "Ya-fei fa-lu kung-tso-che hui-i ti tsung-ta ch'eng-ch'iu (The Important Accomplishment of the Conference of Asian-African Jurists), *CFYC*, no. 2 (1958): 8.

13. Hsin Wu, "Tui chih-ts'ai chieh-chi kuan-yu kuo-chia lin-tu wen-t'i ti p'i-p'an" (A Critique of the Bourgeois International Law Concerning the Question of State Territory), *Kuo-chi wen-t'i yen-chiu* (Studies in International Problems), no. 7 (1960): 42–51.

14. Wang and Hu, *The Abrogation of China's Unequal Treaties*, quoted in Chiu, "Comparison," p. 249.

15. Shih Sung, Yu-Ta-hsin Lu Ying-lui, and Tsao K'o, "An Initial Investigation into the Old Law Viewpoint in the Teaching of International Law," *Chiao-hsueh yu yen-chiu* (Teaching and Research), no. 4 (1958): 14, quotation in Chiu, "Comparison," p. 259.

16. The expression is used in Chinese literature to refer to people engaging in interpretation, application, and writing law. For the sake of consistency, we use the term here.

17. Mao Tao, "The Important Achievements," p. 8.

18. See Chiu, "Comparison," p. 258.

19. Ibid.

20. Chiang, *China's Destiny*, p. 154.

21. *Selected Works of Mao Tse-tung*, 2: 311.

22. English text of Khrushchev's speech in *The Daily Worker* (New York), Dec. 23, 1962, pp. 1–3.

23. "A Comment on the Statement of the Communist Party of the U.S.A.," an editorial in *Jen-min jih-pao* (People's Daily), Peking, March 8, 1963, English text in Doolin, *Territorial Claims,* p. 30.

24. "Chairman Mao Tse-tung tells the Delegation of the Japanese Socialist Party that the Kuriles Must be Returned to Japan," *Sekai Shuko* (Tokyo, August 11, 1964), English text in Doolin, *Territorial Claims,* p. 44.

25. *PR* 12, no. 22 (May 30, 1969): 6.

26. Ibid.

27. Ibid.

28. *PR* 24, no. 37 (September 14, 1981): 21.

29. See John W. Garver, "The Sino-Soviet Territorial Dispute in the Pamir Mountains Region," *The China Quarterly,* no. 85 (March 1981): 116–17.

30. Quotation in David J. Dallin, *Soviet Russia and the Far East* (New Haven: Yale University Press, 1948), p. 354.

31. Ibid., pp. 354–55.

32. Text of the Protocol in Godfrey E. P. Hertslet, *Treaties between Great Britain and China; and between China and Foreign Powers; and Orders in Council, Rules, Regulations. Act of Parliament, Decrees, and Notifications Affecting British Interests in China; in Force on the 1st January, 1908,* 3rd ed., (London: His Majesty's Stationery Office, 1908), 1: 472–78, cited in George Po-chung Chen, "Some Legal Aspects of the Sino-Soviet Border Disputes," (Ph.D. diss., Southern Illinois University, 1975), pp. 65 & 97.

33. See Chen "Some Legal Aspects," p. 96.

34. Dallin, *Soviet Russia and the Far East,* p. 89.

35. "Report on the Question of the Boundary Line between China and Burma Delivered by Chou En-lai, Premier and Foreign Minister, at the Fourth Session of the First National People's Congress," *Important Documents of the Settlement of the Sino-Burmese Boundary Question* (Peking: Foreign Languages Press, 1960), p. 24.

36. Chen, "Some Legal Aspects," p. 20.

37. Ibid., p. 19.

38. English text of these regulations in H. G. W. Woodhead, ed., *The China Year Book 1932* (Shanghai: The North-China Daily News and Herald, 1932), p. 263.

39. English text of the resolution in Thomas F. F. Millard, *The End of Extraterritoriality in China* (Shanghai: The A.B.C. Press, 1931), pp. 3–10, quotation in Chiu, "Comparision," p. 256.

40. English text of the Declaration in Jane Degras, ed., *Soviet Documents on Foreign Policy,* vol. 1 (London: Oxford University Press, 1951), pp. 158–61.

41. English text of this proposed agreement in ibid., pp. 212–15.

42. League of Nations, *Treaty Series,* no. 955 (1925), vol. 37, pp. 176–79.

43. *PR* 12, no. 22 (May 30, 1969): 6.

44. *PR* 12, no. 41 (Oct. 7, 1969): 3.

45. "Statement of the U.S.S.R. Government on March 29, 1969," *The Current Digest of the Soviet Press* 21, no. 24 (July 9, 1969): 10.

46. Ibid., pp. 10–11.

47. Doolin, *Territorial Claims,* p. 51.

48. V. M. Khvostov, "The Chinese 'account' and historical true," *Meshdunarednaya Zhizn,* no. 10 (October 1964). English text in John Gittings, *Survey of the Sino-*

Soviet Dispute: A Commentary and Extracts from the Recent Polemics 1963–1967 (London: Oxford University Press, 1968), pp. 164–66.

49. *PR* 12, no. 41 (Oct. 7, 1969): 11.

50. F. Nikolayev, "How Peking Falsifies History," *International Affairs* (Moscow), no. 5 (May 1973): 33–34.

51. Doolin, *Territorial Claims,* p. 44.

52. Ibid., p. 43.

53. The text of this political program is in *The Collected Laws of the Chinese Republic* (Shanghai: 1936) 1: 10–14, cited by William L. Tung, *China and the Foreign Powers: The Impact of and Reaction to Unequal Treaties* (Dobbs Ferry, NY: Oceana Publications, 1970), p. 303.

54. Text of the Notes in League of Nations, *Treaty Series,* vol. 163 (1935), pp. 178–83.

55. *Important Documents,* p. 17.

56. Harold C. Hinton, *Communist China in World Politics* (Boston: Houghton Mifflin, 1966), p. 314.

57. *Important Documents,* p. 19.

58. Ibid., p. 25.

6

BOUNDARY TREATIES

INTRODUCTION

Since 1960, the PRC has concluded new boundary treaties with the Mongolian People's Republic, Burma, Nepal, Bhutan, Pakistan, and Afghanistan and has demarcated boundary lines with most of them. Peking has also had disputes with the Soviets and the Indians regarding their boundary treaties. This chapter will analyze the Chinese views and practices regarding all their boundary treaties. The differences and similarities of China's approach and the Western states' approach will also be discussed in terms of treaty law.

Forms of the Boundary Treaty

International law does not prescribe any particular form for all international compacts. They can be termed not only treaties but also agreements, conventions, protocols, exchanges of notes, declarations, etc. The binding force upon the contracting parties is the same in each case.[1] The PRC has used all these forms for concluding boundary treaties with neighbors.

Treaty. "A 'treaty' is a formal instrument of agreement by which two or more States establish or seek to establish a relation under international law between themselves."[2] The PRC used this form to denote the final settlement of boundary questions with Afghanistan, Burma, Nepal, and Mongolia. For example, the boundary treaty between the People's Republic of China and the Union of Burma was signed in 1960.[3]

Agreement. The nature of an international agreement is the same as that of a treaty. Nevertheless, treaty is usually "reserved for the more solemn agreements such as treaties of peace, alliance, neutrality, arbitration."[4] The Chinese used "agreement" to refer to preliminary boundary agreements and to define boundaries provisionally. Examples are (1) the agreement between the government of the People's Republic of China and His Majesty's Government of Nepal (1960),[5] and (2) the agreement between the government of the People's Republic of China and the government of Pakistan on the boundary between China's Sinkiang and the contiguous areas, the defense of which is under the actual control of Pakistan (1963).[6]

Convention. This form is usually used to describe multilateral law-making treaties.[7] China initialled a convention with Britain and Tibet at Simla, 1914, concerning the boundary between Outer Tibet and Inner Tibet.[8] However, the initialling was repudiated promptly by China's Central government.

Protocol. The protocol in a boundary treaty is used to describe the boundary alignments in detail after the demarcation is made. China signed many protocols with her neighboring states. For example, after the conclusion of the Ili Treaty in 1881, China and Russia signed seven protocols to complete the new boundary lines.[9]

Exchange of Notes. This form is "now extremely common; sometimes it may embody a more important agreement than the term suggests."[10] They are documents in which each nation states its own position. For example, an exchange of notes took place between China and Russia in 1894 to denote their boundary lines and to maintain the then status quo in the Pamirs.[11]

Declaration. "The term 'declaration' often denotes a 'law-making treaty' of a general character in which the parties engage themselves to pursue in future a certain line of conduct."[12] The PRC acknowledged that the Cairo and the Potsdam Declaration signed by the Nationalist government with the United States and Great Britain in 1945, which returned Taiwan and the Penhu Archipelago to China, are legally binding international agreements.[13]

DEFINITION OF THE BOUNDARY TREATY

In PRC practice, a boundary treaty consists of three essential elements: (1) It must be formally agreed upon by the contracting parties concerned, (2) the contracting parties must be states, and (3) it must deal explicitly with a boundary question.[14]

Agreement

There are two methods of concluding an agreement: orally or by a written statement. Nevertheless, "in practice treaties take the form of a written document, signed by duly authorized representatives of the contracting parties."[15] The Chinese approach is in accordance with this practice. All boundary treaties are concluded by written documents. I can find no example of China entering into an oral boundary treaty.

An agreement is mutual. A unilateral proposal is not an agreement and is without legally binding force. This is the Chinese position in the Sino-Indian dispute over the territory of Wuje (Barahoti). This incident is simple and illustrates the point. In September 1889, some Tibetans entered into the area of Barahoti. An Indian official gave a letter to two Tibetan officials complaining of the intrusion. The Tibetan officials promised to report the incident to a higher official at Gartok. In 1890, a higher Indian official complained again because nothing had been done despite the promise. He showed the Tibetan officials a map proving that Barahoti was Indian territory. New Delhi, therefore, claimed that both the letter and the map "constitute formal acceptances of the Indian alignment."[16]

The PRC disagreed claiming Wuje as Chinese territory. Peking pointed out that the letter and the map presented by the Indian officials to the Tibetan officials constituted no agreement at all. The letter was unilaterally telling the Tibetans to withdraw from Wuje, the Chinese territory. "It is obvious that no question of any boundary agreement arose here," the PRC added.[17]

Contracting Parties

Differing from the Western jurists' point of view, the Chinese writers asserted that international organizations cannot conclude treaties. As for the dependent political entities such as vassal states and protected states, the Chinese agreed with the Western custom that they are only allowed to conclude commercial treaties and the like.

International Organizations. It is generally agreed among Western Jurists that international organizations as well as states have the capacity to conclude treaties.[18] However, one Chinese writer illustrated in 1960 that this capacity is strictly limited and regulated by their respective member states.[19] International organizations do not have their own territory and therefore have not the need to conclude a boundary treaty.[20] Thus, only sovereign states are in fact parties of boundary treaties. The Chinese government also explained:

> Boundary matters are matters of major importance which involve the sovereignty and territory of a country, and only the country concerned can set forth fully its own standpoint, and only the country concerned is able and in a position to obtain an overall and detailed picture of the boundary through the exercise of administrative jurisdiction and through investigations and studies as well as surveys.[21]

Dependent Political Entities. According to principles of international law, treaty-making power belongs to fully sovereign states, but there are exceptions. States not fully sovereign (protected and vassal states) may become contracting parties to treaties concerning railways, extradition, commerce, and the like. The special relation between the suzerain and the dependent political entities determines the extent to which the latter are allowed (if at all) to enter into treaties with other states.[22] Here, the Chinese and the Western jurists agree.

In China, there is "not a single case of authorizing any local authority to conclude any treaty or agreement concerning the delimitation of the boundary with a foreign government."[23] In 1915, when China had suzerainty over Outer Mongolia, a Sino-Russo-Mongolian tripartite agreement emphasized that Outer Mongolia had no right to conclude any treaty of a political or territorial nature with other states, but might sign commercial and industrial agreements.[24]

China also asserted that Tibet had no right to conclude a boundary treaty with any other state without China's authorization because in 1914 she had sovereignty over Tibet. Therefore, the so-called McMahon Line of that date serving as an Indian-Tibetan boundary, created by the exchange of letters between Tibet and Britain was "illegal," and had no binding force on China.[25]

However, India disagreed by saying that Tibet needed no particular authorization in 1914 to sign a boundary treaty with Britain because Tibet had made boundary treaties with other countries without authorization before and after the Simla Conference of 1914. New Delhi pointed out that in 1684, 1842, and 1852, Tibet signed boundary treaties with Ladakh and Kashmir confirming Tibetan western boundaries.[26] These cases showed that the Chinese Government recognized Tibet's right in the past to have foreign relations on her own and deal with matters concerning her boundaries."[27] Even after the 1914 Simla Conference, between 1921 and 1926, the Tibetan government still entered into certain correspondence with Britain regarding certain minor frontier adjustments.[28]

China answered that the existence of a treaty of 1684 could not be established and, thus, it could not be used as evidence.[29] The PRC recognized the existence of the 1842 Treaty but said that "the then Chinese Central Government did not send anybody to participate in the conclusion of this treaty, nor did it ratify the treaty afterwards."[30] That is to say, China did not really authorize Tibet to conclude a boundary treaty with another country.

The Indian government responded that China did participate in concluding the treaty because "the [1842] treaty was signed by the representatives of both the Dalai Lama and the Emperor of China."[31] K. Krisha Rao, legal advisor to Ministry of External Affairs of India, summarized: " . . . by allowing Tibet to sign the 1842 treaty, China concurred in the former's [Tibet's] right and power to take part in such formal legal transactions."[32]

The Indian government and Mr. Rao might have succeeded in proving the existence of the 1842 treaty, but still failed in proving that China had delegated Tibet a general power to sign boundary treaties independently with neighboring states. Their arguments merely demonstrated that the Chinese Central government "signed" the 1842 treaty and allowed Tibet to "take part" in it in the presence of a Chinese representative.

With regard to the 1852 Agreement between Tibet and Ladakh, China said that it "only referred to the maintenance of the old boundary by the two sides of Ladakh and Tibet, and provided that Ladakhis should pay 'annual tribute' to Tibet, but made no provision whatever about [the precise location of] the boundary between Tibet and Ladakh."[33] Thus, that agreement also fails to prove that Tibet had the power to sign boundary treaties independently.

China answered India concerning the 1921, 1924, and 1926 correspondences by saying:

> The Chinese side already stated that from 1919 to 1927 the British Indian Government had asked the local authorities of China's Tibet many times to delimit the boundary between Ladakh and Tibet. Negotiations were held between the two sides [China and India], but nothing came of them.[34]

The PRC did not mention whether these negotiations were authorized by China's Central government or not, but considered China's participation as evidence to support her theory that a dependent political entity (Tibet) had no right to conclude boundary treaties with foreign countries.

As a matter of fact, Britain always negotiated with the Chinese authorities regarding the Tibetan-Indian boundaries. In 1847, a British official proposed a negotiation for delimiting the Ladakh-Tibetan boundary to the Chinese viceroy of Kwangtung and Kwangsi Provinces. The viceroy refused the proposal.[35] After that, Britain signed three more conventions with China's Central government relating to the Tibetan boundary. They were the convention of 1890 between Great Britain and China relating to the Tibetan-Sikkim boundary, the convention of 1904 between Great Britain and Tibet (participated by an Amban, the Chinese Central governmental representative), and the convention of 1906 between Great Britain and China relating to the Tibetan frontiers.[36]

Thus, China has agreed with traditional international law that a dependent political entity has no right to conclude boundary treaties. Peking rejected the Indian arguments that Tibet had independently signed boundary treaties with her neighbors.

The Nature of Boundary Treaties

The PRC has insisted that four treaties are not boundary treaties because they did not contain any provision for the location of the boundary. They are the treaties between Tibet and Ladakh of 1684, 1842, and 1852, and the Sino-Indian Trade Agreement of 1954.

India argued that the 1684 peace treaty between Tibet and Ladakh had defined the boundary between them because it stated that "the boundaries fixed in the beginning, when Skyid-Ida-ngeema-gon gave a kingdom to each of his three sons, shall still be maintained."[37] The eldest son of Skyid-Ida-ngeema-gon (a Tibetan prince) was conferred the Maryul (Ladakh) fief in the tenth century. Thus, New Delhi said that the 1684 Treaty confirmed the boundary between Tibet and Ladakh.[38]

The PRC took an opposing view. First, China stated that Skyid-Ida-ngeema-gon conferring fiefs on each of his three sons did not mean that the three sons' fiefs became independent kingdoms; it only reflected a change in the ownership of manorial estates among the feudal lords of Tibet. "Therefore, the question of delimiting the boundary between Ladakh and Tibet as between two countries does not at all arise" at that time.[39] Furthermore, China said that in the 1684 treaty "not a word defining the boundary can be found in the articles.... How can it be inferred... that an agreement for the delimitation of the boundaries was reached?"[40]

India also argued that the 1842 treaty between Tibet and Ladakh was a boundary agreement. The treaty was in the form of an exchange of documents. The documents, New Delhi argued, "stated explicitly that the boundary between Ladakh and Tibet was well-known and that this boundary was being confirmed."[41] China disagreed, seeing it as an agreement of mutual nonaggression rather than a boundary agreement. One of the documents indicated that both sides "will refrain from being hostile to each other and live together in peace."[42] Another document said that the territories would be "administered by the sides respectively without infringing upon each other."[43] Peking therefore concluded that "it did not have any provision whatever of the specific location of the boundary."[44]

India also claimed that the boundary between Tibet and Ladakh had been defined by the 1852 Ladakh-Tibetan Agreement because it stipulated that "the boundary between Ladakh and Tibet will remain the same as before."[45] But the Chinese pointed out that "the agreement only referred to the maintenance of the old boundary by the two sides of Ladakh and Tibet... but made no provision whatever about the boundary between Tibet and Ladakh."[46] According to the Chinese conception, all the aforementioned three treaties are not boundary treaties.

China also rejected India's claim that the middle section of the Sino-Indian frontiers was defined by the 1954 Sino-Indian Trade Agreement. Article 4 of the agreement reads: "Traders and pilgrims of both sides may travel by the following passes and routes: (1) Shipki La Pass, (2) Mana Pass, (3) Niti Pass, (4) Kungribingri Pass, (5) Darma Pass and (6) Lipu Pass."[47] Based on this article, India claimed that "it was... clear that the Agreement of the 1954 recognized that the six passes were border passes."[48] Peking disagreed:

> The 1954 Sino-Indian Agreement is an agreement on trade and intercourse between the Tibet region of China and India. Not only does none of the paragraphs in this agreement involve the boundary question but the two sides had an understanding at that time, that is, no boundary question should be touched on in the negotiation. ...Article IV of the 1954 Agreement only provides for the routes by which the traders and pilgrims of one country travel to the other. It does not touch specifically the location of the boundary.[49]

China concluded that the 1954 Agreement on trade has no relation to a boundary agreement at all.

CLASSIFICATION OF BOUNDARY TREATIES

The Preliminary and the Definitive Boundary Treaty

The preliminary treaty, or *pactum de contrahendo,* is a real treaty binding upon the contracting parties. It requires the mutual consent of the parties with regard to certain important points. It does not lay down the agreements in detail. For example, the PRC signed a preliminary boundary treaty with Burma on January 28, 1960, entitled "The Agreement on the Question of Boundary between the Government of the People's Republic of China and the Government of the Union of Burma."[50] By this agreement, China agreed in principle to cede the Namwan Assigned Tract to Burma in exchange for three small villages (Article 2). The two governments agreed to set up a joint committee (Article 1) to work out "solutions for the existing issues . . . ," and to draft "a Sino-Burmese boundary treaty, which shall cover not only all the sections of the boundary . . . but also the sections of the boundary which were already delimited in the past" (Article 3).

A definitive treaty, on the other hand, spells out the details loosely agreed upon in the preliminary treaty. For example, China and Burma signed a definitive boundary on October 1, 1960, entitled "Boundary Treaty between the People's Republic of China and the Union of Burma."[51] This treaty stipulated the details of their earlier preliminary treaty.

The Provisional Boundary Treaty and Boundary Treaty

A provisional boundary treaty is a complete treaty; it is called provisional when one of the contracting party's sovereignty over the boundary territory is questionable. The Sino-Pakistani boundary treaty serves as an example. It deals with the western part of Kashmir, and Pakistan's sovereignty over Kashmir is unresolved. Nevertheless, Peking announced in 1962 that she would negotiate with Pakistan concerning her "Sinkiang and the contiguous area, the defense of which is under the control of Pakistan."[52] The PRC hoped that the two states would be able to sign a provisional agreement. The provisional agreement was signed on March 2, 1963. Article 6 reads:

> The two governments agreed that after the settlement of the dispute between Pakistan and India, the sovereign authorities concerned will reopen negotiations with the Government of the People's Republic of China on the boundary . . . so as to sign a formal boundary treaty to replace the present agreement, provided that, in the event of that sovereign authority being Pakistan, the Provisions of the present Agreement . . . shall be maintained in the formal Boundary Treaty to be signed between the People's Republic of China and Pakistan.[53]

It seems clear, then, that as long as the sovereignty of Kashmir is pending, the treaty remains "provisional."

A boundary treaty differs from a provisional boundary treaty in that with the former the contracting parties at the time of signing have already resolved their differences concerning border territories. The examples of boundary treaties used throughout this book should make this clear, without the need for additional examples here.

PROCEDURES FOR CONCLUDING BOUNDARY TREATIES

In PRC practices, as in Western states' practices, there are three steps to conclude boundary treaties: negotiation, signing, and ratification.

Negotiation

China has maintained that a treaty must be formally negotiated by the representatives of the contracting parties. Before the actual negotiations began, the PRC usually reached a procedural agreement with the other side for facilitating negotiations.[54] In practice, the PRC has issued a certificate of full powers to her representative for negotiating a boundary treaty. This certificate is acknowledged in the preamble of that treaty.[55] If the names of the representatives negotiating a treaty are unknown, China then questioned the existence of that treaty.[56]

In international law, there is no fixed method for negotiations. According to one outstanding treatise, "negotiations may, therefore, take place *viva voce,* or through the exchange of written representations and arguments, or both."[57] Negotiations are often protracted: China and Burma spent four years (1956–1960) negotiating a boundary treaty. During this time, formal proposals were put forth and discussed until an accord was reached.

International negotiation "is the term for such intercourse between two or more states."[58] Accordingly, mere proposals made by one party, not acceptable to the other parties, are not binding.[59] Proposals, therefore, may have nothing to do with negotiations or may be made as a part of the negotiations. In the Sino-Indian dispute over Wuje, Peking denied that negotiations ever took place between India and Tibet in 1889, 1890, and 1914:

> The so-called negotiations between 1889 and 1890 referred only to a local official of the British colonial government telling a Tibetan official stationed at Wuje ... about the British intention to occupy Wuje. This of course was not formal negotiations. As to the so-called 1914 negotiations, they referred only to another official of the British colonial government asking Lochen Shatra of Tibet local Government to withdraw the outposts stationed at the Chinese territory of Wuje.[60]

Negotiations also differ from consultations. The Soviets and the Indians took the position that "negotiation" is a formal term by which the concerned parties intend to conclude a boundary treaty. This concept differs somewhat from practice which takes the position that the purpose of negotiation "may be only an exchange of views . . . or it may be an arrangement as to the line of action to be taken in future with regard to a certain point, or a settlement of differences."[61]

Both the Soviets and the Indians argued that their boundaries with China had been already settled except for a few minor differences. So the Soviets refused to "negotiate" the Sino-Soviet boundary questions. They proposed to have "consultations" which meant they would only agree "to discuss the question of clarifying the location of the border line in certain sectors, taking the existing treaties as a basis."[62]

The Indians too refused to "negotiate" boundary questions with China, but proposed to "talk" with China about their boundary discrepancies. Nehru said:

> There is a difference between negotiations and talks, there is a world of difference. . . . Negotiation is a very formal thing, it requires a very suitable background, it should not be taken up unless a suitable background comes. . . . Talking is an entirely different matter. Talking may not yield any result.[63]

China has also been flexible, as is shown by the fact that she agreed to "talk" with India. On April 19, 1960, Chou En-lai told his welcomers in New Delhi that "the Chinese Government has always advocated the holding of *talks* between the Prime Ministers of the two countries to seek avenues to a reasonable settlement of the boundary questions" (emphasis added).[64] Their joint communique issued on April 25 indicated that "the two Prime Ministers had several long, frank and friendly talks between them."[65] The word "negotiation" was avoided here.

The PRC also accepted the traditional principle of *punctations,* which means "mere negotiations on the items of a future treaty without the parties entering into an obligation to conclude that treaty."[66] The aforementioned joint communique of April 25 set up a meeting to study the Sino-Indian boundary questions.

> The two Prime Ministers . . . agreed that officials of the two Governments should meet and examine, check and study all historical documents, records, accounts, maps and other material relevant to the boundary question, on which each side relied in support of its stand, and draw up a report for submission to the two Governments.[67]

The report on the boundary question containing approximately 600 pages was published by the Indian government in 1961. No agreement was mentioned.

Signing

After negotiation, a treaty has to be signed by the proper representatives. In China, international boundary treaties have been signed either by the foreign minister, premier, or chairman of the PRC.[68] Signature is a necessary part of a treaty. Because of the lack of any signature by a proper representative, the PRC questioned the existence of the 1684 treaty between Tibet and Ladakh. China asked: "Who were the representatives who signed it? When and where was it signed?... There cannot be such a strange treaty [without signatures] in the world."[69]

A signature differs from an initialling as far as treaties are concerned. Wei Liang in the PRC wrote:

> Initialling and formal signature are two completely different matters. Ordinarily, the representatives only put down an abbreviation of their names when initialling a draft treaty, such an act merely indicates that the initialling representative temporarily signed and confirmed the draft treaty. His initialling does not represent the formal consent of his government to the draft, and he must await the final instruction of his government before he can formally sign the draft.[70]

During the Simla Conference in 1914, the Chinese representative Chen I-fan initialled the draft of the convention and the attached map, but it was "on the clear understanding that to initial and to sign them were two separate actions."[71] And on the same day China repudiated Chen's initialling.

Initialling does not necessarily mean abbreviating a representative's name on the draft treaty. Chen initialled the Simla Convention by writing his name in full.[72] The Tibetan representative, Lonchen Shatra, also wrote his name in full as there are no abbreviations in the Tibetan writing system.[73] Initialling is thus seen as a provisional acceptance by a negotiator, pending approval by someone qualified to make the more definitive decision.

Ratification

In international law, whether a treaty requires ratification or not depends upon the internal laws of the contracting parties. In the PRC, a boundary treaty does not necessarily require ratification. For example, the Chinese-Pakistani Boundary Agreement (1963), the Chinese-Afghan Boundary Treaty (1963), and the Chinese-Nepalese Boundary Treaty (1961) came into force on the day of their signatures.[74] However, Article 12 of the Sino-Burmese Boundary Treaty of 1960 required that "the present treaty is subjected to ratification and the instruments of ratification will be exchanged in Rangoon as soon as possible."[75] The PRC ratified this treaty and has ratified other boundary treaties as required. Still others have been regarded as binding without ratification.

If there is no record indicating when and how a treaty went into effect, the binding force of that treaty may be doubtful. Thus, the PRC questioned the binding force of the 1684 treaty between Tibet and Ladakh because India could not prove when and how it came into force.[76]

Reservation

According to international law, "no state can be bound by any treaty provision unless it has given its assent."[77] Reservation is based on this principle of assent.[78] Harvard Research Article 13 laid down the definition of a reservation:

> A "reservation" is a formal declaration by which a State, when signing, ratifying or acceding to a treaty, specifies as a condition of its willingness to become a party to the treaty certain terms which will limit the effect of the treaty in so far as it may apply in the relations of that State with the other State or States which may be parties to the treaty.[79]

It is very unusual for a state to make reservations in a bilateral boundary agreement. However, China did so in the 1894 exchange of notes between herself and Russia regarding the boundary in the Pamir area. In 1892, Russian troops occupied the western part of the Sarikol range in the Pamirs, which, according to the 1884 boundary protocol between China and Russia, belonged to China. At that time, the Russian and the Chinese troops faced each other along the Sarikol range. In 1894, the two countries agreed, via an exchange of notes, to maintain temporarily the respective positions of the troops until reaching a final settlement of the Pamir question. However, the Ch'ing government declared that "in adopting the above-mentioned measure, the Chinese Government does not at all mean to abandon the right China possesses over the territories of the Pamirs which are situated beyond the positions occupied by the Chinese troops at present."[80] The PRC called this declaration a "reservation."[81] Comparing the Chinese declaration and the above-mentioned definition of reservation, it appears that the declaration is consistent with international practice.

INTERPRETATION AND ABROGATION

Interpretation

A general rule for interpreting treaties was given in Article 31 of the Vienna Convention on the Law of Treaties in 1969. A part of the article reads:

1. A treaty shall be interpreted in good faith in accordance with the ordinary meaning to be given to the terms of the treaty in their context and in the light of its object and purpose.
2. The context for the purpose of the interpretation of a treaty shall comprise, in addition to the text, including its preamble and annexes:

    a. any agreement relating to the treaty which was made between all the parties in connexion with the conclusion of the treaty.[82]

The PRC satisfied this rule when interpreting the 1842 treaty between Tibet and Ladakh and the 1954 Sino-Indian Trade Agreement.

The 1842 treaty between Tibet and Ladakh has been interpreted by India as a boundary agreement between them because it stipulated that "the boundary between Ladakh and Tibet will remain the same as before."[83] On the contrary, the PRC, looking at the treaty as a whole, interpreted it as a pact of mutual nonagression which did not define any specific location of the boundary; it is "a guarantee of respect by each other for the other's territory."[84]

In interpreting the 1954 Sino-Indian Trade Agreement, the Indians insisted that the treaty had delimited the middle section of the disputed frontiers. Article 4 of the treaty reads: "Traders and pilgrims of both countries may travel by the following passes and routes: (1) Shipi La Pass, (2) Mana Pass, (3) Niti Pass, (4) Kungribingri Pass, (5) Darma Pass and (6) Lipu Lekh Pass."[85] The Indians saw these six "passes" as "border passes" and concluded that "the use of these six passes did not involve ownership because they were border passes."[86] For them, "border pass" means "boundary pass."[87] The PRC argued that the record of negotiations showed the purpose of the treaty. Thus, she interpreted the treaty as not involving the boundary at all. Peking stated that the record showed that the representatives of the two countries for negotiating the 1954 Trade Agreement did not intend to solve all the outstanding questions between the two countries.[88] Thus, during the negotiations, China told the Indian representatives that she did not wish to discuss the boundary question.[89]

Moreover, the Chinese original draft for Article 4 of the agreement stated that "the Chinese Government *agrees to open* the following mountain passes [the six referred to above] in the Ari district of the Tibetan region of China for entry and exit by traders and pilgrims of both parties" (emphasis added).[90] The Indian representatives rejected the draft because it denoted that China owns these passes. After discussion, China and India decided to adopt what became the final text, which "does not involve the ownership of these passes" at all.[91]

It appears that the above-mentioned Chinese approach to interpreting the 1842 and 1954 treaties agrees with the general rules recognized by international society. In both treaties the PRC concluded that the interpretation should be based on the spirit of the agreements, the real contents and the process in which the agreements were reached.[92]

Abrogation

It is an accepted principle that whoever concludes a treaty can lawfully terminate it by agreement either expressed or implied,[93] but abrogation has been a matter of conflict in Chinese relation with the Soviet Union.

Both the Soviets and the Chinese were aware that their boundary lines were the results of tzarist expansionism. After the October revolution, "the Soviet Government . . . renounced the conquests made by the Tzarist Government which deprived China of Manchuria and other areas."[94] On the Soviet initiative, an agreement for the settlement of questions between the two states was signed on May 31, 1924, in Peking.[95] The two governments agreed to hold a conference to carry out detailed arrangements relative to the questions (Article 2). The two governments also agreed to annul all conventions, treaties, agreements, protocols, contracts, etc., concluded between China and tzarist Russia (Article 3). Accordingly, a conference was held in Peking later in 1924, but for unknown reasons, after the Soviet representatives returned to the Soviet Union, future conferences were never rescheduled.[96] The PRC deemed that the Sino-Russian boundary treaties were abrogated by the above-mentioned 1924 Agreement. However, the Soviets argued that the 1924 Agreement annulled only the unequal treaties unrelated to boundaries.[97] The matter has remained unsolved.

But the PRC has jointly abrogated previous boundary treaties with Nepal without difficulty. The two countries had fixed their boundaries in 1792. In 1856, a treaty again acknowledged the general configuration of the boundary between Nepal and Tibet.[98] Nevertheless, the PRC pointed out that "the entire boundary between the two countries has not been scientifically delimited and formally demarcated and certain discrepancies exist."[99] In 1956, the two countries signed a boundary treaty, demarcated their boundary, and *abrogated* "all treaties and documents which existed in the past between China and Nepal including those between the Tibet Region of China and Nepal."[100]

TREATIES RELATED TO THIRD STATES, STATE SUCCESSION, AND CHANGE OF GOVERNMENT

Treaties Related to Third States

Generally, "according to the principle of *pacta tertiis nec nocent nec prosunt*, a treaty concerns the contracting states only; neither right nor duties, as a rule, arise under a treaty for third states which are not parties to the treaty."[101] However, there are exceptions. Article 18(b) of the Harvard Research Draft Convention on Treaties indicates:

> If a treaty contains a stipulation which is expressly for the benefit of a State which is not a party or a signatory to the treaty, such State is entitled to claim the benefit of that stipulation so long as the stipulation remains in force between the parties to the treaty.[102]

The PRC took advantage of this Draft Convention in order to deny the validity of the McMahon Line between Tibet and British India because Great Britain in 1907 signed a Convention with Russia at St. Petersburg, which stipulated: "In conformity with the admitted principle of the suzerainty of China over Tibet, Great Britain and Russia engage not to enter into negotiations with Tibet except through the intermediary of the Chinese Government."[103] In a dispute with India, Peking in 1959 said that according to the 1907 British-Russian Convention, Britain should not negotiate a boundary treaty with Tibet except through the intermediary of the Chinese government. Thus, China asserted that the exchange of letters between Britain and Tibet on April 25–27, 1914, which created the so-called McMahon Line, was invalid.[104]

But China, as a nonsignatory third party, has also *accepted* disadvantages. Here, the PRC's attitude differs from previous Chinese governments. In 1895, for example, Great Britain and Russia created a buffer zone, the Wakhan Corridor, in the Pamirs, which was disputed by China and Russia and not delimited. China traditionally treated the Pamirs as her territory. However, according to the Anglo-Russian Agreement (1895), the Chinese-Russian boundary in the Pamirs extended southward from Kizil Dawan Pass located approximately 38°40' North and 73°50' East to peak Povalo Shveikovski along the main ranges. Therefore, the area west of the main ranges—the Wakhan Corridor—was left in Afghan hands as a buffer between the Russian and British Empires[105] (see map 2). By that agreement, China lost seven of the eight Pamirs; only one remained as Chinese territory.[106] The Ch'ing dynasty of China refused to recognize the Anglo-Russian Treaty of 1895 and the Republic of China also refused to recognize it. But, in the Sino-Afghan Boundary Treaty of 1963, the PRC accepted the Wakhan Corridor as Afghan territory. The Sino-Afghan boundary was hereforth to be at the eastern end of the Wakhan Corridor.[107] The PRC had thus accepted disadvantages created by an 1895 treaty to which she had not been a party.

State Succession

When India became independent in 1947, she assumed the same boundaries as had been established under British rule. The Indians, therefore, asserted that the territory south of the McMahon Line was her territory by succession from British India.

The Chinese held that the so-called McMahon Line "is void of any legal validity," because it was drawn by "the exchange of letters in 1914 between the British representative and the representative of the Tibet local authorities behind the back of the Chinese Government."[108] Since the McMahon Line is illegal, there could be no right of succession to territory south of the line. A Chinese writer, Wei Liang, emphasized this principle:

> According to international custom, new states inherit some rights of the parent states. However, the objects they inherited must be legal. If the objects are illegal, and never recognized by the government of the other side or actually not existed, they cannot become the objects of succession.[109]

Change of Government

According to international law, changes of government have no effect whatever upon the binding force of boundary treaties.[110] Questions have been raised, however, when governments have been regarded as illegal and not the valid representative of the states in whose names they have acted. This has been the case in both China and the USSR.

The revolutions in Russia and China (1949) have been characterized as class revolutions raising questions about the true authority of the governments overthrown. Lin Piao, vice-chairman of the Chinese Communist Party, had this to say: "The Sino-Soviet boundary question is the product of the tsarist Russian imperialist aggression against China . . . when power was not in the hands of the Chinese and Russian peoples."[111] It is not clear from this paragraph that he was advocating the nullification of Sino-Soviet boundaries. But in view of such a possible interpretation, the Soviet government took a precautionary stand against China by saying: "The C.P.R. (The Chinese People's Republic) government is in essence seeking to . . . draw the conclusion that the borders of the Russian state should have collapsed in conjunction with the downfall of the Tsarist autocracy."[112] Here the matter has rested however, and it seems that neither party is prepared to reject traditional international practice.

ESTOPPEL AND ACQUIESCENCE

"Estoppel" is a term used by Anglo-American lawyers in common law cases while "preclusion" is the term used in the Continental legal system. It was originally a procedure in municipal law: "a rule of evidence which precludes a person from denying the truth of some statement previously made by himself."[113] This rule was elaborated in detail by a judge in an English common law case, *Pichard* v. *Sears*:

> Where one by his words or conduct wilfully causes another to believe in the existence of a certain state of things, and induces him to act on that belief so as to alter his own previous position, the former is concluded from averring against the latter a different state of things as existing at the same time.[114]

One's conduct could be action, inaction, or silence. When "silence, on an occasion where there was a duty or need to speak or act, implies agreement or a waiver of right," it means acquiescence;[115] and acquiescence may operate as a preclusion or estoppel in certain cases.[116]

The principle of estoppel has been used in international law cases. For example, in the Costa Rican-Nicaraguan boundary case, Nicaragua argued that a treaty of 1858 defining the boundary was not binding because a third state (El Salvador), as a guarantor, had not ratified. The arbitrator (a president of the United States), in rejecting this contention, said: "The Government of Nicaragua was silent [for ten or twelve years] when it ought to have spoken, and so waived the objection now made. It saw fit to proceed to the exchange of ratification without waiting for San Salvador."[117] Simple silence does not ipso facto mean acquiescence, but Nicaragua's silence in the past ten or twelve years meant acquiescence because it had a duty to speak and failed to do so and it was ready to exchange the ratifications. Thus, Nicaragua was estopped from denying the binding force of the 1858 treaty.

This principle of estoppel was also invoked by India in the Sino-Indian boundary disputes. India claimed that there has been a traditional Chinese-Indian boundary line, which "had . . . on many occasions been publically and authoritatively affirmed by the Government of India,"[118] and was not disputed by China until 1959. China's silence could only be regarded as acquiescence. The Indian government then concluded: "There is no doubt that under the accepted canons of international usage China must be held to have accepted and acquiesced in the Indian alignment and to be now estopped from raising claims to Indian territory."[119]

China first argued that silence does not always equal acquiescence. Peking said that "the contention that silence [necessarily] means acquiescence reflects not at all the accepted principles of international law."[120] If there was not a duty or a need to speak of the boundary question, that silence does not mean acquiescence. The PRC then asked India:

> Is it that the boundary question must be raised even at occasions not at all meant for discussing the boundary question? Is it that the Chinese side must raise the Sino-Indian boundary question on all occasions, otherwise it would imply that the Chinese side has acquiesced in the assertation that there is no question about the Sino-Indian boundary and thus, according to international law, it can no longer raise the boundary question?[121]

The PRC even went beyond this general statement. She rejected Indian claims of estoppel in all three sections of their disputed frontiers.

Concerning the eastern section of the disputed frontiers, an Indian writer argued that the McMahon Line is a valid international boundary line because "China has acquiesced in the McMahon Line for over 45 years."[122] Thus, "China is, on the basis . . . of a definite treaty—the Simla Convention of 1914—estopped from asserting another boundary at this time."[123] China denied having acquiesced. The PRC told India that, "the assertion that China did not raise any objection to the so-called McMahon Line . . . is . . . inconsistent with the fact."[124] She pointed out that in 1947 the Tibetans formally demanded that India return to Tibet certain territories south of the McMahon Line occupied by India,[125] and in 1949 the Nationalist government delivered a note to the Indian Ministry of External Affairs repudiating the Simla Convention and the so-called McMahon Line.[126]

Concerning the middle section of the disputed frontiers, the Indians argued that during the negotiations and after the conclusion of the 1954 Trade Agreement, China did not raise the question of the fixed boundary. Thus, India concluded that the Chinese government thereby had been estopped from raising such claims under international law.[127] The PRC denied India's claims. In this case, however, Peking cited documents to prove that she had a previous agreement with India not to discuss the Sino-Indian boundary question at that time.[128]

Concerning the western section of the disputed frontiers, the PRC challenged Indian territorial claims based on the 1842 Ladakh-Tibetan Treaty. The treaty only ambiguously indicated that their boundary was "fixed from ancient times" without mentioning the locations of the boundary. The territory India claims (based on that treaty) is mostly a part of Chinese Sinkiang rather than Tibet. Sinkiang neither participated in the negotiations nor gave consent to the treaty later. How was Sinkiang's territory involved in the Ladakh-Tibetan Treaty? Obviously, India's territorial claims are much further beyond the boundary "fixed from ancient times" between Tibet and Ladakh. The PRC stated:

> The greatest part about 80 percent of the area now disputed by the Indian Government is part of China's Sinkiang which was no part to the treaty. It is obviously inconceivable to hold that, judging by the treaty, vast areas of Sinkiang have ceased to belong to China but have become part of Ladakh.[129]

K. Krishna Rao, legal advisor to the Ministry of External Affairs of India, instead of admitting excessive claims of territory, asserted that the boundary which had been "fixed from ancient times" was in Sinkiang. He then argued that "China had never before raised the question of Sinkiang's consent," and therefore, the PRC "is estopped from now advancing any alleged claim of Sinkiang."[130] To date, there is no record of a Chinese response to the Indian argument.

SUMMARY

From this study, we see that China's position regarding the procedures for concluding boundary treaties, their forms as well as the interpretation of boundary treaties, has been in agreement with traditional international practice. The PRC specifically emphasized that only sovereign states have the right to conclude boundary treaties. Treaties signed by third states which created advantages for China were considered valid by the PRC. Even if a treaty created disadvantages for China, the PRC, differing from previous Chinese governments, accepted the fait accompli. Regarding state succession, the PRC held that a state has no right to inherit a boundary which had been defined "illegally" and never recognized by the other state.

NOTES

1. See L. Oppenheim, *International Law,* 8th ed. Revised by Hersch Lauterpacht. (London: Longmans Green and Co., 1955), vol. 1, pp. 879–99; Arnold McNair, *The Law of Treaties* (London: Oxford University Press, 1961), pp. 22–26. Neither Oppenheim nor McNair referred to aide-memoires in their treatises. However, the PRC referred to aide-memoire as a form of treaty. For example, aide-memoires exchanged between China and the Soviet Union in 1926 agreeing with each other on the need of re-demarcation in the Pamirs was called a "treaty" by the PRC, *Peking Review* 24, no. 37 (September 14, 1981): 23 (hereafter *PR*).

2. This definition is given in Article 1 of Harvard Draft Convention, cited by McNair, *The Law of Treaties*, p. 4.
3. English text of this treaty in *PR* 3, no. 40 (October 4, 1960): 33–34.
4. McNair, *The Law of Treaties*, p. 22.
5. English text of the Agreement in *PR* 3, no. 40 (October 4, 1960): 8–9.
6. English text of the Agreement in *PR* 6, nos. 10 & 11 (March 15, 1963): 67–70.
7. McNair, *The Law of Treaties*, p. 22.
8. English text of the convention printed in Alastair Lamb, *The McMahon Line: A Study in the Relations between India, China and Tibet, 1904 to 1914* (London: Routledge and Kegan, 1966), vol. 2, pp. 620–24.
9. Tai-Sung An, *The Sino-Soviet Territorial Dispute* (Philadelphia: The Westminster Press, 1973), p. 43.
10. McNair, *The Law of Treaties*, p. 24.
11. A partial text of the protocol was referred in *PR* 24, no. 37 (September 14, 1981): 21–23.
12. Oppenheim, *International Law*, vol. 1, p. 899.
13. It was expressed in 1950 by Prime Minister Chou En-lai in a cablegram to the president of the Security Council of the UN (U.N. Doc. No. S/1715, 1950), quotation in Hungdah Chiu, "The Theory and Practice of Communist China with Respect to the Conclusion of Treaties," *The Columbia Journal of Transnational Law* 5, no. 1 (1960): 7.
14. A treaty, in accordance with a Chinese writer's treatise, is "an agreement between two or among more states. It must be unanimously consented by all the contracting parties," Wei Liang, "Ts'ung kuo-chi-fa chueh-tu k'an shu-wei McMahon hsien" (From the Angle of International Law to look at the So-called McMahon Line), in *Kuo-chi wen-t'i yen-chiu* (Studies in International Problems), no. 6 (1959): 47–52. The Chinese government also expressed that a boundary treaty must deal with the location of a boundary. Ref. *Report of the Officials of the Governments of India and the People's Republic of China on the Boundary Question* (New Delhi: Government of India, 1961), pp. CR–14–15. ("CR" precedes all page numbers in the section which contains the report of the PRC officials, hereafter *Report*).
15. Oppenheim, *International Law*, vol. 1, p. 898; also McNair, *The Law of Treaties*, p. 7.
16. *Report*, p. 84.
17. Ibid., p. CR–18.
18. Oppenheim, *International Law*, vol. 1, p. 877.
19. K'ung Meng, "A Critique of the Theories of Bourgeois International Law on the Subject of International Law," in *Studies of International Problems*, no. 2 (1960): 50–51, quotation in Chiu, "The Theory and Practice," p. 3, note 8.
20. The land that the UN headquarters is located upon is in New York City, which is the territory of the United States; see Agreement between the United Nations and the United States of America Regarding the Headquarters of the United Nations, signed June 26, 1947, United Nations, *Treaty Series* 11, no. 147 (1947): 11–42.
21. *Report*, p. CR–53.
22. Oppenheim, *International Law*, vol. 1, pp. 882–83.
23. *Report*, p. CR–25.
24. Text of the agreement in John V.A. MacMurray, *Treaties and Agreements With and Concerning China, 1894–1919* (London: Oxford University Press, 1921) 2: 1239–

44, quotation in George Po-chung Chen, "Some Legal Aspects of the Sino-Soviet Border Dispute," (Ph.D. diss., Southern Illinois University, 1974), p. 86.

25. See "Note of the Ministry of Foreign Affairs of the People's Republic of China to the Indian Embassy in China, December 26, 1959, in *The Sino-Indian Boundary Question,* enlarged ed. (Peking: Foreign Languages Press, 1962), pp. 53–57 (hereafter cited as *SIBQ*); also in *Notes, Memoranda, and Letters Exchanged and Agreements Signed Between the Governments of India and China: White Paper* (New Delhi: Ministry of External Affairs, 1961–1963) 3: 61–63 (hereafter *White Paper*).

26. "Letter from the Prime Minister of India to the Prime Minister of China, 26 September 1959," *White Paper,* 2: 35–36, and "Note of the Government of India to the Chinese Government, 12 February 1960," *White Paper,* 3: 83–84.

27. *Report,* p. 115.

28. Ibid., p. 115.

29. Ibid., p. CR–12.

30. "Letter from the Prime Minister of China to the Prime Minister of India, September 8, 1959," *White Paper,* 2: 28.

31. "Letter from the Prime Minister of India to the Prime Minister of China, September 26, 1959," *White Paper,* 2: 35.

32. K. Krisha Rao, "The Sino-Indian Boundary Question and International Law," *The International and Comparative Law Quarterly* (London) 2, pt. 2 (April 1962): 395.

33. *Report,* p. CR–15.

34. Ibid., p. CR–16.

35. Ibid., pp. 54, CR–15–16.

36. Rao, "The Sino-Indian Boundary," pp. 397–99.

37. *Report,* p. 51.

38. Ibid., p. 51.

39. Ibid., p. CR–14.

40. Ibid., pp. CR–12–13.

41. Ibid., p. 53.

42. Ibid., p. CR–14.

43. Ibid., p. CR–14.

44. Ibid., p. CR–14.

45. Ibid., p. 54.

46. Ibid., p. CR–15.

47. Text of the agreement in *White Paper,* 1: 98–101; also in Arthur Lall, *How Communist China Negotiates* (New York: Columbia University Press, 1968), pp. 262–68.

48. *Report,* p. 87.

49. Ibid., p. CR–18.

50. English text of the treaty in *PR* 3, no. 5 (February 2, 1960): 14–15.

51. English text of the treaty in *PR* 3, no. 40 (October 1960): 33–34.

52. *PR,* 5, no. 19 (May 11, 1962): 10.

53. English text of the agreement in *PR* 6, nos. 10 & 11 (March 15, 1963): 67–70.

54. For example, China and Pakistan reached a procedural agreement on October 2, 1962, for negotiating their boundary treaty, see *PR* 5, no. 52 (December 28, 1962): 8.

55. For example, in the preamble of the boundary treaty between the PRC and Burma, signed on October 1, 1960, it stated that the two states "appointed their respective plenipotentiaries as follows: Chou En-lai, Premier of the State Councial, for the Chairman

of the People's Republic of China, and U Nu, Prime Minister, for the President of the Union of Burma, who, having mutually examined their full powers and found them in good and due form," in *PR,* 3, no. 40 (October 4, 1960): 29.

56. The PRC denied the existence of the 1684 treaty between Tibet and Ladkh because the representatives of the two sides were unknown, see *Report,* p. CR–12.

57. Oppenheim, *International Law,* vol. 1, p. 868.

58. Ibid., p. 867.

59. Ibid., p. 890.

60. *Report,* p. CR–18.

61. Oppenheim, *International Law,* vol. 1, p. 868.

62. See "Statement of USSR, on June 14, 1969," in *The Current Digest of the Soviet Press* 21, no. 24 (July 9, 1969): 12.

63. *Prime Minister on Sino-Indian Relations,* 3: 115–16, quotation in Neville Maxwell, *India's China War* (New York: Doubleday, 1962), p. 142.

64. "Premier Chou En-lai in India," *PR* 3, no. 17 (April 26, 1960): 40.

65. "Joint Communique of Chinese and India Premiers," *PR* 3, no. 18 (May 3, 1960): 17.

66. Oppenheim, *International Law,* vol. 1, p. 890.

67. *Report,* p. 1.

68. For example, the Sino-Burmese Boundary Treaty (1960) was signed by Prime Minister Chou En-lai, see *PR* 3, no. 40 (October 4, 1960): 33–34; the Sino-Afghan Boundary Treaty (1963) was signed by Minister of Foreign Affairs Chen Yi, with the Minister of Foreign Affairs of Afghanistan A. Kayeum, see *PR* 6, no. 48 (November 29, 1963): 8; the Sino-Nepalese Boundary Treaty (1961) was signed by Chairman Liu Shao-chi of the PRC and his Majesty the King of Nepal, Mahendra Bir Bikram, see *PR* 4, no. 42 (October 20, 1961): 5–8.

69. *Report,* p. CR–12.

70. Wei Liang, "Looking at the So-called McMahon Line," p. 48. This paragraph was translated into English by Chiu in "The Theory and Practice," p. 11.

71. Quotation in Lamb, *The McMahon Line,* p. 505.

72. Ibid.

73. Wei Liang, "Looking at the So-called McMahon Line," p. 49.

74. Text of the Sino-Pakistani Boundary Treaty in *PR* 6, nos. 10 & 11 (March 15, 1963): 67–70; the Sino-Afghan Boundary Treaty in *PR* 6, no. 41 (November 29, 1963): 7; the Sino-Nepalese Boundary Treaty in *PR* 6, no. 42 (October 20, 1961): 5–8. The Sino-Nepalese Boundary Treaty also in Lall, *How Communist China Negotiates,* pp. 262–68.

75. *PR* 3, no. 40 (October 4, 1960): 33–34.

76. See *Report,* p. CR–12.

77. McNair, *The Law of Treaties,* p. 162.

78. Concerning the relationship between consent and reservation, see Oppenheim, *International Law,* vol. 1, p. 913.

79. McNair, *The Law of Treaties,* p. 158.

80. *PR* 12, no. 41 (October 7 1969): 14.

81. Ibid.

82. Text in *The American Journal of International Law* 63 (1963): 875–903.

83. *Report,* p. 54.

84. Ibid., pp. CR–14–15.

85. *White Paper*, 1: 98–101; also Lall, *How Communist China Negotiates*, pp. 262–68.

86. *Report*, p. 85.

87. The Indian government read the word "border" as the same meaning as "boundary." For example, the phrase "to stabilize Chinese-Indian border" was read by the Indian government as that the Chinese-Indian boundary had been fixed and the two countries' only need was to maintain the stability of their "boundary," see the Chinese criticism in *Report*, p. CR–30. By the same token, the Indian government read the six "border passes" in the 1954 Sino-Indian Trade Agreement the same meaning as six "boundary passes."

88. "Note Given by the Ministry of Foreign Affairs, Peking, to the Embassy of India in China, 3 April 1960," *White Paper*, 4: 10.

89. "Memorandum Given by the Ministry of External Affairs, New Delhi, to the Embassy of China in India, 20 October 1959," *White Paper*, 2: 61.

90. "Note Given by the Ministry of Foreign Affairs of China to the Embassy of India in China, 26 December 1959," *White Paper*, 3: 60.

91. *White Paper*, 3: 61. For the Chinese, "border passes" in the agreement has no relations to "boundary" at all; border does not mean boundary. In the negotiations of the 1954 Agreement, the two countries agreed to open the border passes for the traders and pilgrims and leave the boundary question to be settled in the future. The Chinese argument of the connotations of the border and boundary are in *White Paper*, 3: 60.

92. *White Paper*, 3: 61.

93. McNair, *The Law of Treaties*, p. 506.

94. "Declaration Signed by Karakhan to the Chinese People and to the Governments of North and South China, 25 July 1919," in Jane Degras, ed., *Soviet Documents on Foreign Policy*, vol. 1, 1917–1924 (London: Oxford University Press, 1951), p. 159.

95. League of Nations, *Treaty Series*, no. 955 (1925), vol. 37, pp. 176–82.

96. Wang Shih-chieh and Hu Ching-yu, *Ch'ung-kuo pu-p'ing-teng t'iao-yueh chih fei-ch'u* (The Abrogations of the Chinese Unequal Treaties), cited by Chiu, "The Theory and Practice," p. 252.

97. See "Statement of USSR, on June 14, 1969," in *The Current Digest of the Soviet Press* 21, no. 24 (July 9, 1969): 11.

98. Alfred P. Rubin, "The Sino-Indian Border Disputes," *The International and Comparative Law Quarterly* 9, part 1 (January 1960): 96–125, at 96.

99. Editorial of the *People's Daily,* March 25, 1960, printed in English in *PR* 3, no. 13 (March 29, 1960): 6.

100. Text of the treaty printed in *Documents of International Affairs, 1956* (London: Oxford University Press), p. 740.

101. Oppenheim, *International Law*, vol. 1, pp. 925–26.

102. Citation in McNair, *The Law of Treaties*, p. 309. The principle of Article 18(b) of the Harvard Research Draft Convention on Treaties appears in Vienna Convention on the Law of Treaties in 1969. A part of the article of the Vienna Convention reads: "I. A right arises for a third state from a provision of a treaty if the parties to the treaty intend the provision to accord that right either to the third state, or to a group of states to which it belongs, or to all states, and the third state assents thereto. Its assent shall be presumed so long as the contrary is not indicated, unless the treaty otherwise provides," text in 63 *AJIL* 875–903.

103. Article 2 of the St. Petersburg Convention, which is printed in Lamb, *The McMahon Line*, pp. 251–57.

104. See note 25.

105. See An, *The Sino-Soviet Territorial*, pp. 43–44.

106. Tien-fong Cheng, *A History of Sino-Russian Relations* (Washington, D.C.: Public Affairs Press, 1957), p. 50.

107. English text of the treaty in *PR* 7, no. 48 (November 29, 1963): 7–9. Concerning the history and location of the Wakhan Corridor, see Chapter 4 and Map 2 of this book.

108. "Note Given by the Ministry of Foreign Affairs of China to the Embassy of India in China, 26 Dec. 1959," *White Paper*, 3: 60.

109. Wei Liang, "Looking at the So-called McMahon Line," p. 53.

110. See McNair, *The Law of Treaties*, p. 590.

111. Lin Piao's political report to the Ninth Congress of the Chinese Communist Party, April 11, 1969, in Peter Berton, ed., "The Border Issue: China and the Soviet Union, March-October 1969," *Studies in Comparative Communism* 2, nos. 3 & 4 (July/October 1969): 188.

112. See "Statement of USSR, on June 14, 1969," *The Current Digest of the Soviet Press* 21, no. 24 (July 9, 1969): 12.

113. L. J. Lindley in *Low* v. *Bouverie* (1891) 3 Ch. at p. 101, cited by Arnold D. McNair, "The Legality of the Occupation of the Ruhr," *The British Yearbook of International Law,* 5 (1924), p. 34.

114. (1837) 6 Adolphus and Ellis at p. 474, in ibid.

115. This is Sir Gerald Fitsmaurice's definition in the Temple case in International Court of Justice *Reports* (1962), p. 62, cited by R. Y. Jennings, *Acquisition of Territory in International Law* (Manchester: Manchester University Press, 1963), p. 45.

116. D. W. Bowett, "Estoppel before International Tribunals and Its Relation to Acquiescence," in *The British Yearbook of International Law* (1957) 33: 202.

117. Ibid., p. 198.

118. *Report*, p. 271.

119. Ibid., p. 274.

120. Ibid., p. CR–31.

121. Ibid.

122. Surya P. Sharma, "The Indian-China Border Dispute: An Indian Perspective," *AJIL* 59: 16–47.

123. Ibid.

124. *White Paper*, 3: 62; also *SIBQ*, p. 60.

125. See note 105 of Chapter 4.

126. *White Paper*, 3: 60; also *SIBQ*, p. 55.

127. *Report*, p. 87.

128. See *White Paper*, 3: 61 and 4: 10; also *SIBQ*, p. 57.

129. *White Paper*, 3: 60; also *SIBQ*, p. 55.

130. Rao, "The Sino-Indian Boundary Question," p. 387.

7

DETERMINANTS OF BOUNDARIES

INTRODUCTION

Since the PRC has been ambitious to define all her boundaries, in this chapter we will discuss: (1) Why the PRC wanted formal boundary delimitations in legal form, (2) the elements that help the Chinese in boundary claims and settlements, and (3) the procedures the Chinese used for defining boundaries with their neighbors.

THE NEED OF DELIMITATION AND DEMARCATION

The PRC claims that there are two kinds of international boundary lines: lines formally delimited and traditional customary boundary lines. "A formally delimited boundary must be one jointly negotiated (sometimes also jointly surveyed) by the countries concerned and with its alignment and location explicitly and concretely defined in a certain treaty (usually the conclusion of a boundary treaty or agreement); this is an international recognized principle."[1] The "traditional customary line was gradually formed and made clear through a long process of historical development according to the extent up to which each side has all along exercised administrative jurisdiction, and it was not mechanically defined or predetermined by some geographical principle."[2]

India claims that the customary boundary line has been clear, but in reality it is an approximate line and disputes over it easily arise. In 1960, China and India studied their boundary question. During the meetings the Indian delegation asked China many questions about the exact locations of the Chinese-claimed boundary.

Some questions were answered in detail by China; some, in part; and some others were not answered at all. The Chinese delegation asked questions of the Indian representatives who did not supply completely satisfactory answers either.[3] These were not deliberate evasions but instead the result of a lack of needed geographical knowledge in the disputed areas. Thus, a customary boundary line is definitely not a precise line. A good example to further clarify this is the Sino-Indian dispute over Chuva and Chuje. India claimed these areas as parts of Spiti.[4] The PRC disagreed and said that both Chuva and Chuje are separate places from Spiti.[5] India also said at one time that Poling was known as Puling-Sumda,[6] but China disagreed, averring that Poling and Puling-Sumda were two entirely different places.[7]

Sometimes places referred to on customary boundary lines may not exist. For example, India once claimed that a part of her boundary line in the western section of a disputed frontier ran along a watershed from a point east of 80°E to Lanak Pass.[8] However, a Chinese investigation showed that there is no such watershed in that area.[9]

Because of all these defects in the customary boundary line, the Chinese have insisted on a formal delimitation of the boundary with India and Burma. In addition to delimitation, the Chinese insist that it is also necessary to demarcate the ground. Demarcation, according to a Western scholar's view, means "to comprise the actual laying down of a boundary line on the ground, and its definition by boundary pillars or other similar physical means."[10]

In some areas along China's international boundaries, surveys had been completed and lines had been agreed upon, but no markers had been erected. The PRC insists that markers be erected. An exchange of notes in 1941 between Great Britain and China fixed a boundary line in the Kawa region along the Sino-Burmese border. However, the PRC still insisted on erecting demarcation pillars there.[11] The pillars were finally erected after they concluded a new boundary treaty in 1960.

The PRC also wants to redefine and redemarcate the entire Sino-Soviet boundaries. The existing boundaries were the results of tzarist expansion, and parts of their boundaries have not been demarcated.[12] In 1924, China and the Soviet Union signed the Agreement on General Principles for the Settlement of the Questions between China and the Soviet Union. But it has not been possible to go beyond agreement on general principles. The PRC said:

> In pursuance of the 1924 Agreement, China and the Soviet Union held talks in 1926 to discuss the re-demarcation of the boundary and the conclusion of a new treaty. Owing to the historical conditions at the time, no agreement was reached by the two sides on the boundary question, no re-demarcation of the boundary between the two countries was made and no new equal treaty was concluded by the two countries.[13]

Nevertheless, the Chinese were unwilling to give up in their efforts to redefine and redemarcate boundaries with the USSR. Negotiations were again entered into in 1964, to no avail. In February 1987, a Chinese team led by Deputy Foreign Minister Qian Qichen went to Moscow to resume their boundary talks. No information has been received on their progress as of yet.[14]

THE DETERMINANTS OF CLAIMING AND DEFINING BOUNDARIES

An international boundary line may be drawn up by using either natural features or geometrical methods or other factors or by any combination of them.[15]

Natural features include rivers, mountains, lakes, deserts, and their like. The British invoked the doctrine of natural frontiers when they drew a line along the crest of the Himalayas and referred to it as the ideal Indian-Chinese boundary line. She likewise drew a line along the watershed of the Irrawaddy-Salween and referred to that as the ideal Burmese-Chinese boundary line. India, after becoming independent, made use of this doctrine in her disputes with China over boundaries.

The Chinese claimed that natural features are not the most important factor in determining a nation's boundary. In practice, the PRC used other elements in addition to natural features when she disputed or settled boundaries with neighbors.

Former Treaties

Many of China's new international boundary treaties are based on her boundary treaties signed in the past. Regarding the Sino-Burmese boundaries, the PRC pointed out that "the question of the boundary line between China and Burma is the result of the policy of aggression carried on over the years by the imperialists," when Burma was a British colony.[16] However, the new boundary treaty in 1960 virtually accepted all the boundary lines fixed in the former treaties, equal or unequal, with only minor adjustments.

As early as 1957, Chou En-lai reported to the National Congress that "on the question of boundary lines, demands on the basis of formal treaties should be respected according to general international practice."[17] The new boundary treaty with Burma (1960) accepted the alignments from the High Conical Peak south to the junction of the Nam Hpa and the Nam Ting rivers and from the junction of the Nam Hka and the Nam Yung rivers to the southeastern extremity.[18] These two alignments had been decided by the Chinese-British Convention of 1894 and confirmed by the Convention of 1897. Between these two alignments was the "1941 Line." Both the Republic of China and the PRC complained that the British had taken advantage of China's involvement in the war with Japan to extract consent to this line. However, when Peking signed the new boundary treaty (1960), she accepted this "1941 Line" with only minor adjustment.[19] Even the extreme northern sector of the Sino-Burmese boundary which constitutes the eastern part of the "illegal" McMahon Line has also been accepted by the PRC in the new boundary treaty.[20]

The PRC also accepted the existing Sino-Nepalese boundary line acknowledged by the 1856 boundary treaty. The two countries in the 1956 treaty abrogated all their previous treaties,[21] but the boundary alignment remained the same and was accepted by the 1961 boundary treaty.[22]

Concerning the Sino-Sikkimese boundary, the PRC recognized the existing boundary line which had been formally delimited in 1890 and demarcated in 1895.[23]

Customary Boundaries

The PRC, in her new boundary treaties, has accepted the customary boundary lines claimed by Nepal, Burma, Pakistan, and Afghanistan.

In dealing with the Sino-Burmese customary boundary lines, China's basic policy involved examining historical data and focusing on the actual boundary situation.[24] Thus, Chou En-lai told the Burmese that the Sino-Burmese boundary line from "Izurazi Pass northward to Diphu Pass can be demarcated along the customary boundary line."[25] The 1960 boundary treaty confirmed Chou's proposal.[26]

Concerning the Sino-Pakistani boundary, it was announced in 1962 that "an agreement in principle has been reached on the location and alignment of the boundary actually existing between the two countries."[27] This actually existing boundary was written into the Sino-Pakistani provisional boundary agreement of 1963.[28]

China also recognized the customary boundary line with Afghanistan. By the boundary treaty of 1963, the PRC recognized the Wakhan Corridor, which was created by Russia and Great Britain in the late nineteenth century and had never been previously recognized by the Chinese.[29]

The Sino-Nepalese Boundary Treaty of 1961 was also made "on the traditional customary boundary line" with minor adjustments.[30]

Areas Important to National Defense

When defining boundary lines, some areas the PRC deemed important to her national defense were also taken into consideration in China's boundary policy-making. This case can be illustrated by the Sino-Burmese boundary negotiations and treaty. Chou En-lai suggested that the Sino-Burmese boundary between the Izurazi Pass and the High Conical Peak could be demarcated along the Irrewaddy-Salween watershed. However, the PRC was unwilling to give up three villages—Hpimaw, Kangfang, and Gawlun—near the Hpimaw Pass[31] because the Hpimaw Pass provides access to China's Yunnan Province. Since holding this pass safeguards Yunnan against possible military invasion,[32] China insisted it be written into the boundary treaty.

Anthropogeographical Components

Anthropogeographical components have closer and stronger ties with the human element. An anthropogeographical boundary line is based on tribal, linguistic, religious, economic, historical, and cultural factors, administrative jurisdiction, or some combination of the above. Unlike the Indians, who emphasized the natural features (that is, the Himalaya ranges) as the most important factor in determining the eastern section of their disputed frontiers, the Chinese in disputes with India emphasized the anthropogeographical factors. Peking collected administrative and legal documents and maps, proving that "the Chinese Government has always exercised extensive administrative jurisdiction" south of the Himalayas, and therefore claimed that the Himalayas are in Chinese territory.[33]

Defining the Sino-Burmese boundaries, the Chinese have also considered tribal ties. Peking cared for historical ties and the integrity of the Panhung and Panlao tribes. She therefore demanded that Burma turn the territory under the jurisdiction of both the Panhung and Panlao tribes to her.[34] The two governments also made minor adjustments regarding the intra-tribal relationship, production, and livelihood of the local inhabitants. Thus, along the boundary line, some small villages went to China, others to Burma, "so that these boundary-line-intersected villages will no longer be intersected by the boundary line."[35]

This does not mean that the Chinese always take anthropogeographical components into consideration prior to other elements when defining boundaries. When the PRC demanded three villages during the Sino-Burmese negotiations, Chou En-lai realized that "it will be hard to avoid separating the nationalities concerned by the boundary line."[36] But Peking insisted on having these three villages, and the Kahins living there were eventually separated from the Kahins in Burma.

After the conclusion of the Sino-Burmese Boundary Treaty in 1960, the two governments completed the transfer of border territories in the next year. The villages of Hpimaw, Kangfang, and Gawlun, the areas under the jurisdiction of the Panhung and Panlao tribes, and the Yawng Hok and Lunghai villages were transferred to China. The Umpo, Pan Hung, Pan Nawng, and Pan Wai villages were handed over to Burma.[37]

Natural Features

In claiming boundaries and concluding boundary treaties with neighbors, the PRC also used natural features as boundary lines.

Mountains. States use mountains as boundary lines not only because mountains are easy to recognize, but also because they are usually the barriers separating the inhabitants on either side. China has also considered mountains as boundary lines. For example, in the western section of the Sino-Indian disputed frontiers, China claimed a boundary line between the Karakoram Pass and the

Kongka Pass that more or less follows the Karakoram Mountains as the proper boundary. One sector of that line was described by the PRC as the line from the Chipochap River that "turns south-east along the mountain ridge and passes through peak 6,845 (approximately 78° 12'E, 34° 57'N) and peak 6,598 (approximately 78° 13'E, 34° 54'N). From peak 6,598 it runs along the mountain ridge southwards until it crosses the Galwan peak 6,556 (approximately 78° 26'E, 34° 32'N)."[38]

The PRC also inserted mountains as boundary alignments in boundary treaties. For example, Article 1 (10) of the Boundary Treaty of 1961 between China and Nepal reads:

> From Chomo Pamari (Height 6,208.8 meters), the boundary line runs generally northwards along the mountain ridge to Height 5,914.8 meters. Then generally northeastwards along Shondemo Kangri (sudemo) snowy mountain passing through Height 5,148 meters . . . and then along the mountain.[39]

Watersheds and Passes. Watersheds, *Divortium aquarum*, and passes are other natural features used to delimit international boundaries. The term "watershed" has a double meaning according to its definition:

> The term "watershed" in common language has a double meaning. It is used not only to define the basin or drainage area of a river but also to designate the crest or water-parting line separating two contiguous water-basins. For delimitation purposes, however, the second meaning is usually intended.[40]

The second meaning of watershed is related to pass, and the following definition of "pass" is from the *Encyclopaedia Britannica*:

> Watershed, in physical geography, the line separating the headstreams tributary to two different river systems or basins. Alternative terms are "water-parting" and "divide." . . . In a mountainous country, where two sources adjacent, are both gradually eroding or cutting back the land at their heads, a pass is formed.[41]

China used the second meaning of watershed in a dispute with India, claiming that the Sino-Indian boundary in the western sector follows the Karakoram Mountains, which divides the two major river systems: the Hotien River and the Indus River.[42]

India claimed that the Sino-Indian boundary on this frontier follows the Kun Lun Mountains north of the Karakoram Mountains. The Kun Lun range divides "the greater part of the volume of waters of the two big river system."[43] This definition was criticized by the Chinese as a "creation," different from the definition internationally acknowledged.[44]

In contrast, China adhered to the well-established definition when Chou Enlai proposed a delimitation of the Sino-Burmese boundary from the Izurazi Pass to the High Conical Peak. According to his proposal, the boundary line "can be in principle determined along the watershed between the Nu River, the Shweli

River (otherwise called the Lungchuan River) and the Taiping River on the one side, and the Nmai Hka River on the other."[45]

Moreover, a large river always receives the benefit of a multiplicity of streams pouring into it. The water-parting of these streams has an effect on boundary alignments. India once claimed that the Sino-Indian boundary should follow the main watershed, not the numerous minor watersheds.[46] China did not discuss the multiple streams for determining her boundary lines, but pointed out that "the Himalayas are composed of a number of parallel ranges and are hundreds of kilometers wide."[47]

The PRC also used both watershed and pass to define boundary lines with neighboring states. For example, Article 2 of the Sino-Afghan Boundary Treaty of 1963 reads:

> The Contracting Parties agree that whenever the boundary between the two countries follows a watershed, the ridge thereof shall be the boundary line, and whenever it passes through a daban (pass), the water-parting line thereof shall be the boundary line.[48]

Rivers. Rivers have been advocated as ideal international boundary lines and have been used by many states. China too has used the Ussuri River to dispute with the Soviet Union over the boundary line. The Soviets invoked a map attached to the Sino-Russian Treaty of Peking (1860) and claimed the boundary line passing along the Chinese bank of the River. China rejected the Soviets' claim and asserted that the boundary had not been demarcated and that the map had been unilaterally drawn by tzarist Russia before the boundary was surveyed in 1861.[49] According to China's claim, the boundary line should be drawn in agreement with the principle of *thalweg* in international law.[50]

The PRC also used rivers to define her international boundaries. For example, Article 1 (12) of the Sino-Nepalese Boundary Treaty of 1961 reads: "It follows the Sunchunchu (Shumjung) River to its junction with the track leading from Kimathangka to Chentang, then it runs along the track to the ridge on the Karma tsangpo (Kama) River. . . . "[51]

In her boundary treaties, the PRC has emphasized that if a boundary follows a river, the central line of the main channel of the river shall be the boundary line. She further stipulates that when a river changes its course, natural or artificial, and forms a new one, the new channel does not alter the original boundary line; even without water flowing in the old channel, the boundary remains as it was.[52]

Geometrical Methods

Nations engage in geometrics when they draw lines, meridians of longitude, parallels of latitude, arcs of a circle or lines parallel to or equidistant from rivers to make boundary lines. China has practiced geometrics. In the Sino-Soviet dispute over the Pamirs, the Kashgar Boundary Treaty in 1884 stipulated that "Russia's boundary turns southwest while the Chinese boundary extends straight south" from the Uz Bel Pass.[53] A map published by the PRC shows two straight lines which she claims as the only valid international boundary line.[54] (see Map 2).

THE PROCEDURES OF DEFINING BOUNDARIES

To delimit and demarcate international boundaries, certain procedures were followed by the PRC. These procedures involved signing a preliminary boundary agreement, setting up a joint committee for investigations and survey, concluding a formal boundary treaty, erecting permanent boundary markers, and exchanging a final protocol. A good example is that in which the PRC worked out her boundary line with Nepal.

On March 11, 1960, Prime Minister Bishweshwar Prassad Keirala of Nepal visited Peking. China and Nepal signed a preliminary "Agreement Between the Government of the People's Republic of China and His Majesty's Government of Nepal on the Question of the Boundary Between the Two Countries."[55] According to Article 1 of this agreement, a Joint Sino-Nepalese Boundary Committee was set up on August 11, of the same year, in Kathmandu, to discuss and solve the concrete problems concerning the Sino-Nepalese boundary, to conduct investigations and surveys, to determine the specific alignments, to draft a formal boundary treaty, and to erect permanent boundary markers.

The Joint Committee held its first session in Kathmandu and Rangoon from August through December.[56] They agreed on general arrangements for a speedy settlement of the boundary question. They appointed experts to discuss the execution of the concrete tasks and to make recommendations to the Joint Committee.[57]

According to the preliminary boundary agreement, joint survey teams composed of an equal number of persons from each side were set up. The joint teams were obliged to conduct surveys on the spot, determine the boundary lines, and erect boundary markers. The teams were also authorized "to make adjustments in accordance with the principles of equality, mutual benefit, friendship and mutual accommodation." The first joint team was sent out in November 1960 to carry out these tasks along the Chinese-Nepalese border.[58]

The Joint Committee held its second session in Peking from January 8 to February 15, 1961. Certain agreements were reached:[59]

1. They arrived at a common understanding of the general alignment of the boundary.
2. They reached solutions concerning difficult boundary line sections where delineation on the maps had not been identical, and where there existed jurisdictional differences.
3. A decision was reached to send more joint teams to investigate and survey the key points along the entire Chinese-Nepalese boundary line. These joint teams should submit reports, recommendations and maps to the Joint Committee.

The Joint Committee held its third session in Kathmamdu from July 31 through August 24, and with these reports and recommendations, reached an agreement on the draft boundary treaty.[60] On October 5, 1961, the formal boundary treaty was signed in Peking by the two countries and temporary boundary markers were erected.[61]

According to Article 3 of the Sino-Nepalese Boundary Treaty, "the Chinese-Nepalese Joint Boundary Committee . . . should set up permanent boundary markers as necessary on the boundary line between the two countries, and then draft a protocol setting forth in detail the alignment of the entire boundary line and the location of the permanent boundary markers, with detail maps attached thereto showing the boundary of the permanent boundary markers."[62]

It was reported that the erecting of the permanent boundary markers along the entire Chinese-Nepalese boundary line was started in July 1962 and was completed on schedule.

The same procedures that the PRC used with Nepal were also followed in boundary settlements with the Mongolian People's Republic, but in this case, the PRC signed a formal boundary treaty without a preliminary agreement. A joint commission was set up for making surveys and erecting permanent boundary markers, but it was never implemented because of the deterioration of the two countries' relations.

The PRC also signed a formal boundary treaty with Afghanistan without a preliminary treaty. The Sino-Afghan Joint Boundary Demarcation Committee completed the work. The final protocol was signed, and the permanent boundary pillars were erected.

SUMMARY

The Chinese desired to define their international boundaries with accuracy. Rejecting the advocacy of traditional customary boundary lines, they insisted that boundary lines should be written into formal treaties. In their new boundary treaties, the characteristics of rivers, watersheds and passes were utilized, and boundary markers were erected.

The means employed in boundary claims and in boundary defining were practical, reasonable, and in agreement with the customs in international society.

Conservatism and caution were the watchwords for the Chinese in their boundary settlements. They "followed the rules," step by step, until the final pillars were erected on the ground, the protocols were signed, and the maps in detail were exchanged.

NOTES

1. *Report of the Officials of the Governments of India and the People's Republic of China on the Boundary Question* (New Delhi: Ministry of External Affairs, 1961), p. CR–

157. ("CR" precedes all page numbers of the section which contains the report of the Chinese officials, hereafter cited as *Report*.)

2. *Report*, p. CR–186.

3. Ibid., pp. 7–35.

4. Ibid., pp. 88–89.

5. Ibid., p. CR–17.

6. Ibid., pp. 191–92.

7. Ibid., p. CR–42.

8. Ibid., p. CR–6.

9. Ibid.

10. S. Whittemore Boggs, *International Boundaries: A Study of Boundary Functions and Problems* (New York: Columbia University Press, 1940), p. 32.

11. "Report on the Question of the Boundary Line between China and Burma, Delivered by Chou En-lai, Premier and Foreign Minister, at the Fourth Session of the First National People's Congress," *Important Documents on the Settlement of the Sino-Burmese Boundary Question* (Peking: Foreign Languages Press, 1960), p. 19 (hereafter cited as *Important Documents*).

12. The PRC said that the boundaries in the areas of the Ussuri and the Amur rivers were not demarcated, see "Statement of the Government of the People's Republic of China," *Peking Review* (hereafter *PR*), 12, no. 22 (May 30, 1969): 3. The Pamir region has not been demarcated either, see "China-USSR, the Disputed Area of the Pamirs," *PR*, 24, no. 37 (September 14, 1981): 22.

13. "Statement of the Government of the People's Republic of China," *PR* 12, no. 22 (May 30, 1969): 6.

14. *New York Times*, Feb. 8, 1987, p. 3.

15. See A. O. Cukwurah, *The Settlement of Boundary Disputes in International Law* (New York: Oceana Publications, 1967), pp. 16ff.

16. *Important Documents*, p. 24.

17. Ibid.

18. Article 6 of the Sino-Burmese Boundary Treaty; text in *PR* 3, no. 40 (Oct. 4, 1960): 33–34.

19. Article 1 of the Sino-Burmese Boundary Treaty; text in ibid.

20. Article 6 of the Sino-Burmese Boundary Treaty; text in ibid.

21. Text of the treaty in *Documents of International Affairs* (London: Oxford University Press, 1965), p. 740.

22. Article 1 of the Sino-Nepalese Boundary Treaty (1961), text in *PR* 4, no. 42 (Oct. 20, 1961): 5–8; also in Arthur Lall, *How Communist China Negotiates* (New York: Columbia University Press, 1968), pp. 262–68.

23. Harold C. Hinton, *Communist China in World Politics* (Boston: Houghton Mifflin, 1966), p. 323.

24. *Important Documents*, p. 25.

25. Ibid., p. 21.

26. Article 6 of the Sino-Burmese Boundary Treaty, text in *PR* 3, no. 40 (Oct. 4, 1960): 33–34.

27. *New China News Agency* dispatch, Dec. 28, 1962, quotation in Hinton, *Communist China*, p. 319.

28. Text of the treaty in *PR* 6, nos. 10 & 11 (March 15, 1963): 67–70.

29. Text of the Sino-Afghan Boundary Treaty in *PR* 6, no. 48 (Nov. 29, 1963): 7; concerning the Wakhan Corridor see Chapter 4 of this book.
30. See note 22.
31. *Important Documents*, p. 21.
32. Ref. J. J. G. Syatauw, *Some Newly Established Asian States and the Development of International Law* (The Hague: Martinus Nijhoff, 1961), p. 126.
33. *Report*, p. CR–166. Regarding maps the Chinese government provided, see *The Sino-Indian Boundary Question*, enlarged ed. (Peking: Foreign Languages Press, 1962).
34. Article 2 of the Sino-Burmese Boundary Treaty in *PR* 3, no. 40 (Oct. 4, 1960): 33–34.
35. Ibid.
36. *Important Documents*, p. 26.
37. "Sino-Burmese Joint Press Communique on Transfer of Border Area Territories," *PR* 4, no. 23 (June 9, 1961): 10.
38. *Report*, p. CR–1.
39. See note 22.
40. Cukwurah, *The Settlement of Boundary Disputes*, p. 42.
41. *Encyclopaedia Britannica* 8th ed., S. V. "pass."
42. *Report*, pp. CR–4–5.
43. Ibid., p. CR–38.
44. Ibid., p. CR–177.
45. *Important Documents*, p. 21.
46. *Report*, p. CR–38.
47. Ibid., p. CR–63.
48. *PR* 6, no. 48 (Nov. 29, 1963): 7.
49. *Important Documents*, p. 3.
50. Ibid.
51. See note 22.
52. See Article 2 of the 1961 Sino-Nepalese Boundary Treaty, in *PR* 4, no. 42 (Oct. 20, 1961): 5–8; similar stipulations in Article 3 of the 1963 Sino-Pakistani Boundary Agreement in *PR* 6, nos. 10–11 (March 15, 1963): 67–70, and Article 7 of the 1960 Sino-Burmese Boundary Treaty in *PR* 3, no. 40 (Oct. 4, 1960): 33–34.
53. A partial of the 1884 treaty was cited by the PRC in "China-USSR, the Disputed Area of the Pamirs," *PR* 24, no. 37 (Sept. 14, 1981): 22.
54. Ibid.
55. Text of the agreement in *PR* 3, no. 13 (March 29, 1960): 8–9.
56. *PR* 3, no. 35 (August 30, 1960): 26.
57. *PR* 3, no. 44 (Nov. 1, 1960): 17.
58. *PR* 4, no. 3 (Jan. 20, 1961): 25.
59. *PR* 4, no. 7 (Feb. 19, 1961): 27.
60. *PR* 4, no. 35 (Sept. 1, 1960): 20.
61. Text of the Sino-Nepalese Boundary Treaty in *PR* 4, no. 42 (Oct. 20, 1961): 5–8.
62. Ibid., similar stipulations can be found in Article 3 of the 1963 Sino-Pakistani Boundary Agreement in *PR* 6, nos. 10–11 (March 15, 1963): 67–70, and Article 4 of the 1963 Sino-Afghan Boundary Treaty in *PR* 6, no. 48 (Nov. 29, 1963): 7.

8

METHODS FOR SETTLING BOUNDARY QUESTIONS

INTRODUCTION

International boundary disputes may be settled by peaceful means, by armed intervention,[1] or they may be wilfully disregarded temporarily. The PRC has settled some of her boundary disputes with her neighbors peacefully through negotiations as studied in Chapter 4 and does not intend to raise the Sino-Korean boundary discrepancy at present. She has no intention of having her boundary disputes with India and the Soviet Union become obsolescent; peaceful efforts are still in progress to solve them.[2] But the PRC also fought with India and the USSR over border territories. This chapter will examine how the Chinese used both peaceful and militaristic means to deal with her boundary questions.

PEACEFUL METHODS

There are quite a few methods available under international law for the peaceful settlement of boundary questions. A state may choose one or more of them in accordance with her own particular needs. Article 33 of the Charter of the United Nations records the peaceful means available:

> The parties to any dispute, the continuance of which is likely to endanger the maintenance of international peace and security, shall, first of all, seek a solution by negotiation, enquiry, mediation, conciliation, arbitration, judicial settlement, resort to regional agencies or arrangements, or other peaceful means of their own choice.

In the 1960s, when China's boundary disputes with India and the Soviet Union reached the highest point, Peking was excluded from international organizations except for those organizations of Communist origin. The PRC therefore could not bring her boundary disputes to any regional agency. The choices left to her were negotiation, inquiry and conciliation, mediation, arbitration, and judicial settlement.

Negotiation

Negotiation has been the primary means chosen by the PRC to settle her boundary questions with her neighboring countries. It was formally declared as such and actually put into practice.

The principle of negotiation for solving international disputes was first stated in the well-known Five Principles of Peaceful Coexistence in 1954 issued jointly with India. In 1955, Chou En-lai declared at the Asian-African Conference in Bandung that: "As to the determination of common border which we are going to undertake with our neighboring countries, we shall use only peaceful means and we shall not permit any other kinds of methods."[3]

In 1957, Chou delivered a report to the National Congress saying that, "our government has consistently held that a fair and reasonable settlement of all outstanding questions between China and other countries shall be through peaceful negotiation."[4] The National Congress passed a resolution two years later endorsing this basic policy.[5]

The PRC not only successfully settled her boundary questions with neighboring countries by negotiation, but also stipulated in their treaties that "any dispute concerning the boundary, which may arise after the formal delimitation of the boundary between the two countries, shall be settled through friendly consultation."[6]

With both India and the USSR, the PRC made every effort to solve the boundary questions through negotiation, but here the negotiations failed. Before formally declaring peaceful negotiation as a means of settling her boundary questions, the PRC had already attempted to negotiate with India. In 1951, Chou En-lai proposed a meeting with India to solve "pending problems" between the two countries. In 1956, he flew to New Delhi and took the initiative by discussing the McMahon Line. However, no subsequent negotiations took place after this meeting.

The Nehru administration held that their northern boundary (the Himalayas) should not be opened to negotiation.[7] The Indians believed that their northern boundary was legally delimited by an existing international boundary treaty.[8] Therefore, it did not need to be renegotiated except to make minor clarifications.

Toward the end of 1958 the area of the Sino-Indian boundary disputes extended from the Himalayas (the eastern section) to the Aksai Chin Plateau (the western section). Indians soon discovered that the Chinese had constructed a road in the Indian territory of Aksai Chin, and the dispute worsened.[9] In January 1959,

Chou wrote to Nehru telling him that the PRC found "it necessary to take a more or less realistic attitude towards the McMahon Line," and suggested a "friendly settlement."[10] He implied that China could make a deal with India about the eastern and western frontiers. Chou was heard from again in September, stating that "*an over-all* settlement of the boundary question should be sought by both sides through friendly negotiation" (emphasis added).[11]

In the same year (1959), India's policy of refusing to negotiate was extended to the western section of their frontiers. Nehru wrote to Chou in March denying that any boundary question at all existed between the two countries. He stated that "there is no room for doubt about our frontiers as shown in the published maps," and that the "common frontier was settled to the satisfaction of both sides."[12] Indian refusal to negotiate with China concerning the entire boundary (eastern, middle, and western sections) was hereafter established.

Because the Khamba rebellion in 1956 gradually spread from the east of Tibet to the center and the west in 1959, Chinese troops approached the Himalayas. India too under the "forward policy" pushed her troops toward China's frontiers. Complaints of intrusions were frequently exchanged. But the Indians insisted on a policy of non-negotiation. On September 26, 1959, Nehru sent a long letter to Chou. He affirmed again that "the entire length of the border has been either defined by treaty or recognized by custom or by both,"[13] and ruled out any negotiation to settle the boundary questions. He added: "No discussions can be fruitful unless the posts on the Indian side of the traditional frontier now held by the Chinese forces are first evacuated by them, and further threats and intimidations immediately cease."[14]

In the second half of 1959, the boundary situations worsened: The Longju incident occurred in August, and the Kongka Pass incident in October. China remained anxious to settle all her boundary disputes with India. In November, the Chinese government proposed to New Delhi that "the Prime Ministers of the two countries hold talks in the immediate future" to prevent the escalation of conflicts.[15] On December 17, Chou made a personal appeal to Nehru to meet him on December 26. Chou stated:

If you wish to suggest any other date, I am also willing to give consideration....
Should you find it inconvenient for you to hold talks in China, Rangoon can be fixed as the site of the talks, subject to the consent of the Burmese Government.[16]

Chou's appeal was politely rejected on December 21.[17]

Since the Indians denied the existence of any boundary question between the two countries and refused to negotiate with China, the PRC, in a 5,000-word note, dated December 26, 1959, asked India the following: "Has the Sino-Indian boundary been formally delimited?" If not, "what is the proper way to settle the Sino-Indian boundary dispute?" The Chinese government urged that "the two countries stop quarrelling, [and] quickly bring about a reasonable settlement of the boundary question."[18] Answering the PRC, the government of India stated that she too was anxious for a friendly settlement but could not "possibly accept suggestions which gravely prejudice" India's basic position.[19] That basic position was spelled out in the same note wherein she refused to enter into negotiations "to determine afresh the entire Sino-Indian boundary." However, she was willing to "discuss specific disputes in regard to the location of particular places on the boundary, and to make minor frontier ratifications by agreement, where they may be considered necessary."[20]

The door to negotiation over the entire boundary appeared closed. However, the Indians seemed to change their attitude. They now felt that their interest might be better served by talking with Chou.[21] At the beginning of February 1962, Nehru invited Chou to visit India.[22]

On April 19, 1962, Chou and a large entourage arrived in New Delhi to meet the Nehru administration. However, the Chou-Nehru meeting was destined to fail because India did not change her basic position. After six days of private talks between the two prime ministers, Chou issued a written statement revealing the disagreements between the two governments. Those agreements included the existence of boundary disputes, the line of actual control, the use of certain geographical principles to determine their boundaries, the feelings of the native peoples along the disputed boundaries, restraints from further territorial claims, and the refraining of patrols along their entire boundaries.[23] As a result, entering into negotiations to settle the boundary question was firmly ruled out.

After major armed conflicts in October 1962, Chou suggested again that "in order to seek a friendly settlement of the Sino-Indian boundary question, talks should be held once again by the Prime Ministers of China and India."[24] India answered that "if the Chinese . . . go back at least to the position where they were all along the boundary prior to 8 September 1962, India will then be prepared to undertake talks and discussions."[25] The PRC did not accept this precondition because before September 8, 1962, India occupied some places north of the McMahon Line in the eastern section and greater area of the disputed Aksai Chin Plateau in the western section. Thus, no face-to-face talks and discussions took place between the two countries.

In addition to suggesting that India hold direct negotiations, the PRC also engaged in a circuitous strategy to encourage India to enter the conference room. She sought to demonstrate by her policies elsewhere that a settlement could be reached through negotiations. In October 1960, she recognized the eastern end of the so-called McMahon Line (that is, from Diphu Pass to Izrazi Pass) as the customary boundary line between China and Burma in the Sino-Burmese Boundary Treaty (1960). The PRC also reached a boundary agreement in 1961 with Nepal, legalizing their customary boundary line. China also negotiated a boundary settlement with Pakistan in 1962. China's friendly and reasonable settlement of boundary questions with these nations was intended to invoke world public opinion to press India to settle her boundary with China. Peking did not hide her purpose. A note in 1962 to India said:

Since the Burmese and Nepalese Governments can settle their boundary questions with China in a friendly way through negotiations and since the Government of Pakistan has also agreed with the Chinese Government to negotiate a boundary settlement, why is it the Indian Government cannot negotiate and settle its boundary question with the Chinese Government?[26]

Again, the PRC's circuitous strategy failed in bringing India to the negotiation table.

With the Soviet Union, China twice negotiated boundary questions—in 1926 and 1964. In pursuance of the 1924 Agreement, China and the Soviet Union in 1926 held negotiations in Peking to discuss the redemarcation of their boundary and to conclude a new boundary treaty. However, these negotiations soon were discontinued and produced no result.[27]

The PRC in 1960 twice took the initiative, proposing to the USSR that negotiations be held to solve the boundary question.[28] Negotiations began in Peking in February 1964. The Soviet negotiator was a colonel-general (*sic*) of the border guards and the Chinese negotiator, in contrast, was Deputy Foreign Minister Cheng Yung-chuan.[29] Sending a minor official meant that the Soviets would not be interested in changing the entire boundary, but would make only minor adjustments of existing boundaries. Later on, the Soviets characterized the 1964 meetings as "bilateral consultations" rather than "negotiations"[30] because the Soviet government denied any "territory problem" between the two countries.[31] Since the two countries held totally different expectations about their international boundary lines, the negotiations in 1964 ceased. However, negotiations for solving local problems, such as commercial navigation along boundary waterways, investigation and utilization of natural resources, etc., took place and were successful.[32]

For the Chinese, "there [still] exists a boundary question between China and the Soviet Union"[33] because tzarist Russia annexed more than 1.5 million square kilometers (approximately 580,000 square miles) of Chinese territory by the unequal treaties it imposed on China. The Russians also crossed over some of the boundary lines stipulated by the unequal treaties and occupied additional Chinese territory. As late as 1969, Peking stated this in a note to the Soviet government and again emphasized the importance of peaceful negotiation:

The treaties relating to the present Sino-Soviet boundary are unequal treaties.... In consideration of the actual conditions, China will take these treaties as the basis for an overall settlement of the Sino-Soviet boundary question through peaceful negotiation and for determining the entire alignment of the boundary line... and will conclude a new equal Sino-Soviet treaty to replace the old unequal Sino-Soviet treaties.[34]

Inquiry and Conciliation

The definition of inquiry was given by Article 9 of the Hague Convention for the Pacific Settlement of International Disputes (1899), which stipulated that in case of disputes arising out of differences of opinion on points of fact and involving neither honor nor vital interests, which the parties could not settle by negotiation, they should institute an International Commission of Inquiry to elucidate the facts underlying the differences by investigation.[35]

Investigating the boundaries claimed by China and India would not only reveal the details of the Khamba rebellion in Tibet, but also the secrecy of the roads across the Aksai Chin Plateau, which has a high military value to the PRC. It would take years to overcome tremendous physical difficulties to accomplish the task. This method was absolutely impractical for Peking. Investigation of the Sino-Soviet border, along which both countries had stationed heavy military forces, was equally unacceptable to both nations.

According to the Chinese concept, "boundary matters are matters of major importance which involve the sovereignty and territory of a country."[36] The Sino-Indian boundary disputes involve about 130,000 square kilometers (50,000 square miles) of territory;[37] and the Sino-Soviet boundary disputes involve about 1,360,000 square kilometers (600,000 square miles).[38] These disputes, of course, involve vital interests and are not suitable for international inquiry.

Conciliation differs from inquiry which only involves an investigation of the facts. Conciliation entails not only an investigation of the facts, but the making of proposals to the parties concerned as well.[39] Without the investigated facts, conciliation was ruled out to settle China's boundary disputes with her neighbors.

Mediation

Mediation is an acceptable method to the PRC because disputed parties, who are brought together by the mediator, negotiate directly.[40]

Mediation was the method used by the PRC trying to solve the Sino-Indian boundary question. During the first major armed conflict between these two countries in October 1962, President Nasser of the United Arab Republic, a close friend of India, proposed to China and India a four-point resolution to solve their boundary question: a cease-fire, the demarcation of a demilitarized buffer zone, negotiation, and the withdrawal of troops "to the positions they held prior to the recent clashes which began on the 20th October, that is, behind the line where their forces stood on the 8th September last."[41] Before September 8, Indian troops occupied some areas north of the McMahon Line. The PRC could not accept this proposal, and the mediation failed.

During the time of the second major armed conflict between the two countries, Chou En-lai wrote to the leaders of the Asian and African countries on November 15, 1962, asking them to uphold justice and to exercise "distinguished influence to promote a peaceful settlement of the Sino-Indian boundary question."[42] President Nasser suggested a conference of Asian-African governments to discuss the cease-fire and a possible basis for bilateral negotiation. In December, delegates of six nonaligned countries—Burma, Cambodia, Ghana, Ceylon, Indonesia, and the United Arab Republic—called together by Mrs. Bandaranaike, prime minister of Ceylon, met in Colombo to discuss the Chinese-Indian conflict. After discussion and compromise, the Colombo Conference proposed three points to serve as the basis of bilateral negotiation between China and India.

With regard to the western section of the disputed frontiers, the conference suggested that China fulfill her commitment to withdraw her troops 20 kilometers (12 miles) away from the military posts. The Indian government was to keep her existing military positions there. With regard to the eastern section of the disputed frontiers, the Colombo Conference suggested that the line of actual control before the armed conflicts serve as the cease-fire. This meant that the Indian troops would move up to the McMahon Line. The Colombo Conference rejected China's desire to have both sides keep their troops 20 kilometers back from the McMahon Line. The conference also suggested that the middle section of the disputed frontiers be solved by peaceful means.[43]

Both China and India accepted these proposals in principle.[44] However, India accepted them only after the Indian Ministry of External Affairs had drafted, and Mrs. Bandaranaike had released, a "clarifications" of the original proposals.[45] China accepted them conditionally as well with "two points of interpretations" which were in fact reservations.[46]

New Delhi declared that China must accept the Colombo powers' proposals in toto without "interpretations" before bilateral negotiations could begin.[47] Peking argued with India by saying that India did not accept the Colombo powers' proposals in toto either. India did accept the proposals but attached her own drafted "clarifications."[48] Peking answered that bilateral negotiations could be started now between the two countries because the Colombo powers' proposals were suggestions, not arbitration:

> The task of the Colombo Conference was to mediate and not to arbitrate. Its proposals are only a recommendation for the consideration of China and India and not a verdict or arbitral award which China and India must accept *in toto*.... There is no need for China and India to agree to all the Colombo proposals before going to the Conference [*sic*] table.[49]

Nevertheless, no agreement between China and India to confer was reached, and the Colombo Conference powers' mediation failed.

Arbitration and Judicial Settlement

Both arbitral award and judicial settlement are legal decisions. The Chinese have been and are reluctant to submit their grievances to legal decisions. To go before a tribunal of law not only is contrary to Chinese philosophy and thinking, but also to their upholding sovereignty which a revolutionary state such as China holds dear. In addition, lacking trust in the World Court, the PRC ruled out any judicial settlement of the International Court of Justice.

Confucianism, dear to traditional Chinese values, discourages people from becoming involved in legal battles even when the grievance is legitimate.[50] Chinese people are urged to respect one another by the Confucian code of ethics (*li*); only the "moral midgets" (*hsiao-jen*) and "pettifoggers" (*sung-shih*) gravitate toward litigation.[51] Therefore, the Chinese have traditionally preferred to settle their disputes "by negotiation, mediation or conciliation rather than by courts."[52] This philosophy and thinking has had a significant influence on their behavior on the international level; China has never submitted her disputes to international adjudication by the application of positive international law.

"Emancipated" from the big powers' oppression, the PRC has emphasized state sovereignty in international relations, believing that there is nothing higher than sovereignty. Theories that work to limit sovereignty are limitations placed on the weak by the "imperialist" nations.[53] Richard A. Falk has observed: "It is hardly surprising that revolutionary nations are reluctant to participate at all in international judicial proceedings, and refuse, for example, to settle disputes in the World Court."[54]

Through this quote we are able to understand the PRC's rejection of India's suggestion to submit the Sino-Indian boundary disputes "to the International Court of Justice at the Hague and agree to abide by the Court's decision."[55] The PRC pointed out:

> The Chinese Government is of the opinion that complicated questions involving sovereignty, such as the Sino-Indian boundary question, can be settled only through direct negotiations between the two parties concerned, and absolutely not through any form of arbitration.[56]

Sovereignty alone did not account for the PRC's unwillingness to submit her boundary disputes to the International Court of Justice in the 1960s. During that time, the Nationalist government of the Republic of China was still the sole representative of China in the United Nations. The Nationalist government but not the PRC was a member of the International Court of Justice, an organ of the UN. Thus, the PRC declared that the "Chinese Government could not agree to referring the Sino-Indian boundary question to international arbitration"[57] under the auspices of the United Nations, which had "degenerated into a tool of American imperialism."[58]

THE USE OF ARMED FORCES

War has been outlawed not only by virtue of the 1928 Kellogg-Briand Pact and the United Nations Charter, but also by virtue of the Five Principles of

Peaceful Coexistence initiated by China and India. Nevertheless, the PRC has had borders wars with India and the USSR.

The border wars between China and India had both a remote cause as well as an immediate one. The remote cause was that the boundary question was left over from the former British policy of expansion, and China never recognized the boundary lines drawn by the British. The immediate cause was provoked by India's "forward policy." India, after it became independent, established administrative centers in the disputed frontiers, set check posts along her claimed boundary lines and pushed troops even beyond them. China, during the Khamba rebellion in the late 1950s, also moved troops to the border. Conflicts started and then increased.

After the wars broke out in 1962, the PRC was able to push her troops forward, but later she chose an alternate way. Peking unilaterally declared a cease-fire and withdrew her troops back to the Chinese-claimed customary line in the western section and the McMahon Line in the eastern section. These actions suggest that the Chinese use of force was not intended to make India sign a boundary agreement favorable to her needs.

Along the Sino-Soviet 6,700-kilometer (4,150-mile) border, conflicts have been a chronic phenomenon. Many minor conflicts took place without world notice. However, a major armed conflict that attracted world attention took place in March 1969 on the small uninhabited Chenpao Island in the Ussuri River. The clashes were inevitable because the two inimical armies moved forward too close with each other. It is generally thought that the first conflict there on March 2, 1969, was provoked by the Chinese, and the subsequent conflict of March 14–15, by the Soviets.[59] Here the Chinese provocation was interpreted as not for the purpose of territorial recovery, but possibly the result of an internal power struggle.[60] China was no match for the Soviets, who had superior nuclear power. Therefore, she limited the conflicts to the Chenpao Island even though she had questioned the legality of the whole Sino-Soviet boundary.

The PRC justified her border wars with India and the USSR as wars of self-defense.[61] Such wars she claimed were not in violation of international law.

SUMMARY

The methods the PRC has chosen to settle her boundary questions are all defined by international law. Even though there are many methods for solving boundary disputes available, the PRC chose only two: negotiation and mediation. She did not choose inquiry, conciliation, arbitration and judicial settlement because of her traditional philosophy and/or objective limitations (not a member of the United Nations and not suitable to international investigation).

The Chinese border wars were defined as self-defense fought in the face of invasion. The war against India was not fought to reach a definitive settlement of boundary questions but, rather, to restore an undefined but provisional status quo which had been altered through India's "forward policy." The wars against the Soviets were not fought to recover China's "lost territories" but, rather, to defend her territory—the Chenpao Island—against the Soviets' invasion.

NOTES

1. This author has borrowed the concept for the settlement of boundary disputes from the work of Quincy Wright, who wrote: "Disputes may be settled by dictation, by negotiation, by obsolescence, or by adjudication, that is, in accord with the will of one, of both, of no one, or of third party," in *The Role of International Law in the Elimination of War* (New York: Oceana Publications, 1961), p. 77.

2. China and India held border talks on Peking on July 21, 1986, trying to settle their boundary questions, see *New York Times*, July 22, 1986, p. 5; China and the Soviet Union also resumed border talks on February 9, 1987, in Peking, by Deputy Foreign Ministers Igor A. Rogachev of the Soviet Union and Qian Qichen of China, see *New York Times*, Feb. 10, 1987, p. 5.

3. "Speech by Premier Chou En-lai to the Political Committee of the Asian-African Conference, April 23, 1955," George McTurnan Kahin, *The Asian-African Conference, Bandung, Indonesia, April 1955* (Ithaca: Cornell University Press, 1956), pp. 59–60.

4. "Report on the Question of the Boundary Line Between China and Burma Delivered by Chou En-lai, Premier and Foreign Minister, at the Fourth Session of the First National People's Congress," *Important Documents of the Settlement of the Sino-Burmese Boundary Question* (Peking: Foreign Languages Press, 1960), p. 17.

5. See "The Crux of the Boundary Question," *Peking Review* 2, no. 37 (Nov. 15, 1959): 5 (hereafter cited as *PR*).

6. Article 11 of the 1960 Sino-Burmese boundary treaty, *PR* 3, no. 40 (Oct. 4, 1960): 33–34; similar stipulations in Article 4 of the 1961 Sino-Nepalese boundary treaty, *PR* 4, no. 42 (Oct. 10, 1961): 5–8, Article 4 of the 1963 Sino-Afghan boundary treaty, *PR* 6, no. 48 (Nov. 29, 1963): 7–8, and Article 5 of the 1963 Sino-Pakistani boundary treaty, *PR*, nos. 10–11 (March 15, 1963): 67–70.

7. Regarding the formation of this policy, see Neville Maxwell, *India's China War* (New York: Doubleday & Co., 1972): 76.

8. See, for example, *Report of the Officials of the Governments of India and the People's Republic of China on the Boundary Question* (New Delhi: Ministry of External Affairs, 1961), p. 233 (hereafter cited as *Report*).

9. "Informal Note Given by the Foreign Secretary to the Chinese Ambassador, 18 Oct. 1958," *Notes, Memoranda and Letters Exchanged and Agreements Signed Between the Governments of India and China; White Paper* (New Delhi: Ministry of External Affairs, 1959–1963), 1: 26 (hereafter cited as *White Paper*).

10. "Letter from the Prime Minister of China to the Prime Minister of India, 23 January 1959," *White Paper*, 1: 53.

11. "Letter from the Prime Minister of China to the Prime Minister of India, 8 Sept. 1959," *White Paper*, 2: 27–33.

12. "Letter from the Prime Minister of India to the Prime Minister of China, 22 March 1959," in *White Paper*, 1: 55–57.

13. "Letter from the Prime Minister of India to the Prime Minister of China, 26 September 1959," in *White Paper*, 2: 35.

14. Ibid.

15. "Letter from the Prime Minister of China to the Prime Minister of India, 7 Nov. 1959," *White Paper*, 3: 45.
16. "Letter from the Prime Minister of China to the Prime Minister of India, 17 Dec. 1959," *White Paper*, 3: 55.
17. "Letter from the Prime Minister of India to the Prime Minister of China, 21 Dec. 1959," *White Paper*, 3: 56–57.
18. "Note Given by the Ministry of Foreign Affairs of China to the Embassy of India in China, 26 Dec. 1959," *White Paper*, 3: 58–79; also in *The Sino-Indian Boundary Question*, enlarged ed. (Peking: Foreign Languages Press, 1962), pp. 51–92 (hereafter cited as *SIBQ*).
19. "Note of the Government of India to the Chinese Government, 12 Feb. 1960," *White Paper*, 3: 94.
20. Ibid., p. 83.
21. See Maxwell, *India's China War*, p. 50.
22. "Letter from the Prime Minister of India to the Prime Minister of China, 5 Feb. 1960," *White Paper*, 3: 80–81.
23. The entire text see "Premier Chou En-lai's Written Statement," *PR* 5, no. 18 (May 3, 1962): 18–19; also in Dorothy Woodman, *Himalayan Frontiers: A Political Review of British, Chinese, Indian and Russian Rivalries* (London: The Cresset Press, 1969), pp. 256–57.
24. "Letter from the Premier Chou En-lai to the Prime Minister of India, 24 Oct. 1962," *White Paper*, 8: 1.
25. "Annexure to Letter from the Prime Minister of India to Premier Chou En-lai, 27 Oct. 1962," *White Paper*, 8: 6–7.
26. "Note Given by the Ministry of Foreign Affairs, Peking, to the Embassy of India in China, 31 May 1962," *White Paper*, 7: 101.
27. See Chapter 5 of this book.
28. "Statement of the Government of the People's Republic of China, May 24, 1969," *PR*, 7, no. 22 (May 30, 1969): 7.
29. Peter Berton, "The Border Issue: China and the Soviet Union, March-October 1969," in *Studies in Comparative Communism* 2, nos. 3 & 4 (July/Oct. 1969): 144. However, according to the Soviet governmental statement of March 29, 1969, the Soviet delegation was led by a Soviet Plenipotentiary with a rank of deputy minister, P. I. Zyryanon, see ibid., p. 186.
30. "Soviet Statement of March 29, to the C.P.R.," in ibid., p. 186.
31. Ibid., pp. 181–87. This denial was repeated on June 14, 1969, in *The Current Digest of the Soviet Press* 21, no. 24 (July 9, 1969) 2: 9–13.
32. For example, they signed an agreement relating to navigation and construction along boundary waterways in 1951, an agreement on the joint investigation and comprehensive utilization of national resources in the Amur Valley in 1956, and an agreement opening up the boundary rivers and lake to commercial navigation in 1957, see Berton, "Background to the Territorial Issue," pp. 145–46.
33. "Statement of the Government of the People's Republic of China, May 24, 1969," *PR* 12, no. 22 (May 30, 1969): 5.
34. "Statement of the Government of the People's Republic of China, Oct. 7, 1969," *PR* 21, no. 41 (Oct. 10, 1969): 3.
35. Text of the convention in Clive Perry, ed., *The Consolidated Treaty Series*, vol. 187 (1898–1899) (Dobbs Ferry, NY: Oceana Publications, 1979), pp. 410–28.

36. *Report*, p. CR–53. ("CR" precedes all page numbers in the section which contains the report of the PRC officials.)

37. *Report*, Summary, p. 1.

38. Tai-Sung An, *The Sino-Soviet Territorial Dispute* (Philadelphia: The Westminster Press, 1973), p. 114.

39. Regarding the difference between inquiry and conciliation, see L. Oppenheim, *International Law*, 7th ed. Revised by Hersch Lauterpacht. (London: Longmans Green and Co., 1952), vol. 2, pp. 12–13.

40. Concerning the definition of "mediation," see ibid., vol. 2, p. 10.

41. "China and Aggression and India," *International Studies* (New Delhi: Indian School of International Studies, July-October, 1963), cited by G. H. Jansen, *Nonalignment and the Afro-Asian States* (New York: Praeger, 1966), p. 331.

42. *SIBQ*, pp. 6–36; also in *PR* 5, nos. 7–8 (Nov. 21, 1962): 7.

43. For detail of the conference, see Jansen, *Nonalignment*, pp. 336–43. The text of the Colombo powers' proposals was printed in *White Paper*, 9: 184–85.

44. For India's acceptance, see "Letter from the Prime Minister of India, to the Prime Minister of Ceylon, 26 January 1963," *White Paper*, 9: 186–87. For China's acceptance, see "Premier Chou En-lai Replies to Madame Bandaranaika [sic]," in *PR* 6, no. 5 (Feb. 1, 1963): 10–11.

45. "Letter from Mrs. Bandaranaike, Prime Minister of Ceylon, to Chou En-lai," citation in Maxwell, *India's China War*, p. 461. Text of the "clarifications" in *White Paper*, 9: 185–86.

46. "Premier Chou En-lai Replies to Madame Bandaranaike," *PR* 6, no. 5 (Feb. 1, 1963): 10–11.

47. "Letter from the Prime Minister of India, to the Prime Minister of Ceylon, 26 January 1963," *White Paper*, 9: 186–87.

48. "Letter from Premier Chou En-lai, to the Prime Minister of India, 20 April 1963," *White Paper*, 9: 10–13.

49. "Text of Chinese Government Note Dated the 9th October, 1963 and the 6th September, 1963," *White Paper*, 10: 9.

50. Jerome Alan Cohen, "Chinese Mediation on the Eve of Modernization," *The California Law Review* 54, no. 3 (August 1966): 1,206.

51. James Chieh Hsiung, *Law and Policy in China's Foreign Relations* (New York: Columbia University Press, 1972), p. 310.

52. Quincy Wright, "The Influence of the New Nations of Asia and Africa upon International Law," *Foreign Affairs Reports* 7 (1958): 38, cited by R. P. Anand, "Role of the 'New'- Asian-African Countries in the Present International Legal Order," *The American Journal of International Law* 56, no. 2 (April 1962): 395.

53. See Yang Hsin and Ch'en Chien, "Hsieh-nu ho p'i-p'an ti-kuo-chu-i-che kuan-yu kuo-chia chu-ch'uan wen-t'i ti miu-nun (Exposing and Criticizing the Imperialists' Absurd Theories Concerning the Question of State Sovereignty), *Chen-fa yen-chiu* (Studies in Political Science and Law), no. 4 (1964): 6–11; Ying T'ao, "Tui chih-ts'an chieh-chi kuo-chi-fa kuan-yu kuo-chia chu-ch'uan wen-t'i ti p'i-p'an" (A Critique of Bourgeois International Law Concerning the Question of National Sovereignty), *chen-fa yen-chiu* (Studies in Political Science and Law), no. 3 (1960): 47–52; Chou Keng-sheng, *Hsien-dai ying-mei kuo-chi-fa shih-hsiang t'ung-hsiang* (Trends in Thought of Modern Anglo-American International Law) (Peking: World Knowledge Press, 1963), p. 53.

54. Richard A. Falk, "Revolutionary Nations and the Quality of International Legal

Order,'' Morton A. Kaplan, ed., *The Revolution in World Politics* (New York: John Wiley and Sons, 1962), p. 317.

55. "Note Given by the Ministry of External Affairs, New Delhi, to the Embassy of China in India, 6 Sept. 1963," *White Paper*, 10: 7.

56. "Letter from Premier Chou En-lai, to the Prime Minister of India, 20 April 1963," *White Paper*, 9: 11–12.

57. See *White Paper*, 10: 11.

58. "International Court of Justice—A Shelter for Gangsters," *Jen-min jih-pao* (People's Daily), July 27, 1966.

59. An, *Sino-Soviet Territorial Dispute*, p. 94; Thomas W. Robinson, *The Sino-Soviet Border Dispute: Background, Development, and the March 1969 Clashes* (New York: Rand Co., 1970), pp. 35–40. Robinson's article was reprinted in *The American Political Science Review* 66, no. 4 (Dec. 1972): 1175–1202.

60. Robinson, *Sino-Soviet Border Dispute*.

61. "Note Given by the Ministry of Foreign Affairs, Peking, to the Embassy of India to China, 9 January 1963," *White Paper*, 9: 90; "Chinese Government Lodges Strong Protest with Soviet Government," *PR* 27, no. 28 (July 11, 1969): 6; "Chinese Government Lodges Strong Protest with Soviet Government." *PR* 27, no. 33 (August 15, 1969): 3.

9

CONCLUSION

Territorial integrity has been one of several causes of the Chinese revolutions since 1911. After the establishment of the PRC in 1949, Peking has been emphasizing state sovereignty and attempting to define or redefine all her land boundaries with her neighbors. Political forces, economic forces, and international law all have a role to play in this process. However, this book limits itself to the role played by international law.[1]

First, boundary claims: The Chinese have based their boundary claims on international law. They have never claimed territories over which China at one time had suzerainty or even lesser relations as a tributary system, albeit they describe these territories as "lost territories." Thus, their boundary claims have been limited to those treaties stipulated and to those territories that they have jurisdiction over; such territories make up what are called traditional customary boundaries.

The present Sino-Soviet boundaries, except for the Pamir area (according to the PRC's governmental statement), were delimited by "unequal treaties." Territories ceded to Russia under "unequal treaties" comprise the Ili Valley in Sinkiang, the area of Lake Baikal and north of the Amur River, and the area east of the Ussuri River to the Sea of Japan. The Chinese concept of the "unequal treaty" has resulted from her feelings of national humiliation. China has regarded these treaties as being in violation of international law. Accepting the fait accompli, Peking has not claimed wider boundaries beyond the lines stipulated by the unequal treaties; all she wants is to conclude a new treaty based on the present "actual situation" on the border, but she insists that the USSR must admit that the old treaties are unequal in nature. Yet, there is no agreement among the

Chinese themselves as to which treaties are actually unequal in nature. One boundary delimited by treaty which was signed under duress—the 1941 Line of the Sino-Burmese boundary—has been accepted as an effective boundary and has been incorporated into a new boundary treaty. Boundaries delimited by valid treaties have been respected. The PRC has recognized both the Sino-Burmese boundary treaties and the Sino-Nepalese boundary treaties of the past.

In the case of frontiers not defined by treaty, the PRC accepts the customary boundaries. Peking defined her customary boundaries with Burma, Nepal, Pakistan, and Afghanistan by treaties. The Chinese are still in dispute with India over their customary boundaries; both sides are claiming that they have jurisdiction over the disputed frontiers.

Second, boundary alignments: The exact boundary alignments should be determined in accordance with international practice. There are a number of ways to determine a nation's boundary lines. China has used the artificial methods (geometrics and anthropogeographics) as well as the natural features (mountain, river, watershed, and pass). Natural features, for example, mountains, do not necessarily make international boundary lines just because they are natural. The PRC also uses anthropogeographical components to define international boundaries, and which of these two elements takes priority in determining her international boundary in question depends on what territorial interests are at stake.

Third, boundary policy: To maintain boundary tranquility has been the PRC's basic policy. Peking has successfully written the Five Principles of Peaceful Coexistence, which have been interpreted as the fundamental principles of international law, into treaties with neighboring countries. It was also specifically stipulated in her boundary treaties that any future boundary disputes would be solved peacefully by negotiation.

Fourth, boundary settlements: In solving questions, the PRC has chosen mediation and negotiation. Mediation was tried in the Sino-Indian boundary disputes but it did not work. Negotiation, however, worked well with China's neighbors, excluding India and the USSR. Peking has successfully concluded boundary treaties through negotiations with Mongolia, Burma, Nepal, Pakistan, and Afghanistan. While concluding these boundary treaties, the PRC followed established international practices, such as negotiation, signing, ratification, demarcation, etc., step by step.

In cases where the sovereignty of an adjacent territory was uncertain, Peking signed provisional boundary agreements (the Sino-Pakistani boundary agreement). If a disputed area is not significant, Peking has chosen not to raise the issue of boundary (the Sino-Korean boundary). In order to obtain some strategic villages, Peking has gone so far as to trade her own territory (the Hpimaw Pass and the Namwan Assigned Tract in the Sino-Burmese Boundary Treaty).

Fifth, armed conflicts: The PRC has fought with the Soviet Union and India along respective disputed borders, but here the Chinese said that the use of force was justified as self-defense. It was not designed to "recover lost territories" or to gain new territory.

NOTE

1. For China, there is a necessity to use international law to advance her boundary interest. Benjamin I. Schwartz once observed that the Chinese "government appeals to international law whenever it finds it to its advantage to do so." See "The Chinese Perception of World Order, Past and Present," in John K. Fairbank, ed., *The Chinese World Order: Traditional China's Foreign Relations* (Cambridge: Harvard University Press, 1968), p. 288.

SELECTED BIBLIOGRAPHY

PRIMARY SOURCES

Treaties, Collections of Documents, Relevant Legal
Enactments, Selected Works, Translated and Bibliographical
Sources

Berton, Peter. "Background to the Territorial Issue, Documents." *Studies in Comparative Communism* 2, nos. 3 & 4 (July/October 1969).
Blanstein, Albert P., ed. *Fundamental Legal Documents of Communist China*. South Hackensack, NJ: Fred B. Rothman & Co., 1962.
Bowie, Robert R., and John K. Fairbank. *Communist China 1955–1959: Policy Documents with Analysis*. Cambridge: Harvard University Press, 1962.
Chen, Theodore, ed. *Chinese Communist Regime*. New York: Praeger, 1967.
Cheng, Chester, ed. *The Politics of the Chinese Red Army: A Translation of the Bulletin of Activities of the People's Liberation Army*. Stanford: Hoover Institute Publications, Stanford University Press, 1966.
China and the Afro-Asian Conference. Peking: Foreign Languages Press, 1955.
Chung-hua jen-min kung-ho-kuo hsien-fa hsieh-hsi ts'an-k'ao tsu-liao (Reference Materials for the Study of the People's Republic of China's Constitution). Peking: Law Press, 1957.
Committee for the Publication of the Selected Works of Mao Tse-tung, Central Committee of the Communist Party of China, ed. *Selected Works of Mao Tse-tung*. 5 vols. Peking: Foreign Languages Press, 1951–1977.
Degras, Jane, ed. *Soviet Documents on Foreign Policy*. 3 vols. London: Oxford University Press, 1951.
Documents of International Affairs. London: Oxford University Press, 1949–1963.

Doolin, Dennis J. *Territorial Claims in the Sino-Soviet Conflicts: Documents and Analysis*. Stanford: Hoover Institute on War, Revolution and Peace, Stanford University Press, 1956.
Fan, K., ed. *Post-Revolutionary Writings: Mao Tse-tung and Lin Piao*. Garden City, NY: Anchor Books, 1972.
Gittings, John. *Survey of the Sino-Soviet Dispute: A Commentary and Extracts from the Current Polemics 1963–1967*. London: Oxford University Press, 1968.
Hidson, G. F., Richard Louentual, and Roderick MacFarquhar. *The Sino-Soviet Dispute*. New York: Praeger, 1963.
Important Documents of the First Plenary Session of the Chinese People's Political Consultative Conference. Peking: Foreign Languages Press, 1949.
Important Documents of the Settlement of the Sino-Burmese Boundary Question. Peking: Foreign Languages Press, 1960.
Johnson, Douglas M., and Chiu, Hungdah, eds. *Agreements of the People's Republic of China, 1949–1967: A Calendar*. Cambridge: Harvard University Press, 1968.
League of Nations. *Treaty Series*, 1925 and 1935.
Mayers, William Frederick, ed. *Treaties Between the Empire of China and Foreign Powers*. London: Taubfer & Co., 1877. Reprint. Taipei: Ch'eng-wen Publishing Co., 1966.
Notes, Memoranda, and Letters Exchanged and Agreements Signed Between the Governments of India and China, 1954–1959: White Paper. 2 vols. New Delhi: Ministry of External Affairs, 1963.
Perry, Clive, ed. *The Consolidated Treaty Series*. vol. 187 (1898–1899). Dobbs Ferry, NY: Oceana Publications, 1979.
Report of the Officials of the Governments of India and the People's Republic of China on the Boundary Question. New Delhi: Ministry of External Affairs, 1961.
Selected Works of Chou En-lai. Vol. 1. Peking: Foreign Languages Press, 1981.
The Sino-Indian Boundary Question. Peking: Foreign Languages Press, 1962.
United Nations. *United Nations Treaty Series*. Vol. 299.
A Victory for the Five Principles of Peaceful Coexistence. Peking: Foreign Languages Press, 1960.

Periodicals and Newspapers

Chung-hua jen-min kung-ho-kuo tui-wai kuang-hsi wen-chien-chi (Collection of Documents Relating to the Foreign Relations of the People's Republic of China), *1954–1955, 1955–1956*. Peking: World Knowledge Press.
The Current Digest of the Soviet Press. 1956, 1957, 1961, 1963, 1969.
The Daily Worker. New York, 1962.
Indian Affairs Records. New Delhi, 1969.
Jen-min jih-pao (People's Daily). 1950, 1954, 1956, 1957, 1960, 1963, 1967, 1969.
New York Times. 1949, 1951, 1960, 1963, 1969, 1970, 1986, 1987.
Peking Review. 1958–1987.
Washington Post. 1969.

SECONDARY SOURCES

Books, Monographs, and Dissertations

Allison, Graham T. *Essence of Decision: Explaining the Cuban Missile Crisis.* Boston: Little, Brown, 1971.
An, Tai Sung. *The Sino-Soviet Territorial Dispute.* Philadelphia: The Westminster Press, 1973.
Baade, Hans W., ed. *The Soviet Impact on International Law.* New York: Oceana, 1965.
Barnett, A. Doak. *Communist China and Asia: Challenge to American Policy.* New York: Harper, 1960.
Bell, Charles. *Tibet: Past and Present.* London: Oxford University Press, 1924.
Bhat, Sudhaker. *India and China.* New Delhi: Popular Book Services, 1967.
Blum, Yehuda Z. *Historic Titles in International Law.* The Hague: Martinus Nijhoff, 1965.
Boggs, Samuel Whittemore. *International Boundaries: A Study of Boundary Functions and Problems.* New York: Columbia University Press, 1940.
Boker-Szego, Hanna. *New States and International Law.* Budapest: Akademial Kiado, 1970.
Bowie, Robert R., and John K. Fairbank, eds. *Communist China, 1955–1959: Policy Documents with Analysis.* Cambridge: Harvard University Press. 1962.
Brierly, James L. *The Law of Nations.* 6th ed. London: Oxford University Press, 1963.
Bunge, Frederica M., and Rinn-Sup Shinn, eds. *China: A Country Study.* 3rd ed. Area Handbook Series. Washington, D.C.: Government Printing Office, 1981.
——, eds. *North Korea: A Country Study.* 3d ed. Area Handbook Series. Washington, D.C.: Government Printing Office, 1981.
Chai, Winberg, ed. *The Foreign Relations of the People's Republic of China.* New York: Capricorn Books, 1972.
Chakravarti, P. C. *India's China Policy.* Bloomington: Indiana University Press, 1962.
Chawla, Sudershan, Gurtov and Alsin-Gerard Marsat, eds. *Southeast Asia under the New Balance of Power.* New York: Praeger, 1974.
Chen, George Po-chung. "Some Legal Aspects of the Sino-Soviet Border Dispute." Ph.D. diss., Southern Illinois University, 1974.
Chen, Vincent. *Sino-Russian Relations in the Seventeenth Century.* The Hague: Martinus Nijhoff, 1966.
Cheng, Peter, ed. *A Chronology of the People's Republic of China, from October 1, 1949.* Totowa: Rowman and Littlefield, 1972.
Cheng, Tien-fong. *A History of Sino-Russian Relations.* Washington, D.C.: Public Affairs Press, 1957.
Chiang, Kai-shek. *China's Destiny.* 1943. (An unauthorized translation with notes by Philip Jaffe, *China's Destiny and Chinese Economic Theory.* New York: Roy Publishers, 1947).
Chin, Szu-k'ai. *Communist China's Relations with the Soviet Union, 1949–1957.* Kowloon, Hong Kong: Union Research Institute, 1961.
China Yearbook 1975. Taipei: China Publishing Co., 1976.
Chiu, Hungdah. *The People's Republic of China and the Law of Treaties.* Cambridge: Harvard University Press, 1972.

Chou, Keng-sheng. *Hsien-dai ying-mei kuo-chi-fa shih-hsiang tung-hsiang* (Trends in Thought of Modern Anglo-American International Law). Peking: World Knowledge Press, 1963.

Clubb, O. Edmund. *China and Russia: The "Great Game."* New York: Columbia University Press, 1971.

Cohen, A. Jerome, ed. *China's Practice of International Law: Some Case Studies.* Cambridge: Harvard University Press, 1972.

———. *Contemporary Chinese Law: Research Problems and Perspectives.* Cambridge: Harvard University Press, 1970.

———, ed. *Dynamics of China's Foreign Relations.* Cambridge: Harvard University Press, 1970.

Cohen, A. Jerome, and Hungdah Chiu. *People's China and International Law: A Documentary Study.* 2 vols. Princeton: Princeton University Press, 1974.

Corbett, Percy E. *Law in Diplomacy.* Princeton: Princeton University Press, 1959.

Cukwurah, A. O. *The Settlement of Boundary Disputes in International Law.* New York: Oceana Publications, 1967.

Dallin, David J. *Soviet Russia and the Far East.* New Haven: Yale University Press, 1948.

Dalvi, J. P. *Himalayan Blunder.* Bombay: Thacher & Co., 1969.

Doolin, Dennis J. *Territorial Claims in the Sino-Soviet Conflict.* Stanford: Hoover Institute on War, Revolution, and Peace, Stanford University Press, 1965.

Ellison, Herbert J. *The Sino-Soviet Conflict: A Global Perspective.* Seattle: University of Washington, 1982.

Fisher, Margaret W., Leo E. Rose, and Robert A. Huttenback. *Himalayan Battleground: Sino-Indian Rivalry in Ladakh.* New York: Praeger, 1963.

Garthoff, Raymond L., ed. *Sino-Soviet Military Relations.* New York: Praeger, 1966.

Ginsburgs, George. *Communist China and Tibet, the First Dozen Years.* The Hague: Martinus Nijhoff, 1964.

Griffith, Williams E. *Sino-Soviet Relations.* Cambridge: The M.I.T. Press, 1967.

Gupta, Karunakar. *India in World Politics: A Period of Transition.* Calcutta, India: Scientific Book Agency, 1966.

Gupta, S. K. *The Hidden History of the Sino-Indian Frontier.* Calcutta, India: Minerva Associates, 1974.

Handbook on People's China. Peking: Foreign Languages Press, 1957.

Henderson, John W., ed. *Area Handbook for Burma.* Washington, D.C.: U.S. Government Printing Office, 1971.

Hinton, Harold C. *The Bear at the Gate: Chinese Policy-Making under Soviet Pressure.* Washington, D.C.: American Enterprise Institute for Public Policy Research, 1971.

———. *Communist China in World Politics.* Boston: Houghton Mifflin, 1966.

———. *The Sino-Soviet Confrontation: Implication for the Future.* New York: Cranes, Russak & Co., 1976.

Hook, Brian, ed. *The Cambridge Encyclopedia of China.* London: Cambridge University Press, 1982.

Horris, George L. et al., eds. *Area Handbook for Nepal, Bhutan and Sikkim.* 2nd ed., Washington, D.C.: U.S. Government Printing Office, 1972.

Hsiung, James Chieh. *Law and Policy in China's Foreign Relations: A Study of Attitude and Practice.* New York: Columbia University Press, 1972.

Hsu, Immanuel C. Y. *China's Entrance into the Family of Nations*. Cambridge: Harvard University Press, 1960.
Huck, Arthur. *The Security of China: Chinese Approaches to Problems of War and Strategy*. New York: Columbia University Press, 1970.
Hutchings, Robert L. *Soviet-East European Relations: Consolidation and Conflict 1968–1980*. Madison: University of Wisconsin Press, 1983.
Jackson, W. A. Douglas. *Russo-Chinese Borderlands: Zone of Peaceful Contact or Potential Conflict?* Princeton: Van Nostrand, 1962.
Jansen, G. H. *Nonalignment and the Afro-Asian States*. New York: Praeger, 1966.
Jennings, R. Y. *Acquisition of Territory in International Law*. Manchester: Manchester University Press, 1963.
Johnstone, William C. *Burma's Foreign Policy: A Study in Neutralism*. Cambridge: Harvard University Press, 1963.
Kahin, George McTurnan. *The Asian-African Conference, Bandung, Indonesia, April 1955*. Ithaca: Cornell University Press, 1956.
Kaplan, Morton A., ed. *The Revolution in World Politics*. New York: John Wiley and Sons, 1962.
Karnik, V. B., ed. *China Invades India: The Story of Invasion against the Background of Chinese History and Sino-Indian Relations*. Bombay: Allied Publishers, 1963.
Kim, Samuel S. *China, the United Nations, and World Order*. Princeton: Princeton University Press, 1979.
Kozhevnikov, F. I., ed. *International Law: A Text Book for Use in Law Schools*. Translated by Dennis Ogden. Moscow: Academy of Sciences of the U.S.S.R. Institute of State and Law, Foreign Languages Publishing House, 1961.
Lall, Arthur. *How Communist China Negotiates*. New York: Columbia University Press, 1968.
Lamb, Alastair. *Asian Frontiers: Studies in a Continuing Problem*. New York: Praeger, 1968.
———. *The McMahon Line: A Study in the Relations between India, China and Tibet, 1904 to 1914*, 2 vols. London: Routledge and Kegan, 1966.
———. *The China-India Border: The Origins of the Disputed Boundaries*. London: Oxford University Press, 1964.
———. *The Sino-Indian Border in Ladakh*. Asian Publications Series. Canberra: Australian National University, 1973.
Leng, Shao-chuan, and Hungdah Chiu, ed. *Law in Chinese Foreign Policy: Communist China and Selected Problems of International Law*. New York: Oceana Publications, 1972.
Li, Tieh-tseng. *The Historical Status of Tibet*. New York: Columbia University Press, 1956.
———. *Tibet: Today and Yesterday*. New York: Bookman Association, 1960.
Lissitzyn, Oliver J. *International Law: Today and Tomorrow*. Dobbs Ferry, NY: Oceana Publications, 1965.
Luard, Evan, ed. *The International Regulation of Frontier Disputes*. London: Thames and Hudson, 1970.
Macridis, Roy C., ed. *Foreign Policy in World Politics*. 4th ed. Englewood Cliffs, NJ: Prentice-Hall, 1972.
Maxwell, Neville. *India's China War*. New York: Doubleday, 1972.
McNair, Arnold D. *The Law of Treaties*. London: University Press, 1961.

Misra, K. P. *India's Policy of Recognition of States and Governments*. Bombay: Allied Publishers, 1966.

Morgenthau, Hans J. *Politics Among Nations*. 5th ed. New York: Alfred A. Knopf, 1973.

Moseley, George. *A Sino-Soviet Cultural Frontier: The Ili Kazakh Autonomous Chou*. Cambridge: Harvard University Press, 1966.

Nyrop, Richard F. et al., eds. *Area Handbook for Pakistan*. Washington, D.C.: U.S. Government Printing Office, 1975.

O'Connell, D. P. *The Law of State Succession*. London: Cambridge University Press, 1956.

Ojha, Ishwer. *Chinese Foreign Policy in an Age of Transition: The Diplomacy of Cultural Despair*. Boston: Beacon Press, 1969.

Oppenheim, Lassa F. L. *International Law*. 8th ed. Vol. 1. Revised by Hersch Lauterpacht. London: Longmans, 1955.

Patterson, George N. *Peking Versus Delhi*. New York: Praeger, 1964.

―――. *Tragic Destiny*. New York: Praeger, 1959.

Philips, C. H., and Mary Doreen Wainwright, eds. *The Partition of India*. Cambridge: The M.I.T. Press, 1970.

Ram, Mohan. *Politics of Sino-Indian Confrontation*. New Delhi: Vikas Publishing House, 1973.

Ramundo, Barnard. *Peaceful Coexistence*. Baltimore: Johns Hopkins University Press, 1967.

Rao, Gondker Narayana. *The India-China Border: A Reappraisal*. London: Asia Publishing House, 1968.

Richardson, Hugh E. *Tibet and Its History*. London: Oxford University Press, 1962.

Robinson, Thomas W. *The Border Negotiations and the Future of Sino-Soviet-American Relations*. New York: Rand Corp., 1971.

Rowland, John. *A History of Sino-Indian Relations: Hostile Co-existence*. Princeton: D. Van Nostrand, 1967.

Shabad, Theodore. *China's Changing Map: National and Regional Development 1949–1971*. New York: Praeger, 1972.

Sherwani, Latif Ahmed. *India, China and Pakistan*. Karachi: Council for Pakistan Studies, 1967.

Smith, Harvey H. et al., eds. *Area Handbook for North Vietnam*. Washington, D.C.: U.S. Government Printing Office, 1967.

Snow, Edgar. *The Other Side of the River—Red China Today*. London: Gollancz, 1963.

Starke, J. G. *An Introduction to International Law*. 5th ed. London: Butterworths, 1963.

Syatauw, J. J. G. *Some Newly Established Asian States and the Development of International Law*. The Hague: Martinus Nijhoff, 1961.

Tang, Peter S. H. *Russia and Soviet Policy in Manchuria and Outer Mongolia, 1911–1931*. Durham, NC: Duke University Press, 1959.

Taylor, Jay. *China and Southeast Asia: Peking's Relations with Revolutionary Movements*. New York: Praeger, 1974.

Tung, William L. *China and the Foreign Powers: The Impact of and Reaction to Unequal Treaties*. Dobbs Ferry, NY: Oceana Publications, 1970.

Ulam, Alam Bruno. *Expansion and Coexistence: Soviet Foreign Policy 1917–1973*. 2nd ed. New York: Praeger, 1974.

Urban, G. R., ed. *Détente*. New York: Universe Books, 1976.

Van Eckelen, W. P. *Indian Foreign Policy and the Border Dispute with China.* The Hague: Martinus Nijhoff. 1964.
Van Ness, Peter. *Revolution and Chinese Foreign Policy: Peking's Support for Wars of National Liberation.* Berkeley: University of California Press, 1971.
Varma, Shanti Prasad. *Struggle for the Himalayas: A Study in Sino-Indian Relations.* New Delhi: Sterling Publishers, 1971.
Whiting, Allen S. *Sinkiang: Pawn or Pivot?* East Lansing: Michigan University Press, 1958.
———. *Soviet Policies in China, 1917–1924.* New York: Columbia University Press, 1954.
Who is Who in Communist China. Kowloon, Hong Kong: Union Research Institute, 1966.
Willoughby, Westel W. *Foreign Rights and Interests in China.* 2 vols. New York: Paragon Book Gallery, 1966.
Woodhead, H. G. W., ed. *The China Year Book, 1932.* Shanghai: The North-China Daily News and Herald, 1932.
Woodman, Dorothy. *Himalayan Frontiers: A Political Review of British, Chinese, Indian and Russian Rivalries.* London: The Cresset Press, 1969.
———. *The Making of Burma.* London: Cresset, 1962.
Wright, Quincy. *The Role of International Law in the Elimination of War.* New York: Oceana Publications, 1961.
Wu, Yuan-li, ed. *China: A Handbook.* New York: Praeger, 1973.
Young, Kenneth T. *Negotiating with the Chinese Communist: The United States Experience, 1953–1968.* New York: McGraw Hill Book Co., 1968.
Zagoria, Donald S. *The Sino-Soviet Conflict, 1956–1961.* Princeton: Princeton University Press, 1962.

Articles

Alexandrowicz-Alexander, C. H. A. "The Legal Position of Tibet." *American Journal of International Law* 48 (1954): 265–74.
Anand, R. P. "Role of the 'New' Asian-African Countries in the Present International Legal Order." *American Journal of International Law* 56, no. 2 (April 1962): 383–406.
Ashmed, Nasim. "China's Himalayan Frontiers, Pakistan's Attitude." *Foreign Affairs* 38, no. 4 (October 1962): 478–84.
Aspaturian, Vernon V. "The Soviet Union and International Communism." In *Foreign Policy in World Politics*, 4th ed. edited by Roy C. Macridis, pp. 238–387. Englewood Cliffs, NJ: Prentice-Hall, 1972.
Berton, Peter. "The Border Issue: China and the Soviet Union, March-October 1969." *Studies in Comparative Communism* 2, nos. 3 & 4 (July-October 1969): 130–382.
Bowett, D. W. "Estoppel before International Tribunals and Its Relation to Acquiescence." *The British Yearbook of International Law*, 33 (1957): 176–202.
Bradsher, Henry S. "The Sovietization of Mongolia." *Foreign Affairs* 50, no. 3 (April 1972): 545–53.
Chacko, C. J. "Peaceful Coexistence as a Doctrine of Current International Affairs." *Indian Yearbook of International Affairs* 4 (1955): 14–39.
Ch'ien, Ssu. "P'i-p'an chih-ts'an chieh-chi kuo-chi-fa tsai chu-ming wen-t'i shang ti

chu-chang" (A Critique of the Advocacy Regarding the Question of Residents in Bourgeois International Law). *Kuo-chi wen-t'i yen-chiu*, no. 5 (1960): 40–49.

Chiu, Hungdah. "Certain Legal Aspects of Communist China's Treaty Practice." *Proceedings of the American Society of International Law* (1967): 117–26.

———. "Communist China's Attitude Toward International Law." *American Journal of International Law* 60, no. 2 (April 1966): 245–67.

———. "Concept and Practice of International Law." In *China: A Handbook*, edited by Yuan-li Wu, pp. 393–421. New York: Praeger, 1973.

———. "Hsi-fang 'kuo-chi-fa' hsu-ju chung-huo ti chin-ko" (The Introduction of Western 'International Law' to China). *Tung-fang cha-chih* (The Eastern Miscellany) 1, no. 12 (June 1, 1968): 28–34.

———. "The Theory and Practice of Communist China with Respect to the Conclusion of Treaties." *The Columbia Journal of Transnational Law* 5, no. 1 (1966): 1–13.

Chou, Keng-sheng. "Ts'ung kuo-chi-fa nun ho-p'ing kung-ch'u ti yuan-che" (On the Principle of Peaceful Coexistence in International Law). *Cheng-fa yen-chiu* (Studies in Political Science and Law), no. 6 (1955): 37–41.

Chu, Ch'i-wu. "Tan-tan kuo-chi-fa ti ting-i wen-t'i" (Talking about the Question of the Definition of International Law). *Fa-hsueh yen-chiu* (Studies in the Science of Law), no. 3 (1981): 51–53.

Cohen, Jerome A. "Chinese Mediation on the Eve of Modernization." *The California Law Review* 54, no. 3 (August 1966): 1201–6.

Falk, Richard A. "Revolutionary Nations and the Quality of International Legal Order." In *The Revolution in World Politics*, edited by Morton A. Kaplan, pp. 30–52. New York: John Wiley and Sons, 1962.

Fang, Ch'ao. "Wo-kuo shih-nien-lai wai-chiao chan-hsien-shang ti chu-ta sheng-li" (Great Victories in China's Diplomacy Over the Past Decade). *Kuo-chi wen-t'i yen-chiu* (Studies in International Relations), no. 6 (1959): 1–12.

Feuerwerker, Albert. "Chinese History and the Foreign Relations of Contemporary China." *The Annals of the American Academy of Political and Social Science* 402 (July 1972): 1–14.

Field, A. R. "Bhutan, Kham, and the Upper Assam Line." *Orbis* 3, no. 2 (Summer 1959): 92–100.

Fifield, Russel H. "The Five Principles of Peaceful Coexistence." *American Journal of International Law* 52 (July 1958): 504–10.

Fisher, Margaret W., and Leo E. Rose. "Ladakh and the Sino-Indian Border Crisis." *Asian Survey* 2, no. 8 (October 1962): 27–37.

Garver, John W. "The Sino-Soviet Territorial Dispute in the Pamir Mountains Region." *The China Quarterly*, no. 85 (March 1981): 107–18.

Ginsburg, George. "The Dynamics of Sino-Soviet Territorial Dispute: The Case of the River Islands." In *The Dynamics of China's Foreign Relations*, edited by Jerome A. Cohen, pp. 1–20. Harvard Asian Monographs, no. 39. Cambridge: Harvard University Press, 1970.

Gittings, John. "Guessing with Guns." *Far Eastern Economic Review*, August 21, 1969.

Green, L. C. "Legal Aspects of the Sino-Indian Border Dispute." *The China Quarterly*, no. 3 (July-September 1960): 42–58.

———. "Communist China's Demands on the World." In *The Revolution in World*

Politics, edited by Morton A. Kaplan, pp. 233–48. New York: John Wiley and Sons, 1962.
———. "Communist China and Peaceful Coexistence." *The China Quarterly*, no. 3 (July-September 1960): 16–32.
Hinton, Harold C. "Conflict on the Ussuri: A Clash of Nationalism." *Problems of Communism* 20, nos. 1–2 (January-April 1971): 45–59.
———. "Sino-Soviet Relations in the Brezhnev Era." *Current History* 61, no. 361 (September 1971): 135–41.
———. "The United States and the Sino-Soviet Conflict." *Orbis* 19, no. 1 (September 1975): 25–46.
Ho, Wu-shuang, and Ma Chun. "P'i-p'an Ch'en T'i-ch'ien tsai kuo-chi-fa-hsueh fang-meng ti fan-t'ung kuan-tien" (A Critique of Ch'en T'i-ch'ien's Reactionary Viewpoint on the Science of International Law). *Chen-fa-yen-chiu* (Studies in Political Science and Law), no. 6 (1957): 35–38.
Hsia, Tao-tai. "Chinese Legal Publications: An Appraisal." In *Contemporary Chinese Law: Research Problems and Perspectives*, edited by Jerome A. Cohen, pp. 1–19. Cambridge: Harvard University Press, 1970.
Hsin, I. "Chih-ts'an chieh-chi kuo-chi-fa tsai kan-se wen-t'i-shang shao-ming-liao sheng-mo" (What Did the Bourgeois International Law Say About the Question of Intervention?) *Chen-fa yen-chiu* (Studies in Political Science and Law), no. 4 (1960): 47–54.
Hsin, Wu. "Tui chih-ts'an chieh-chi kuan-yu kuo-chia lin-tu wen-t'i ti p'i-p'an" (A Critique of the Bourgeois International Law Concerning the Question of State Territory). *Kuo-chi wen-t'i yen-chiu* (Studies in International Problems), no. 7 (1960): 42–51.
Hsiung, James C. "China's Foreign Policy: The Interplay of Ideology, Practical Interests, and Polemics." In *China Today*, edited by William Richardson, pp. 20–55. New York: Maryknoll, 1969.
Hudson, G. F. "The Frontier of China and Assam: Background to the Fighting." *The China Quarterly*, no. 12 (October-December 1962): 203–6.
Hutterback, R. A. "A Historical Note on the Sino-Indian Dispute over the Aksai Chin." *The China Quarterly*, no. 18 (April-June 1964): 201–7.
Jacquet-Francillon, Jacques. "The Borders of China: Mao's Bold Challenge to Khrushchev." *The New Republic*, April 20, 1963, pp. 18–22.
Kan, Sheng. "On the Current International Situation." *Peking Review* 3, no. 6 (February 9, 1960): 6–8.
Karpov, Victor P. "The Soviet Concept of Peaceful Coexistence and Its Implications for International Law." *Law and Contemporary Problems* 29, no. 4 (Autumn 1964): 858–64.
Kripalani, Acharya J. B. "For Principled Neutrality." *Foreign Affairs* 38, no. 1 (October 1959): 46–60.
Kuns, Josef L. "The Changing Law of Nations." *American Journal of International Law* 51 (1957): 77–83.
K'ung, Meng. "Tui chih-ts'an chieh-chi kuo-chi-fa kuan-yu kuo-chi-fa chu-t'i ho kuo-chia ch'en-jeng ti li-nun ti p'i-p'an" (A Critique of the Bourgeois International Law Regarding Subjects of International Law and Theories of Recognition of States). *Kuo-chi wen-t'i yen-chiu* (Studies in International Problems), no. 2 (1960): 44–53.

Li, P'ing. "Ho-p'ing kung-ch'u fa-chan" (A Further Development of the Five Principles of Peaceful Coexistence). *Chen-fa yen-chiu* (Studies in Political Science and Law), no. 1 (1960): 35–36.
Li, Tieh-tseng. "The Legal Status of Tibet." *American Journal of International Law* 50 (1956): 394–404.
Li, Yu-chao. "Excellent Situation for the Struggle for Peace." *Peking Review* 3, no. 1 (January 5, 1960): 15–19.
Li, Ta-kuang. "U.S. Espionage and Subversion against China." *People's China*, no. 3 (February 1, 1955): 9–12.
Malodtsov, S. "Frontiers and International Law." *International Affairs*, (Moscow), no. 4 (1964): 9–14.
Mancall, Mark. "The Persistence of Tradition in Chinese Foreign Policy." *The Annals of the American Academy of Political and Social Science* 349 (September 1963): 15–26.
Mao, Tao. "Ya-fei fa-lu kung-tso-tse fei-i ti tsung-ta ch'eng-ch'iu" (The Important Accomplishment of the Conference of Asian-African Jurists). *Chen-fa yen-chiu*, no. 2 (1958): 3–9.
Maxwell, Neville. "Why the Russians Lifted the Blockade at the Bear Island." *Foreign Affairs* 57, no. 1 (Fall 1978): 138–45.
May, Ernest R. "The Nature of Foreign Policy: The Calculated versus the Axiomatic." *Daedalus* (Fall 1962): 653–67.
McNair, Arnold. "The Legality of the Occupation of the Ruhr." *British Yearbook of International Law* 5 (1924): 17–37.
McWhinney, Edward. "Peaceful Coexistence and Soviet-Western International Law." *American Journal of International Law* 56, no. 4 (October 1962): 951–70.
Michael, Franz. "Is China Expansionist? A Design for Aggression." *Problems of Communism* 20, no. 1–2 (January-April 1970): 62–67.
Nikolayev, F. "How Peking Falsifies History." *International Affairs* (Moscow), no. 5 (May 1973): 33–34.
Patterson, George N. "China and Tibet: Background to the Revolt." *The China Quarterly*, no. 1 (January-March 1960): 97–99.
———. "The Himalayan Frontier." *Survival* 5, no. 5 (September-October 1963): 107–208.
———. "Recent Chinese Policies in Tibet and Towards the Himalayan Border States." *The China Quarterly*, no. 12 (October-December 1962): 191–202.
Rao, K. Krisha. "The Sino-Indian Boundary Question and International Law." *The International and Comparative Law Quarterly* 11, part 2 (April 1962): 375–415.
Robinson, Thomas W. "The Sino-Soviet Border Dispute: Background, Development, and the March 1969 Clashes." *The American Political Science Review* 66, no. 4 (December 1972): 1175–1203.
Rubin, Alfred P. "The Position of Tibet in International Law." *The China Quarterly*, no. 35 (July-September 1968): 110–54.
———. "The Sino-Indian Border Disputes." *The International and Comparative Law Quarterly* 9, part 1 (January 1960): 96–125.
Schapiro, Leonard. "Communists in Collision." *Studies in Comparative Communism* 2, nos. 3 & 4 (July-October 1969): 121–29.
Schwartz, Benjamin I. "The Chinese Perception of World Order, Past and Present." In

The Chinese World Order: Traditional China's Foreign Relations, edited by John K. Fairbank. Cambridge: Harvard University Press, 1968.
Seth, S. P. "Sino-Indian Relations: Changing Perspectives." *Problems of Communism* 23, no. 2 (March-April 1974): 14–26.
Sharma, Surya P. "The Indian-China Border Dispute: An Indian Perspective." *American Journal of International Law* 59, no. 1 (January 1965): 16–47.
Shelvankar, K. S. "China's Himalayan Frontier: India's Attitude." *Foreign Affairs* (London) 38, no. 4 (October 1962): 472–77.
Smith, Jay Holmes. "The Truth About the China-India Border." *New York Times*, July 17, 1981, p. 22.
Snyder, Earl A., and Hans Werner Bracht. "Coexistence and International Law." *The International and Comparative Law Quarterly* 7 (1958): 54–71.
Steiner, H. Arthur. "The Mainsprings of Chinese Communist Foreign Policy." *American Journal of International Law* 44, no. 1 (January 1950): 69–99.
Stern, Robert W. "The Sino-Indian Border Controversy and the Communist Party in India." *The Journal of Politics* 27, no. 1 (February 1965): 66–86.
Tsou, Tang, and Morton Halperin. "Mao Tse-tung's Revolutionary Strategy and Peking's International Behavior." *The American Political Science Review* 59, no. 1 (March 1965): 80–99.
Wang, Chao-tsai. "Tear off the Wrappings from the Soviet Revisionists' 'Definition of Aggression'." *Peking Review* 12, no. 22 (May 24, 1969): 13–15.
Wang, Jinqing. "Why the Sino-Soviet Strains?" *Peking Review* 27, no. 28 (July 9, 1984): 32.
Wei, Liang. "Lueh-nun ti-erh-ch'ih szu-chieh-ta-chan-hou ti kuo-chi tiao-yueh" (On the Post Second World War International Treaties). *Kuo-chi tiao-yueh chi* (International Treaty Series) *1953–1955*, pp. 660–88. Peking: World Knowledge Press, 1961.
———. "Ts'ung kuo-chi-fa chueh-tu k'an shu-wei McMahon hsien" (From the Angle of International Law to Looking at the So-called McMahon Line). *Kuo-chi wen-t'i yen-chiu* (Studies in International Problems), no. 6 (1959): 47–52.
Wheeler, Geoffrey. "Sinkiang and the Soviet Union." *The China Quarterly*, no. 16 (October-December 1963): 56–61.
Whiting, Allen S. "Sinkiang and Sino-Soviet Relations." *The China Quarterly*, no. 3 (July-September 1960): 32–41.
———. "The Use of Force in Foreign Policy by People's Republic of China." *The Annals of the American Academy of Political and Social Science* 402 (July 1972): 55–66.
Whittam, Daphne E. "The Sino-Burmese Boundary Treaty." *Pacific Affairs* 34, no. 2 (Summer 1961): 174–83.
Wu, An-yu. "Hsieh-lu chiu-ta-hsueh cheng-chih-hsi ti fan-t'ung pen-chih" (Revelling the Nature of Reaction in Political Science Departments of Old Colleges). *Chen-fa yen-chiu* (Studies in Political Science and Law), no. 6 (1957): 47–49.
Yang, Hsin, and Ch'en Ch'ien. "Hsieh-nu ho p'i-p'an ti-kuo-chu-i-che kuan-yu kuo-chia chu-ch'uan wen-t'i ti miu-nun" (Exposing and Criticizing the Imperialists' Absurd Theories Regarding the Question of State Sovereignty). *Chen-fa yen-chiu* (Studies in Political Science and Law), no. 4 (1964): 6–11.
Yang, Tsui. "Brillant Achievements of China's Policy of Peaceful Coexistence." *Peking Review* 4, no. 5 (February 3, 1961): 6–8.

Ying, T'ao. "Ts'ung chi-ko chi-pen k'ai-nien jeng-shih chih-ts'an chieh-chi kuo-chi-fa ti tseng-mien-mu" (Recognizing the True Face of Bourgeois International Law from Several Basic Concepts). *Kuo-chi wen-t'i yen-chiu* (Studies in International Problems), no. 1 (1960): 42–51.

———. "Tui chih-ts'an chieh-chi kuo-chi-fa kuan-yu kuo-chia chu-ch'uan wen-t'i ti p'i-p'an" (A Critique of Bourgeois International Law Concerning the Question of National Sovereignty). *Chen-fa yen-chiu* (Studies in Political Science and Law), no. 3 (1960): 47–52.

Yu, Chao-li. "Peaceful Competition: An Invitable Trend." *Peking Review* 2, no. 33 (August 18, 1959): 6–8.

INDEX

Afghanistan: boundary with China, 70–71; boundary protocol (1965), 71; boundary treaty (1963), 32, 71, 100, 116, 119; provisional boundary agreement (1963), 71. *See also* Wakhan Corridor
Aksai Chin plateau, 25–27, 62, 65, 68, 72, 126, 128, 130
Amur River, 11, 52, 54. *See also* Bear Island, Chenpao Island

Bandung Conference, 32
Bear (Hei-hsia-tsu) Island, 53–54
Bhutan: boundary with China treaty (1961), 68
Burma: agreement (1897) between Great Britain and China concerning, 58, 83, 115; border situation, 24–25; boundary disputes, 56–58, 115; boundary negotiations, 58–60, 85–86; boundary treaty with China (1960), 31, 32, 59, 91, 97, 100, 115, 117, 128; convention (1894) between Great Britain and China concerning, 58, 115; exchange of notes (1941) between Great Britain and China concerning, 58, 83, 114, 115; (1935), 85; preliminary border agreement (1960), 32, 59. *See also* Iselin Line, U Nu, Unequal boundary treaties

Cairo Declaration, 92
Chacko, C. J., 33, 34
Chang-pei (Everwhite) Mountain, 55
Chen I-fan, 66, 100
Chenpao Island (Damansky), 11, 38, 52, 133, 134
Chiang Kai-shek, 77, 79
Chou En-lai, 12, 25; Bandung Conference, 126; border policy, 31–32; boundary negotiations, 58–60, 115–118; Burmese boundary treaty, 31; complaint of U.S. subversive activities, 29; concerning Namwan Assigned Tract, 58; Five Principles of Peaceful Coexistence with Soviet Union, 37–38; good neighbor policy, 30; Indian boundary talks, 99, 126–128; and leaders of Asian and African, 130; Mongolian boundary, 55; and Nepal, 69; principle for settling boundary questions, 126–128; Sino-Burmese unequal

boundary treaties, 82–83; unequal treaties, 85–86
Chou Keng-sheng, 10, 33–35; on Peaceful Coexistence, 33–34; on unequal treaty, 78
Chuje, 114
Chuva, 114
Colombo Conference, 130
Confucianism, 132
Costa Rican-Nicaraguan boundary case, 105–106; treaty (1858), 105–106

Dalai Lama, 26

Five Principles of Peaceful Coexistence, 14, 30, 32–35, 60, 126, 132–133, 138; applies to Socialist states, 36–39. See also Pancha Shila
Forward policy, Indian, 127, 133

Geneva Convention (1954), 56

Hague Convention for the Pacific Settlement of International Disputes (1899), 130
Harvard Research Draft Convention on Treaties, 103; Article 13, 101
Himalayas, 126–127. See also McMahon Line

India: border situation, 25–29: boundary disputes, 63–67; problem treaties concerning boundary: Kashmir and Ladakh on one side and Tibet and China on the other side (1842), 63, 94–96, 101–102, 107; exchange of letters with Tibet (1914), 65–67, 92, 104, 106; Ladakh and Tibet (1684), 63, 94–96, 100, (1852), 65, 94–96; Trade Agreement (1954), 65, 95–97, 101–102, 106. See also Askai Chin plateau, McMahon Line, Simla Conference, Tibet
International Court of Justice, 132
International law: definition of, 9–10; Five Principles of Peaceful Coexistence and, 33–35, 126; general, 8–9; system of, 8–9; the *Thalweg*, 54, 71, 119; utility of, 14–16
Iselin Line ("1941 Line"), 58, 140

Karakoram Mountains, 118; Pass, 117
Kashmir, 27, 69–70, 97
Kawa region (area), 58, 115
Kellogg-Briand Pact (1928), 132
Khamba revolt, 24–26, 28–29, 31, 127, 130, 133
Kongka Pass, 26, 31, 117; incident, 67, 127
Kun Lun Mountains, 118

Ladakh, 26–27. See also Tibet
Laos: boundary with China defined by a French-Chinese agreement (1887), 56; boundary agreement modified (1895), 56
Law of Treaties, codified by UN International Law Commission (1966), 79
Longju, 31; incident, 67, 127
"lost territories," 56, 77, 134, 138, 140

Manchuria, 35–36, 47
Mao Tse-tung, 12, 14, 35, 77; and unequal treaty, 80
McMahon Line, 26–27, 56, 63, 65–68, 72, 94, 103–104, 106, 116, 126–128, 130–131, 133; formed, 65–67. See also Simla Conference
Mongolia: boundary with Russia, 81–82; and Chinese history, 81; Inner and Outer, 81; Inner Mongolian Autonomous Region, 35; Inner Mongolian People's Revolutionary Party, 35. See Mongolian People's Republic, for Outer Mongolia
Mongolian People's Republic (Outer Mongolia), 35, 45, 55; autonomy from China, 81; boundary procedures with China, 121; independence from China, 82; boundary treaty with China, 55; treaty with Tannu Tuva (1926), 82
Mount Everest, 69

Namwan Assigned Tract (Meng-Mao Triangular area), 32, 58–59, 85–86, 97, 140

Index   157

National sovereignty, 10–13; absolute, 12; limited, 11
Nehru, Jawaharlal, 29, 31–32, 127–128; administration, 126; boundary policy, 126; principle for settlement of boundaries, 67–68
Nepal: agreement with China (1960), 32, 69, 92, 120; boundary, 69; boundary negotiations and erecting markers, 120–121; boundary treaty with China (1961), 32, 69, 100, 116, 118–119, 121, 128; boundary treaty with Tibet (1856), 66–67, 103, 116; protocol (1963), 69
North East Frontier Agency (NEFT), 26–27, 29
North Korea, 35, 125; boundary with China, 55

Opium War (1840), 77–78, 80–81
Oppenheim, L., 9–10

Pakistan: boundary, 69–70; boundary agreement with China (1963), 32, 70, 92, 97, 100, 104; boundary protocol (1965), 70
Pamirs, 49–50, 101, 104, 120, 138
Pancha Shila, 34, 39. *See also* Five Principles of Peaceful Coexistence
Panhung tribe, 117
Panlao tribe, 117
Poling, 114
Potsdam Declaration, 92
Puling-Sumda, 114

Russian agreements: Anglo, 104; Chinese (1727), 47; Sino-Russian-Mongolian (1915), 94
Russian-Chinese boundary treaties: Aigun (1858), 47, 80–81, 84; Bur (Burinsky) (1727), 47, 80–81; Ili (1881), 48–49, 80–81; Kashgar (1884), 71, 81, 120; Kiakhta (Kyakhta) (1727–28), 47; Livadia (1879), 48; Nipchu (Nerchinsk) (1689), 47, 80, 84; Peking (1860), 48, 80–81, 84, 119; Tientsin (1858), 80, 84

Russian-Chinese exchange of notes (1894), 50, 92, 101
Russian-Chinese protocols: Goulimtou (1882), 49; Ili (1882), 49; Kashgar (1882), 49–50, (1884), 49–50, 101, 120; Novi-Margelian (1883), 49; Tarbagatai (1883), 49, (1884), 49

Sarikol Range, 101
Shimonoseki (1895), Treaty of, 78
Sikkim: boundary with China, 116; Convention with Tibet (1890), 69, 95, 110
Simla Conference (1914), 66–67, 94, 100; Convention (1914), 92, 106
Sinkiang, 26, 35, 48, 65, 70, 107
Soviet-Chinese agreements: 1920, 83–84; 1924, 83–84, 102–103, 114–115, 129
Soviet-Chinese boundary: border conflicts (1969), 133; border situation, 35–36; disputes, 49–54; formed, 45–49. *See also* Unequal boundary treaties
Soviet proclamation (1919), 83–84
Soviets: agitating Chinese minorities, 35; peaceful coexistence with, 36–38
Spiti, 114
St. Petersburg, Great Britain and Russian Treaty of (1907), 103
state equality, 13–14
Sun Yat-sen, 13, 77

Taiwan, 24, 29, 33, 77–79, 85, 92.
Tannu Tuva (Tannu Urianghai), 82
Tawang, 26, 67
Territorial acquisition, 13
Tibet: agreement with PRC, 28, 30; boundary with India, 63–67, 95; Convention with Great Britain (1904), 95; Convention with Great Britain (1906), 95; Convention with Sikkim (1890), 95; People's Liberation Army entered, 25, 28; relations with India, 25, 26; relations with Republic of China, 25
Tribute system, 23

UN Charter, 78, 125
U Nu, boundary negotiation, 58–60, 85–86
Unequal boundary treaties, 129, 138;

conception of, 78–79; efforts to revise or abrogate, 83–86; Outer Mongolian-Soviet boundary, 81–82; Sino-Burmese boundary, 82–83; Sino-Russian, 79–81

United States: and Chinese minorities, 25; hostile toward China, 29–30; subversive activities in Tibet, 27–28, 30

Ussuri River, 47–48, 52–54, 119, 133

Vienna Conference on the Law of Treaties (1968, 1969), 79, 101

Vietnam: boundary with China defined by a French-Chinese agreement (1887), 56; boundary agreement modified (1895), 56

Wakhan Corridor, 70–72, 104, 116. *See also* Afghanistan boundary treaty (1963)

Wuje (Barahoti) incident (1889), 93, 98

Yalta agreement concerning Outer Mongolia, 82

ABOUT THE AUTHOR

BYRON N. TZOU, a native Chinese, received a B.A. in law and an M.A. in political science at National Taiwan University, as well as an M.A. in international law from Harvard and a Ph.D. in international politics from The New School for Social Research.

He taught Chinese language at Columbia University and worked as a civil servant in New York City. At present he is a full-time Associate Research Fellow at the Institute of International Relations, Chengchi University, and a part-time Associate Professor at Tsinghua University in Taiwan. He edited seven volumes of *Collections of Chinese-Japanese Diplomatic Documents 1911–1949* and has published articles in *The Annals of the Chinese Society of International Law* (in English) and other academic periodicals (in Chinese).

DATE